A HymnTune Psalter

Book Two

Gradual Psalms: The Season after Pentecost

Revised Common Lectionary Edition

Carl P. Daw, Jr. and Kevin R. Hackett

CHURCH
PUBLISHING
INCORPORATED

Church Publishing Incorporated
19 East 34th Street
New York, NY 10016

CONTENTS

INTRODUCTION

The Psalms are the hymns of ancient Israel. In them, every mood and emotion of the human heart is given voice, from the heights and ecstasy of praise to the depths and darkness of despair. While the texts of Israel's hymns have survived, sadly, the music has not. We can only imagine the rugged marching tune that must have carried a wilderness psalm like Psalm 107 or the delicate, homespun melody to which Psalm 131 must surely have been hummed or the protest song to which Psalm 137 was defiantly sung. Certainly, they must have been tunes that were much loved by the people, and certainly they must have been known by heart.

The early Christian church, springing as it did from Jewish soil, naturally continued the tradition of offering its life to God in song through the prayer and praise of the psalms (which, being hymns, were meant to be sung). Thanks to the eventual development of a convention like standard musical notation, we retain some vestiges of this ancient tradition and its evolution. Plainsong melodies, some of which may be traceable to ancient Jewish origins, have conveyed to us (with Latin texts) a priceless body of Judeo-Christian song. Subsequently, at the Reformation the concern that the sacred texts of the Church be available to ordinary people in the vernacular resulted in two significant developments: Latin chant texts were translated into English, and the melodies adapted to fit; and metrical versions of the psalms (precursors of the modern hymn) gained broad popularity. A further refinement of the chant resulted in the 18th-century development of what is now known as Anglican chant, facilitating the singing of non-metrical translations of the psalms.

Beautiful as plainsong is, however, it is an idiom whose modal tonalities and unfamiliar cadences are foreign to the sensibilities and beyond the capability of many modern worshipers. Anglican chant (even in its simplified form) relies on skillful choral leadership and is inaccessible to many Episcopal congregations. And metrical psalmody, undeniably useful in many settings, is one more step removed from the original text.

This psalter draws upon much of what has gone before; indeed, this collection does not attempt to create a new manner of singing the psalms. Rather, it endeavors to draw together various traditions of psalmody by preserving the refrain/verse pattern of Israel's worship (the responsorial form); by using a hybrid form of the chant (simplified Anglican chant, itself a hybrid of plainsong); and most significantly, by basing its refrains on hymn tunes (many of which carried the texts of early metrical psalms) likely to be already known by heart by most Protestants in North America.

As a general strategy for recovering the experience of the psalms as sung scripture, it seemed fitting that these ancient hymns should be wedded in our day to the hymn tunes that have become familiar in Christian worship. But more particularly, *A HymnTune Psalter* is offered as a pastoral resource for those responsible for planning and leading the Church's worship in congregations that may have felt unable to sing the psalms in any of the available styles. Through the use of varied antiphon tunes and chant tones, it also attempts to convey the distinctive character of each psalm and provides an alternative to the unexpressive monotony of singing every psalm to one or two simplified Anglican chants. By drawing on the hymn melodies already known to them, the congregation can recognize and recover something of the vitality and comprehensiveness of the psalms.

Performance Notes

The translation used in this collection is that of The Book of Common Prayer 1979. The texts of the antiphons are those appointed for each Proper. They are identical to those used in *Gradual Psalms* and in the lectionary-based bulletin inserts used in many congregations. Indeed, given the familiarity of tunes for the antiphons, the availability of the antiphon on the scripture insert may eliminate the need to print the antiphon and its music.

The traditional method for singing this type of psalmody is as follows:

Cantor or choir sings the antiphon;
all repeat.

Cantor or choir sings the first set of verses;
all respond with the antiphon.

And so forth, always concluding with the antiphon.

The Antiphons

At its best, the antiphon of a psalm is the peoples' "take-home-package," the word of scripture that, set to music and committed to memory, "dwells in the heart richly." The tunes of the antiphons are drawn from familiar hymns found in *The Hymnal 1982*. All are in the public domain and most are part of the larger Church's standard repertoire. Wherever possible, tunes traditionally associated with a metrical version of particular psalm (e.g., Psalm 46 and *Ein feste Burg*), have been used as a means of reinforcing that association. Other rationales for tune selections include seasonal associations (e.g., *Easter Hymn*), thematic connections with tune names or texts (e.g., *Light* for Psalm 27), and the necessity of accommodating the sometimes erratic stress patterns of the appointed antiphon. In many cases, it will be appropriate and desirable that the hymn on which the antiphon is based be used in the same liturgical celebration.

In performance, the tempo and accompaniment (if any) of the antiphon should generally approximate that of the tune on which it is based. In some cases, however, in order to accommodate a wordier text, a slightly broader tempo will be in order. Like *The Hymnal 1982*, this psalter provides only a melody line for antiphons intended to be sung in unison and full harmony for those to be sung in parts. If the antiphons are accompanied, it is important that organ registrations or other instrumental accompaniment be chosen that will support and encourage congregational singing.

The Verses and Chant Tones

The chant tones in this psalter are cast as simplified Anglican chant. Each tone features two four-chord progressions (designated A and B). One four-chord sequence usually carries the text of an entire verse. The first and third chords in each progression are reciting chords, and the second and fourth chords function as medial and final cadences. We have avoided slavish adherence to the practice of changing chords on the last word or syllable of a line, opting occasionally to vary the formula in order to convey the meaning more effectively (e.g., Psalm 118:23a, "This is the **Lord's doing**" rather than "This is the Lord's **doing**" or worse, "This is the Lord's do**ing**."). When inner voices have a second note in a cadential chord, it should be reserved for the final syllable if there are more than one or for the second beat of a single sustained syllable.

The customary pattern of singing two psalm verses between antiphons means that the first verse is sung to part A of the chant tone and the second verse to part B. Where the sentence structure or poetic patterns require it, more than two verses may sometimes be sung before an antiphon. In these cases the pattern of singing the first half twice (i.e., AAB) or of singing the full chant tone twice (ABAB) will be marked in the left-hand margin. Similarly, a very long verse may sometimes need to be subdivided and sung to the full chant tone rather than to half of it. In such cases the verse is printed as four lines of text and is sung in the customary AB pattern.

The verses may be chanted in a variety of ways. Ideally, they would be sung unaccompanied in four-part harmony by a quartet or choir. The antiphon may then be accompanied or not, depending on the confidence and skill of the congregation. Alternatively, a solo voice accompanied by an organ, piano, autoharp, or other chordal instrument can provide satisfying leadership for the verses. If possible, some variation from the instrumentation for the antiphon (e.g., change of organ registration or the addition of handbells) would be desirable. To ensure a smooth transition between the verse and the antiphon, a slight elongation of the word or syllable at each cadence will effect a sense of pulse for the congregation and will help to cue their entrance.

Making Copies for Congregational Use

Purchase of this volume carries with it an authorization for congregations to reproduce in service leaflets either the antiphon or the entire setting, as appropriate. Versions of the antiphons suitable for photocopying can be found at the end of this volume, or the antiphons may be downloaded free of charge in EPS or TIF format at **http://www.churchpublishing.org/hymntunepsalterbooktwo**

Regardless of the source from which the antiphon or entire setting is taken, the following copyright notice must be included on each copy:

Commercial reproduction, or reproduction for sale, of any portion of this psalter without permission of the copyright owners is expressly prohibited. Any questions about appropriate use or permission for commercial reproduction should be channeled through Church Publishing, Inc.

Acknowledgments

In the course of preparing the original version and the current revision of this psalter, we have been encouraged and helped by many people, and we welcome the opportunity to express our appreciation to them. The initial positive response to a very sketchy proposal came from Frank Hemlin, and we were grateful for his early assurance that Church Publishing would be interested and for continuing support in the long transition from good idea to actual publication. As the project proceeded, various groups used portions of these materials in order to evaluate their viability, especially the Community of Celebration in Aliquippa, Pennsylvania, and the Society of Saint John the Evangelist in Cambridge, Massachusetts. We are especially indebted to Dr. William Bradley Roberts and the people of St. Philip's in the Hills, Tucson, Arizona, for extended use and much affirmation.

In the preparation for printing, we have been carefully and supportively guided by Marilyn Haskel and Frank Tedeschi of Church Publishing. In this final phase, as throughout its earlier stages, May Bates Daw has been an invaluable source of sound advice and an unfailing support.

Carl P. Daw, Jr.
Kevin R. Hackett, SSJE

RCL Year A

Trinity Sunday
through
Proper 29

RCL Trinity Sunday A Psalm 8

based on "Leoni" (H82–401)

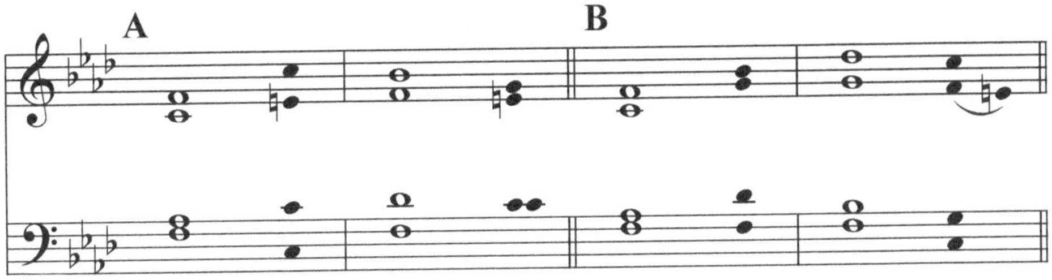

2 Out of the mouths of infants and children *
your majesty is praised above the heavens.
3 You have set up a stronghold against your adversaries, *
to quell the enemy and the avenger. [ANT.]

4 When I consider your heavens, the work of your fingers, *
the moon and the stars you have set in their courses,
5 What is man that you should be mindful of him? *
the son of man that you should seek him out? [ANT.]

A 6 You have made him but little lower than the angels; *
you adorn him with glory and honor;
B 7 You give him mastery over the works of your hands; *
you put all things under his feet:
A 8 All sheep and oxen, *
even the wild beasts of the field,
B 9 The birds of the air, the fish of the sea, *
and whatsoever walks in the paths of the sea. [ANT.]

RCL Trinity Sunday A   Canticle 13

based on "Foundation" (H82–636)

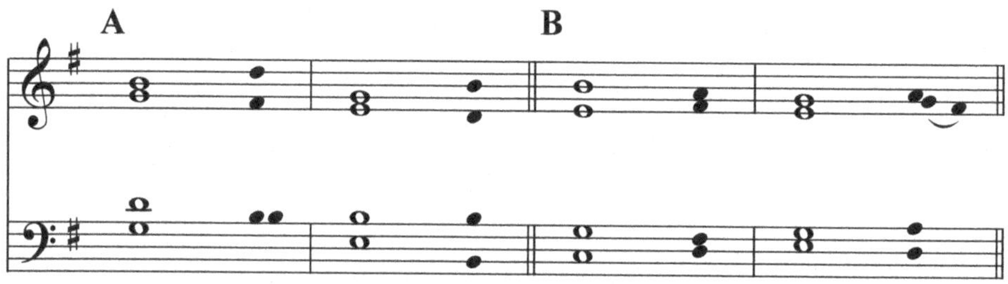

1 Glory to you, Lord God of our fathers; *
you are worthy of praise; glory to you.
2 Glory to you for the radiance of your holy Name; *
we will praise you and highly exalt you for ever. [ANT.]

3 Glory to you in the splendor of your temple; *
on the throne of your majesty, glory to you.
4 Glory to you, seated between the Cherubim; *
we will praise you and highly exalt you for ever. [ANT.]

5 Glory to you, beholding the depths; *
in the high vault of heaven, glory to you.
6 Glory to you, Father, Son, and Holy Spirit; *
we will praise you and highly exalt you for ever. [ANT.]

RCL Proper 1A Psalm 119: 1–8

based on "Hymn to Joy" (H82–376)

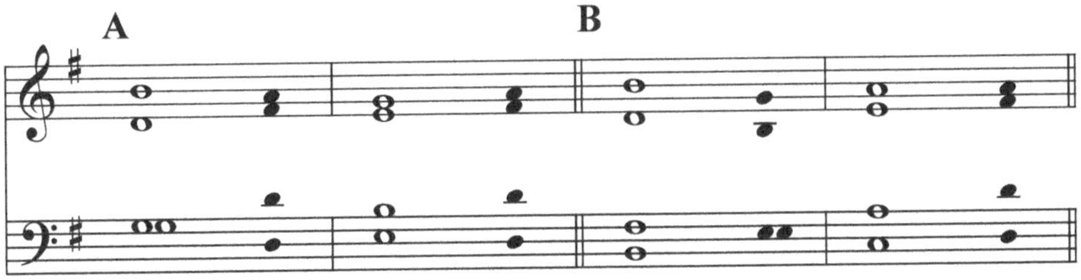

A 1 Happy are they whose way is blameless, *
who walk in the law of the LORD!
A 2 Happy are they who observe his decrees *
and seek him with all their hearts!
B 3 Who never do any wrong, *
but always walk in his ways. [ANT.]

A 4 You laid down your commandments, *
that we should fully keep them.
A 5 Oh, that my ways were made so direct *
that I might keep your statutes!
B 6 Then I should not be put to shame, *
when I regard all your commandments. [ANT.]

7 I will thank you with an unfeigned heart, *
when I have learned your righteous judgments.
8 I will keep your statutes; *
do not utterly forsake me. [ANT.]

RCL Proper 2A Psalm 119: 33–40

based on "Cwm Rhondda" (H82–690)

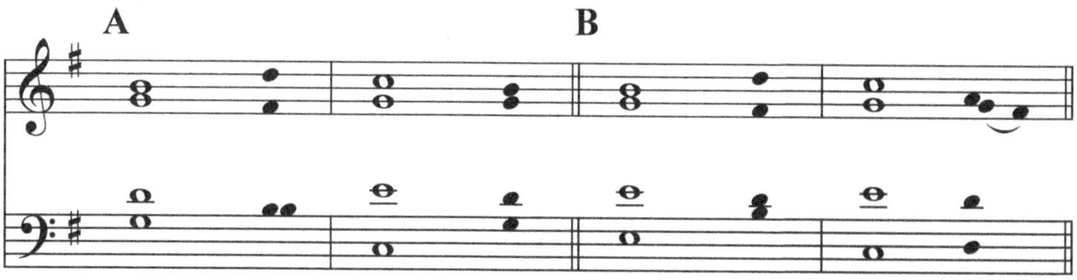

33 Teach me, O Lord, the way of your statutes, *
and I shall keep it to the end.
34 Give me understanding, and I shall keep your law; *
I shall keep it with all my heart. [ANT.]

35 Make me go in the path of your commandments, *
for that is my desire.
36 Incline my heart to your decrees *
and not to unjust gain. [ANT.]

37 Turn my eyes from watching what is worthless; *
give me life in your ways.
38 Fulfill your promise to your servant, *
which you make to those who fear you. [ANT.]

39 Turn away the reproach which I dread, *
because your judgments are good.
40 Behold, I long for your commandments; *
in your righteousness preserve my life. [ANT.]

RCL Proper 3A Psalm 131

based on "Picardy" (H82–324)

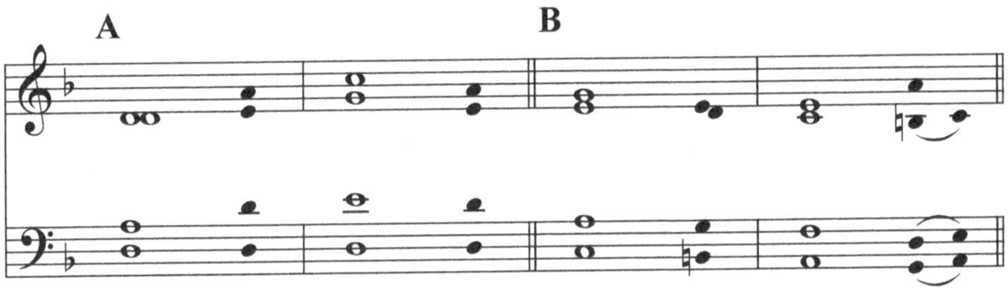

1 O LORD, I am not proud; *
  I have no haughty looks.
2 I do not occupy myself with great matters, *
  or with things that are too hard for me. [ANT.]

3 But I still my soul and make it quiet,
  like a child upon its mother's breast; *
  my soul is quieted within me.
4 O Israel, wait upon the LORD, *
  from this time forth for evermore. [ANT.]

RCL Proper 4A (C Track) Psalm 46

based on "Ein feste burg" (H82–688)

A 1 God is our refuge and strength, *
a very present help in trouble.
A 2 Therefore we will not fear, though the earth be moved, *
and though the mountains be toppled into the depths of the sea;
B 3 Though its waters rage and foam, *
and though the mountains tremble at its tumult. [ANT.]

A 5 There is a river whose streams make glad the city of God, *
the holy habitation of the Most High.
A 6 God is in the midst of her;
she shall not be overthrown; *
God shall help her at the break of day.
B 7 The nations make much ado, and the kingdoms are shaken; *
God has spoken, and the earth shall melt away. [ANT.]

A 9 Come now and look upon the works of the LORD, *
what awesome things he has done on earth.
A 10 It is he who makes war to cease in all the world; *
he breaks the bow, and shatters the spear,
and burns the shields with fire.
B 11 "Be still, then, and know that I am God; *
I will be exalted among the nations;
I will be exalted in the earth." [ANT.]

RCL Proper 4A (G Track) **Psalm 31: 1–5, 19–24**

based on "Pleading Savior" (H82–586)

1 In you, O LORD, have I taken refuge;
let me never be put to shame: *
deliver me in your righteousness.
2 Incline your ear to me; *
make haste to deliver me. [ANT.]

A 3 Be my strong rock, a castle to keep me safe,
for you are my crag and my stronghold; *
for the sake of your Name, lead me and guide me.
A 4 Take me out of the net that they have secretly set for me, *
for you are my tower of strength.
B 5 Into your hands I commend my spirit, *
for you have redeemed me,
O LORD, O God of truth. [ANT.]

19 How great is your goodness, O LORD!
which you have laid up for those who fear you; *
which you have done in the sight of all
for those who put their trust in you.
20 You hide them in the covert of your presence from those
who slander them; *
you keep them in your shelter from the strife of tongues. [ANT.]

21 Blessed be the LORD! *
for he has shown me the wonders of his love in a
besieged city.
22 Yet I said in my alarm,
"I have been cut off from the sight of your eyes." *
Nevertheless, you heard the sound of my entreaty
when I cried out to you. [ANT.]

23 Love the LORD, all you who worship him; *
the LORD protects the faithful,
but repays to the full those who act haughtily.
24 Be strong and let your heart take courage, *
all you who wait for the LORD. [ANT.]

RCL Proper 5A (C Track) Psalm 33: 1–12

based on "Wondrous Love" (H82–439)

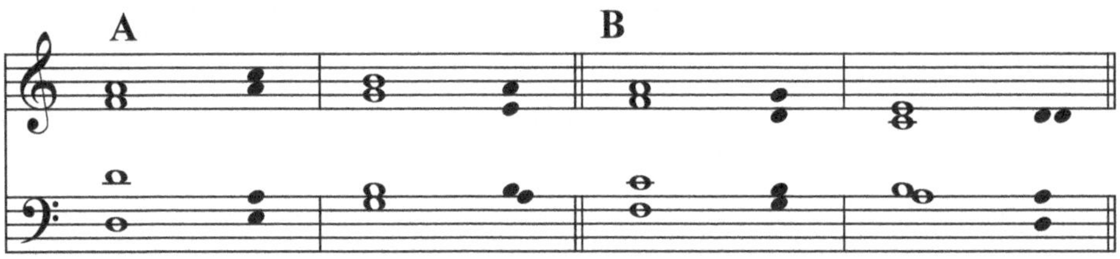

A 1 Rejoice in the LORD, you righteous; *
it is good for the just to sing praises.
A 2 Praise the LORD with the harp; *
play to him upon the psaltery and lyre.
B 3 Sing for him a new song; *
sound a fanfare with all your skill upon the trumpet. [ANT.]

4 For the word of the LORD is right, *
and all his works are sure.
5 He loves righteousness and justice; *
the loving-kindness of the LORD fills the whole earth. [ANT.]

6 By the word of the LORD were the heavens made, *
by the breath of his mouth all the heavenly hosts.
7 He gathers up the waters of the ocean as in a water-skin *
and stores up the depths of the sea. [ANT.]

8 Let all the earth fear the LORD; *
let all who dwell in the world stand in awe of him.
9 For he spoke, and it came to pass; *
he commanded, and it stood fast. [ANT.]

A 10 The LORD brings the will of the nations to naught; *
he thwarts the designs of the peoples.
A 11 But the LORD's will stands fast for ever, *
and the designs of his heart from age to age.
B 12 Happy is the nation whose God is the LORD! *
happy the people he has chosen to be his own! [ANT.]

RCL Proper 5A (G Track) Psalm 50: 7–15

based on "Nyland" (H82–232)

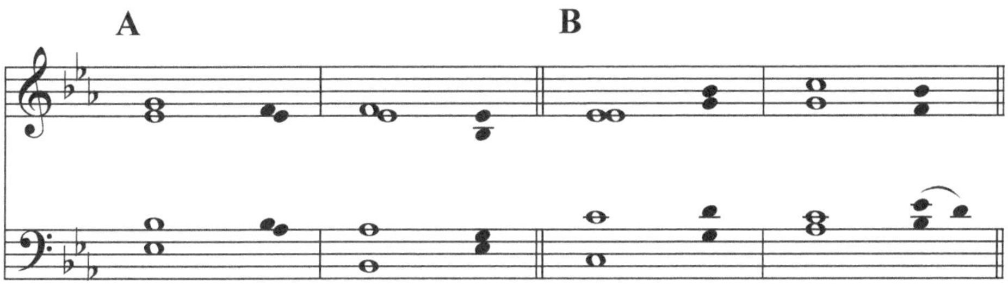

7 Hear, O my people, and I will speak:
"O Israel, I will bear witness against you; *
for I am God, your God.
8 I do not accuse you because of your sacrifices; *
your offerings are always before me. [ANT.]

9 I will take no bull-calf from your stalls, *
nor he-goats out of your pens;
10 For all the beasts of the forest are mine, *
the herds in their thousands upon the hills. [ANT.]

A 11 I know every bird in the sky, *
and the creatures of the fields are in my sight.
A 12 If I were hungry, I would not tell you, *
for the whole world is mine and all that is in it.
B 13 Do you think I eat the flesh of bulls, *
or drink the blood of goats? [ANT.]

14 Offer to God a sacrifice of thanksgiving *
and make good your vows to the Most High.
15 Call upon me in the day of trouble; *
I will deliver you, and you shall honor me." [ANT.]

RCL Proper 6A (C Track) Psalm 116: 1, 10–17

based on "Middlebury" (H82–213)

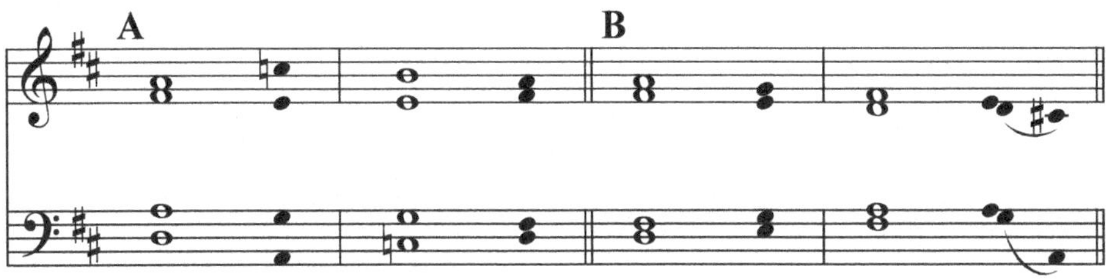

1 I love the LORD,
because he has heard the voice of my supplication, *
because he has inclined his ear to me
whenever I called upon him. [ANT.]

A 10 How shall I repay the LORD *
for all the good things he has done for me?
A 11 I will lift up the cup of salvation *
and call upon the Name of the LORD.
B 12 I will fulfill my vows to the LORD *
in the presence of all his people. [ANT.]

13 Precious in the sight of the LORD *
is the death of his servants.
14 O LORD, I am your servant; *
I am your servant and the child of your handmaid;
you have freed me from my bonds. [ANT.]

A 15 I will offer you the sacrifice of thanksgiving *
and call upon the Name of the LORD.
A 16 I will fulfill my vows to the LORD *
in the presence of all his people,
B 17 In the courts of the LORD's house, *
in the midst of you, O Jerusalem.
Hallelujah! [ANT.]

RCL Proper 6A (G Track) **Psalm 100**

based on "Old 100th" (H82–377)

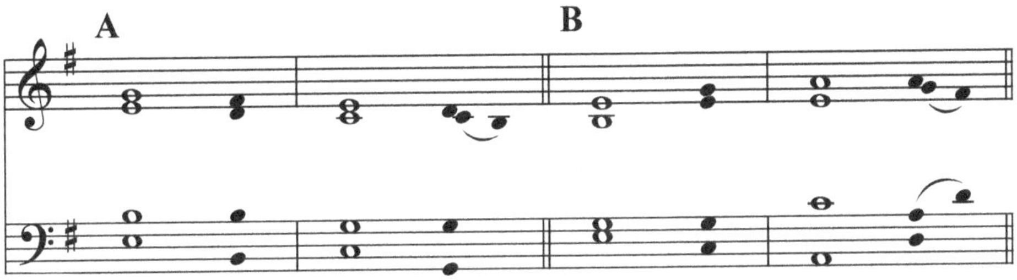

1 Be joyful in the LORD, all you lands; *
serve the LORD with gladness
and come before his presence with a song.
2 Know this: The LORD himself is God; *
he himself has made us, and we are his;
we are his people and the sheep of his pasture. [ANT.]

3 Enter his gates with thanksgiving;
go into his courts with praise; *
give thanks to him and call upon his Name.
4 For the LORD is good;
his mercy is everlasting; *
and his faithfulness endures from age to age. [ANT.]

RCL Proper 7A (C Track) Psalm 86: 1–10, 16–17

based on "Rouen" (H82–360)

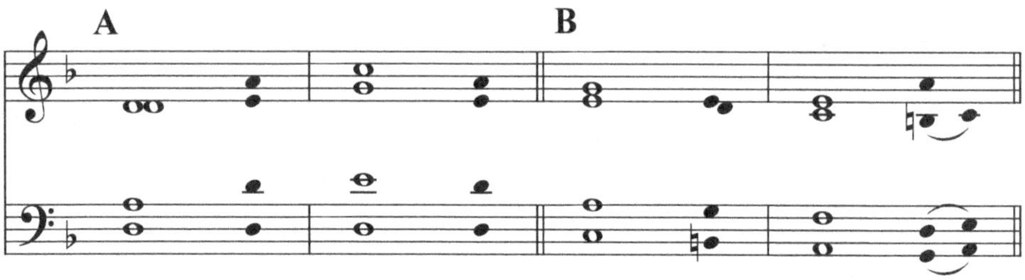

A 1 Bow down your ear, O Lord, and answer me, *
for I am poor and in misery.
A 2 Keep watch over my life, for I am faithful; *
save your servant who puts his trust in you.
B 3 Be merciful to me, O Lord, for you are my God; *
I call upon you all the day long. [ANT.]

A 4 Gladden the soul of your servant, *
for to you, O Lord, I lift up my soul.
A 5 For you, O Lord, are good and forgiving, *
and great is your love toward all who call upon you.
B 6 Give ear, O Lord, to my prayer, *
and attend to the voice of my supplications. [ANT.]

7 In the time of my trouble I will call upon you, *
for you will answer me.
8 Among the gods there is none like you, O Lord, *
nor anything like your works. [ANT.]

9 All nations you have made will come and
worship you, O Lord, *
and glorify your Name.
10 For you are great;
you do wondrous things; *
and you alone are God. [ANT.]

16 Turn to me and have mercy upon me; *
give your strength to your servant;
and save the child of your handmaid.
17 Show me a sign of your favor,
so that those who hate me may see it and be ashamed; *
because you, O Lord, have helped me and comforted me. [ANT.]

RCL Proper 7A (G Track) Psalm 69: 8–11, (12–17), 18–20

based on "Tender Thought" (H82–702)

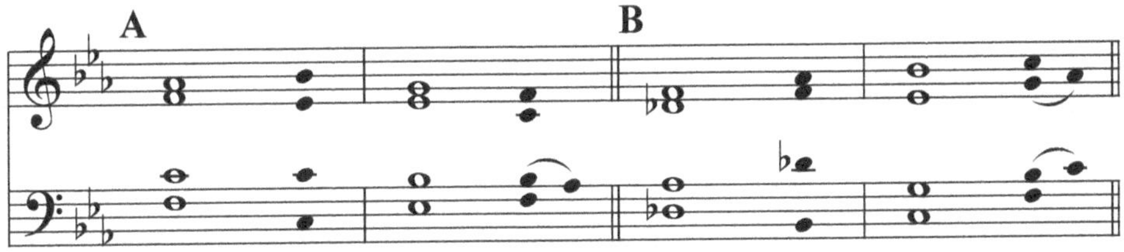

8 Surely, for your sake have I suffered reproach, *
and shame has covered my face.
9 I have become a stranger to my own kindred, *
an alien to my mother's children. [ANT.]

10 Zeal for your house has eaten me up; *
the scorn of those who scorn you has fallen upon me.
11 I humbled myself with fasting, *
but that was turned to my reproach. [ANT.]

(12 I put on sack-cloth also, *
and became a byword among them.
13 Those who sit at the gate murmur against me, *
and the drunkards make songs about me. [ANT.]

14 But as for me, this is my prayer to you, *
at the time you have set, O LORD:
15 "In your great mercy, O God, *
answer me with your unfailing help. [ANT.]

16 Save me from the mire; do not let me sink; *
let me be rescued from those who hate me
and out of the deep waters.
17 Let not the torrent of waters wash over me,
neither let the deep swallow me up; *
do not let the Pit shut its mouth upon me. [ANT.])

A 18 Answer me, O LORD, for your love is kind; *
in your great compassion, turn to me.'
A 19 "Hide not your face from your servant; *
be swift and answer me, for I am in distress.
B 20 Draw near to me and redeem me; *
because of my enemies deliver me. [ANT.]

RCL Proper 8A (C Track) Psalm 13

based on "Aberystwyth" (H82–349, 640, 699)

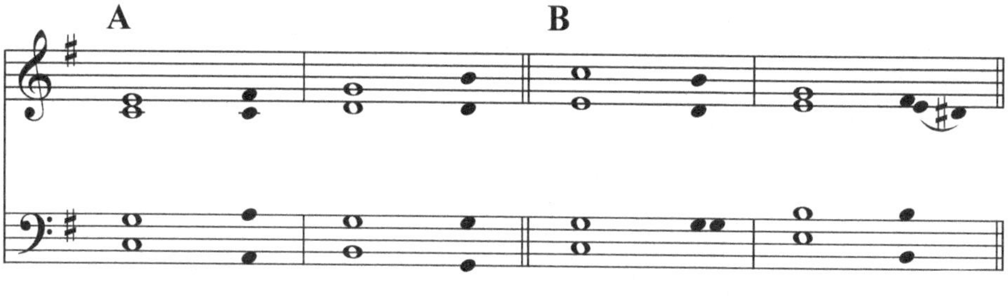

1 How long, O LORD?
will you forget me for ever? *
how long will you hide your face from me?
2 How long shall I have perplexity in my mind,
and grief in my heart, day after day? *
how long shall my enemy triumph over me? [ANT.]

3 Look upon me and answer me, O LORD my God; *
give light to my eyes, lest I sleep in death;
4 Lest my enemy say, "I have prevailed over him," *
and my foes rejoice that I have fallen. [ANT.]

5 But I put my trust in your mercy; *
my heart is joyful because of your saving help.
6 I will sing to the LORD, for he has dealt with me richly; *
I will praise the Name of the LORD Most High. [ANT.]

RCL Proper 8A (G Track) Psalm 89: 1–4, 15–18

based on "Eventide" (H82–662)

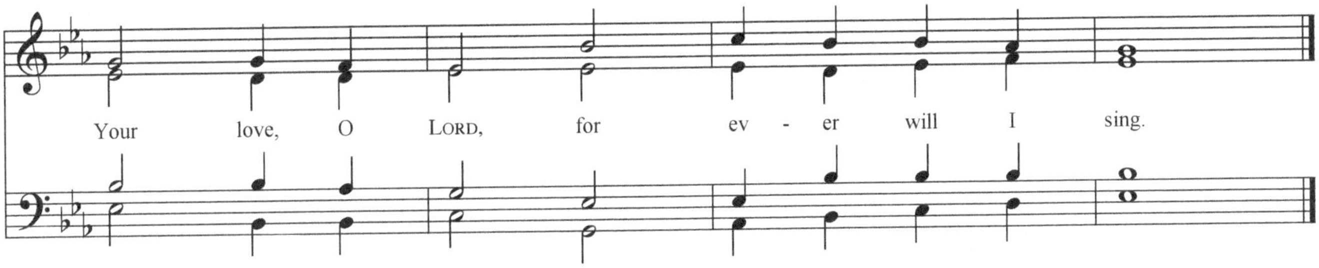

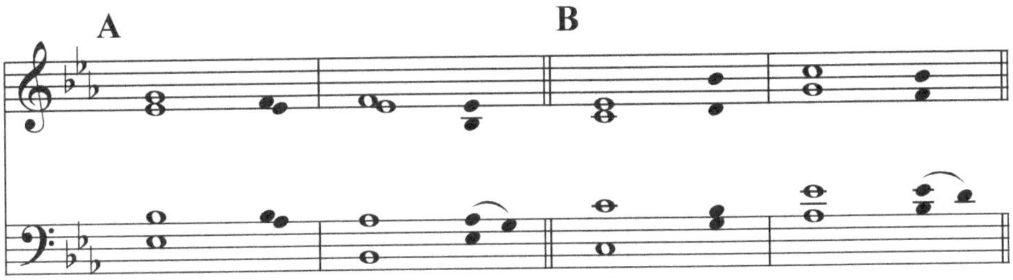

1 Your love, O LORD, for ever will I sing; *
from age to age my mouth will proclaim your faithfulness.
2 For I am persuaded that your love is established for ever; *
you have set your faithfulness firmly in the heavens. [ANT.]

3 "I have made a covenant with my chosen one; *
I have sworn an oath to David my servant:
4 'I will establish your line for ever, *
and preserve your throne for all generations.'" [ANT.]

15 Happy are the people who know the festal shout! *
they walk, O LORD, in the light of your presence.
16 They rejoice daily in your Name; *
they are jubilant in your righteousness. [ANT.]

17 For you are the glory of their strength, *
and by your favor our might is exalted.
18 Truly, the LORD is our ruler; *
the Holy One of Israel is our King. [ANT.]

RCL Proper 9A (C Track) Psalm 45: 11–18

based on "Song 1" (H82–499)

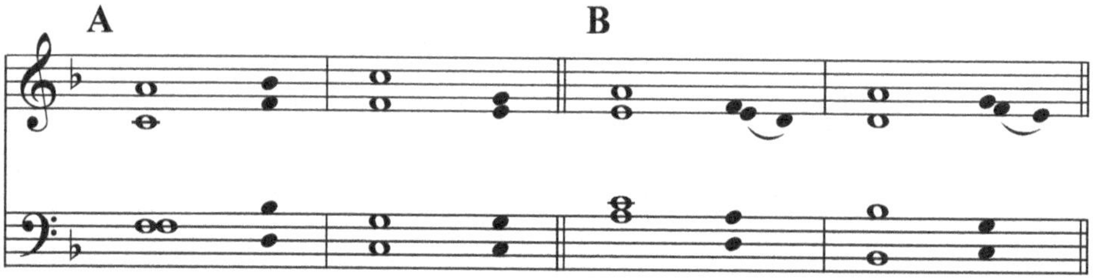

A 11 "Hear, O daughter; consider and listen closely; *
forget your people and your father's house.
A 12 The king will have pleasure in your beauty; *
he is your master; therefore do him honor.
B 13 The people of Tyre are here with a gift; *
the rich among the people seek your favor." [ANT.]

A 14 All glorious is the princess as she enters; *
her gown is cloth-of-gold.
A 15 In embroidered apparel she is brought to the king; *
after her the bridesmaids follow in procession.
B 16 With joy and gladness they are brought, *
and enter into the palace of the king. [ANT.]

17 "In place of fathers, O king, you shall have sons; *
you shall make them princes over all the earth.
18 I will make your name to be remembered
from one generation to another; *
therefore nations will praise you for ever and ever." [ANT.]

RCL Proper 9A (C Track, alt.) The Song of My Beloved (Song of Solomon 2: 8–13)

based on "Middlebury" (H82–213)

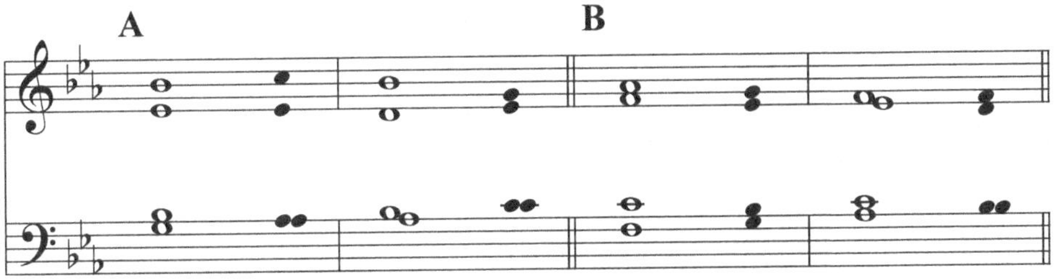

Hear the voice of my belovèd!
    Over the mountains he comes leaping,
    bounding over the hills like a young stag or a gazelle.
See where he stands gazing in at the windows,
    peeking through the lattice. [ANT.]

A My beloved calls to me:
    Rise up, my love, my beauty, come away;
B for now the winter is past,
    the rains are over and gone.
A Flowers appear on the earth
    and the time of singing has come;
B the voice of the turtle-dove
    is heard throughout the land. [ANT.]

The fig tree bends with scented fruit;
    and all the squash-vines blossom,
sending forth their sweet perfume.
    Rise up my love, my beauty, come away. [ANT.]

RCL Proper 9A (G Track) Psalm 145: 8–15

based on "Old 124th" (H82–404)

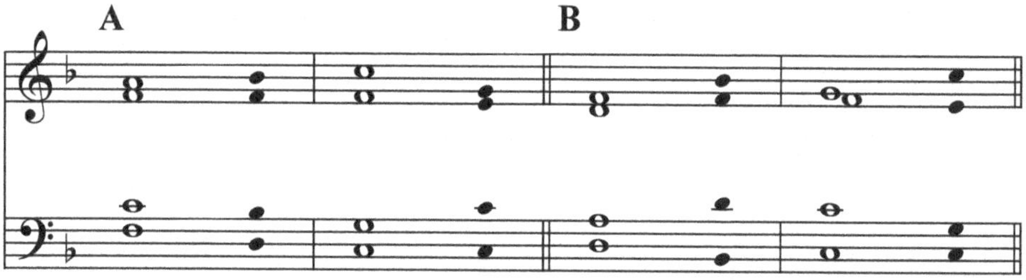

8 The Lord is gracious and full of compassion, *
slow to anger and of great kindness.
9 The Lord is loving to everyone *
and his compassion is over all his works. [ANT.]

A 10 All your works praise you, O Lord, *
and your faithful servants bless you.
A 11 They make known the glory of your kingdom *
and speak of your power;
B 12 That the peoples may know of your power *
and the glorious splendor of your kingdom. [ANT.]

A 13 Your kingdom is an everlasting kingdom; *
your dominion endures throughout all ages.
A 14 The Lord is faithful in all his words *
and merciful in all his deeds.
B 15 The Lord upholds all those who fall; *
he lifts up those who are bowed down. [ANT.]

RCL Proper 10A (C Track) Psalm 119: 105–112

based on "Wondrous Love" (H82–439)

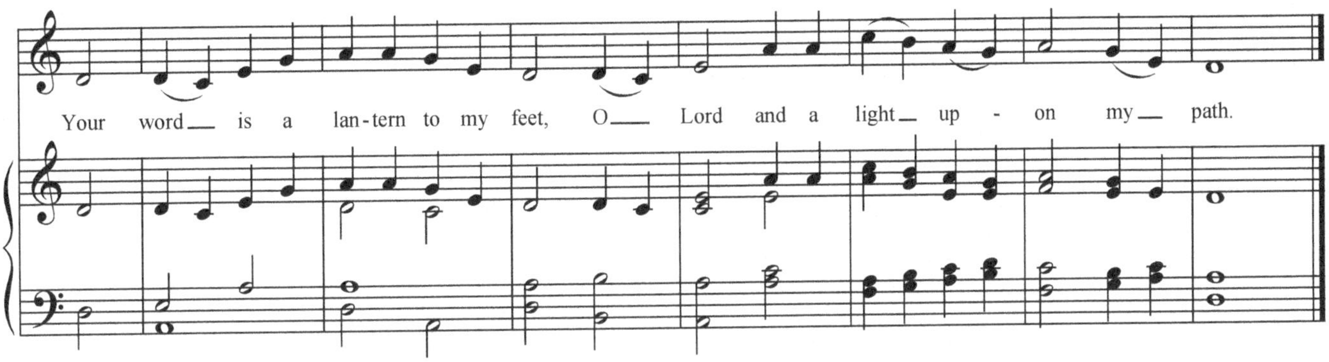

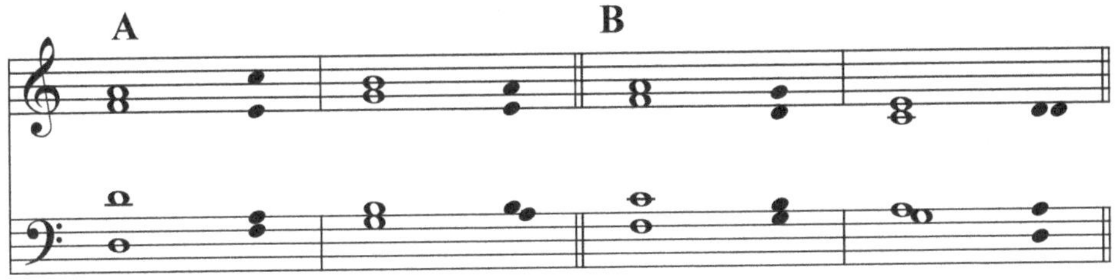

105 Your word is a lantern to my feet *
and a light upon my path.
106 I have sworn and am determined *
to keep your righteous judgments. [ANT.]

107 I am deeply troubled; *
preserve my life, O LORD, according to your word.
108 Accept, O LORD, the willing tribute of my lips, *
and teach me your judgments. [ANT.]

109 My life is always in my hand, *
yet I do not forget your law.
110 The wicked have set a trap for me, *
but I have not strayed from your commandments. [ANT.]

111 Your decrees are my inheritance for ever; *
truly, they are the joy of my heart.
112 I have applied my heart to fulfill your statutes *
for ever and to the end. [ANT.]

RCL Proper 10A (G Track) Psalm 65: (1–8), 9–14

based on "Birmingham" (H82–437)

(A 1 You are to be praised, O God, in Zion; *
to you shall vows be performed in Jerusalem.
A 2 To you that hear prayer shall all flesh come, *
because of their transgressions.
B 3 Our sins are stronger than we are, *
but you will blot them out. [ANT.]

4 Happy are they whom you choose
and draw to your courts to dwell there! *
they will be satisfied by the beauty of your house,
by the holiness of your temple.
5 Awesome things will you show us in your righteousness,
O God of our salvation, *
O Hope of all the ends of the earth
and of the seas that are far away. [ANT.]

A 6 You make fast the mountains by your power; *
they are girded about with might.
A 7 You still the roaring of the seas, *
the roaring of their waves,
and the clamor of the peoples.
B 8 Those who dwell at the ends of the earth will tremble at your
marvelous signs; *
you make the dawn and the dusk to sing for joy. [ANT.])

9 You visit the earth and water it abundantly;
you make it very plenteous; *
the river of God is full of water.
10 You prepare the grain, *
for so you provide for the earth. [ANT.]

11 You drench the furrows and smooth out the ridges; *
with heavy rain you soften the ground
and bless its increase.
12 You crown the year with your goodness, *
and your paths overflow with plenty. [ANT.]

13 May the fields of the wilderness be rich for grazing, *
and the hills be clothed with joy.
14 May the meadows cover themselves with flocks,
and the valleys cloak themselves with grain; *
let them shout for joy and sing. [ANT.]

RCL Proper 11A (C Track) Psalm 139: 1–11, 22–23

based on "Tender Thought" (H82–702)

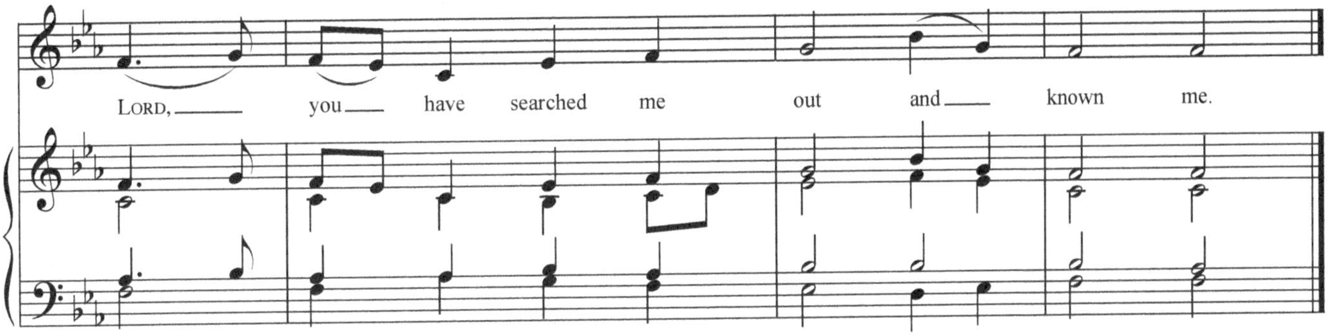

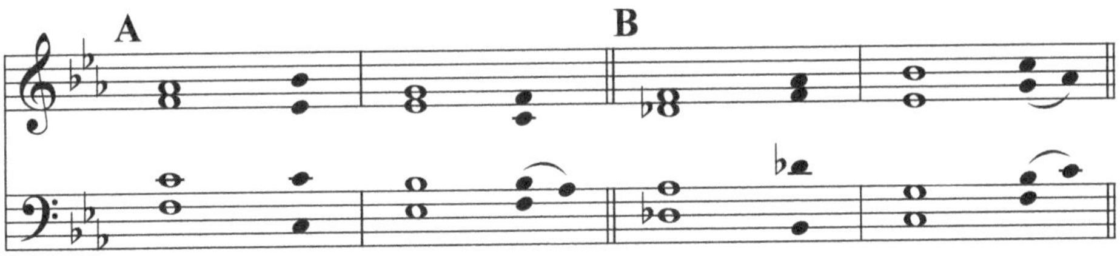

1 LORD, you have searched me out and known me; *
you know my sitting down and my rising up;
you discern my thoughts from afar.
2 You trace my journeys and my resting-places *
and are acquainted with all my ways. [ANT.]

A 3 Indeed, there is not a word on my lips, *
but you, O LORD, know it altogether.
A 4 You press upon me behind and before *
and lay your hand upon me.
B 5 Such knowledge is too wonderful for me; *
it is so high that I cannot attain to it. [ANT.]

6 Where can I go then from your Spirit? *
where can I flee from your presence?
7 If I climb up to heaven, you are there; *
if I make the grave my bed, you are there also. [ANT.]

A 8 If I take the wings of the morning *
and dwell in the uttermost parts of the sea,
B 9 Even there your hand will lead me *
and your right hand hold me fast.
A 10 If I say, "Surely the darkness will cover me, *
and the light around me turn to night,"
B 11 Darkness is not dark to you;
the night is as bright as the day; *
darkness and light to you are both alike. [ANT.]

22 Search me out, O God, and know my heart; *
try me and know my restless thoughts.
23 Look well whether there be any wickedness in me *
and lead me in the way that is everlasting. [ANT.]

RCL Proper 11A (C Track, alt.) A Song of God's Strength in Mercy (Wisdom 12: 13, 16–19)

based on "Foundation" (H82–636)

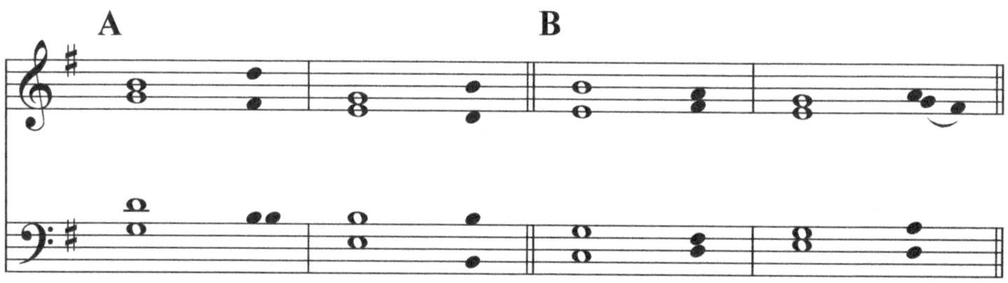

A Your care, O God, encompasses all creation! *
Nor is there any god besides you.
B To whom do you need to prove *
that your judgements are just?
A For your righteousness comes from your strength, *
and your dominion makes way for your mercy;
B for you show your might when mortals doubt your sovereignty; *
you rebuke those who treat it with contempt. [ANT.]

A Although you rule in boundless power, *
you administer justice with mildness;
B you govern us with great forbearance *
though you are free to act without constraint.
A You have taught your people by such deeds *
that all who would be righteous must be kind.
B You have filled your children with good hope *
by stirring them to repent for their sins. [ANT.]

RCL Proper 11A (G Track) Psalm 86: 11–17

based on "Rouen" (H82–360)

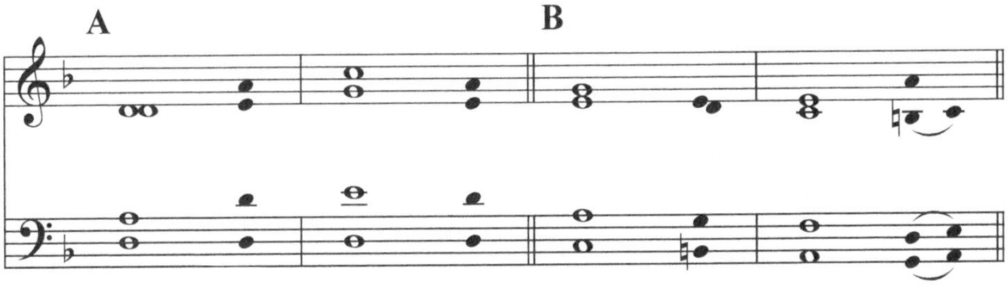

11 Teach me your way, O LORD
and I will walk in your truth;*
knit my heart to you that I may fear your Name.
12 I will thank you, O LORD my God, with all my heart, *
and glorify your Name for evermore. [ANT.]

13 For great is your love toward me; *
you have delivered me from the nethermost Pit.
14 The arrogant rise up against me, O God,
and a band of violent men seeks my life; *
they have not set you before their eyes. [ANT.]

A 15 But you, O LORD, are gracious and full of compassion, *
slow to anger, and full of kindness and truth.
A 16 Turn to me and have mercy upon me; *
give your strength to your servant;
and save the child of your handmaid.
B 17 Show me a sign of your favor,
so that those who hate me may see it and be ashamed; *
because you, O LORD, have helped me and comforted me. [ANT.]

RCL Proper 12A (C Track) **Psalm 105: 1–11, 45b**

based on "Hanover" (H82–388)

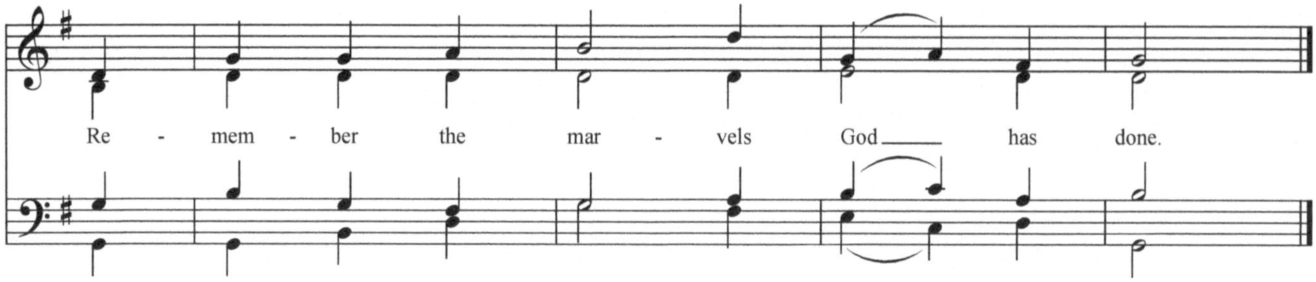

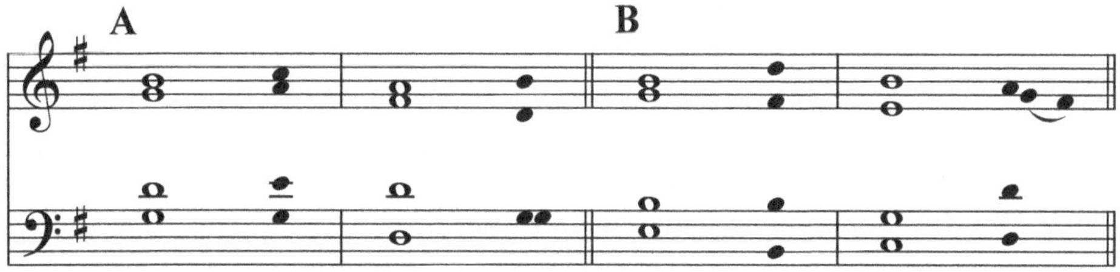

A 1 Give thanks to the LORD and call upon his Name; *
make known his deeds among the peoples.
A 2 Sing to him, sing praises to him, *
and speak of all his marvelous works.
B 3 Glory in his holy Name; *
let the hearts of those who seek the Lord rejoice. [ANT.]

A 4 Search for the LORD and his strength; *
continually seek his face.
A 5 Remember the marvels he has done, *
his wonders and the judgments of his mouth,
B 6 O offspring of Abraham his servant, *
O children of Jacob his chosen. [ANT.]

7 He is the LORD our God; *
his judgments prevail in all the world.
8 He has always been mindful of his covenant, *
the promise he made for a thousand generations: [ANT.]

A 9 The covenant he made with Abraham, *
the oath that he swore to Isaac,
A 10 Which he established as a statute for Jacob, *
an everlasting covenant for Israel,
B 11 Saying, "To you will I give the land of Canaan *
to be your allotted inheritance."
[45b.] Hallelujah! [ANT.]

RCL Proper 12A (C Track, alt.) Psalm 128

based on "Bereden väg för Herran" (H82–65)

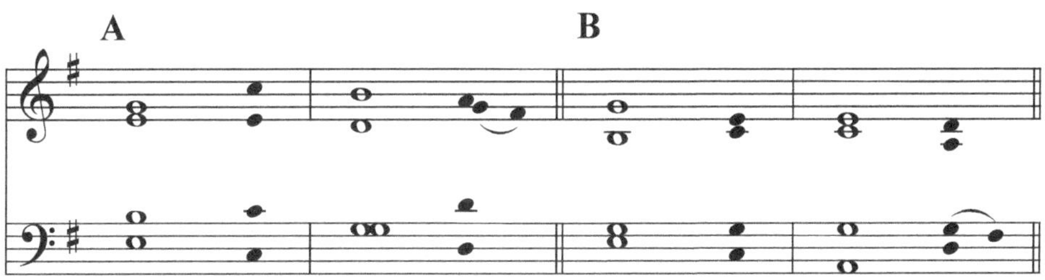

1 Happy are they all who fear the LORD, *
and who follow in his ways!
2 You shall eat the fruit of your labor; *
happiness and prosperity shall be yours. [ANT.]

3 Your wife shall be like a fruitful vine within your house, *
your children like olive shoots round about your table.
4 The man who fears the LORD *
shall thus indeed be blessed. [ANT.]

5 The LORD bless you from Zion, *
and may you see the prosperity of Jerusalem all the days of your life.
6 May you live to see your children's children; *
may peace be upon Israel. [ANT.]

RCL Proper 12A (G Track) Psalm 119: 129–136

based on "Liebster Jesu" (H82–631)

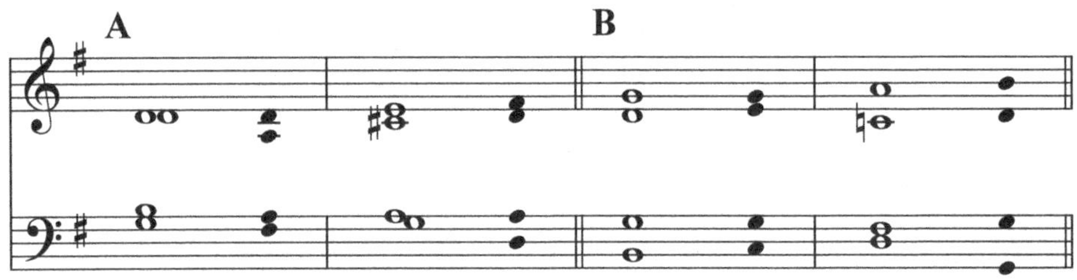

129 Your decrees are wonderful; *
therefore I obey them with all my heart.
130 When your word goes forth it gives light; *
it gives understanding to the simple. [ANT.]

131 I open my mouth and pant; *
I long for your commandments.
132 Turn to me in mercy, *
as you always do to those who love your Name. [ANT.]

133 Steady my footsteps in your word; *
let no iniquity have dominion over me.
134 Rescue me from those who oppress me, *
and I will keep your commandments. [ANT.]

135 Let your countenance shine upon your servant *
and teach me your statutes.
136 My eyes shed streams of tears, *
because people do not keep your law. [ANT.]

RCL Proper 13A (C Track) Psalm 17: 1–7, 16

based on "Tender Thought" (H82–702)

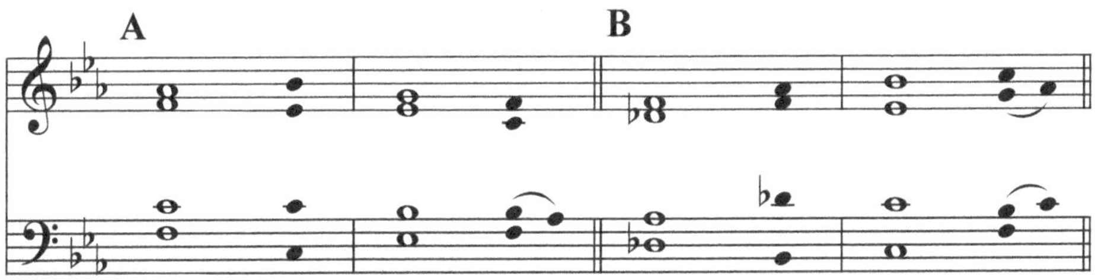

1 Hear my plea of innocence, O LORD;
give heed to my cry; *
listen to my prayer, which does not come from lying lips.
2 Let my vindication come forth from your presence; *
let your eyes be fixed on justice. [ANT.]

3 Weigh my heart, summon me by night, *
melt me down; you will find no impurity in me.
4 I give no offense with my mouth as others do; *
I have heeded the words of your lips. [ANT.]

5 My footsteps hold fast to the ways of your law; *
in your paths my feet shall not stumble.
6 I call upon you, O God, for you will answer me; *
incline your ear to me and hear my words. [ANT.]

7 Show me your marvelous loving-kindness, *
O Savior of those who take refuge at your right hand
from those who rise up against them.
16 But at my vindication I shall see your face; *
when I awake, I shall be satisfied, beholding
your likeness. [ANT.]

RCL Proper 13A (G Track) Psalm 145: 8–9, 15–22

based on "Foundation" (H82–636)

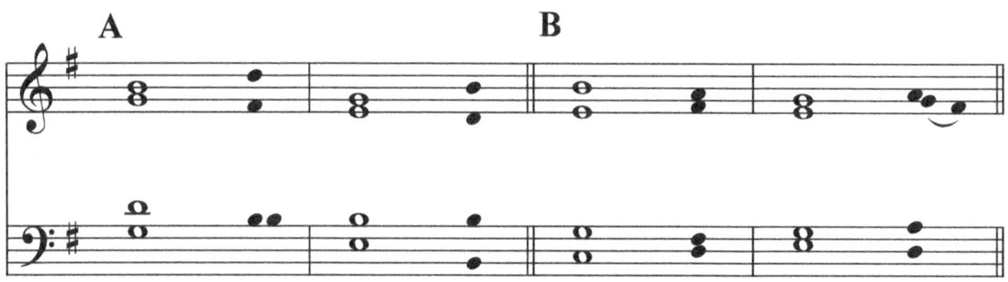

8 The LORD is gracious and full of compassion, *
slow to anger and of great kindness.
9 The LORD is loving to everyone *
and his compassion is over all his works. [ANT.]

A 15 The LORD upholds all those who fall; *
he lifts up those who are bowed down.
A 16 The eyes of all wait upon you, O LORD, *
and you give them their food in due season.
B 17 You open wide your hand *
and satisfy the needs of every living creature. [ANT.]

18 The Lord is righteous in all his ways *
and loving in all his works.
19 The Lord is near to those who call upon him, *
to all who call upon him faithfully. [ANT.]

A 20 He fulfills the desire of those who fear him; *
he hears their cry and helps them.
A 21 The Lord preserves all those who love him, *
but he destroys all the wicked.
B 22 My mouth shall speak the praise of the LORD; *
let all flesh bless his holy Name for ever and ever. [ANT.]

RCL Transfiguration ABC August 6 Psalm 99

based on "Old 124th" (H82–404)

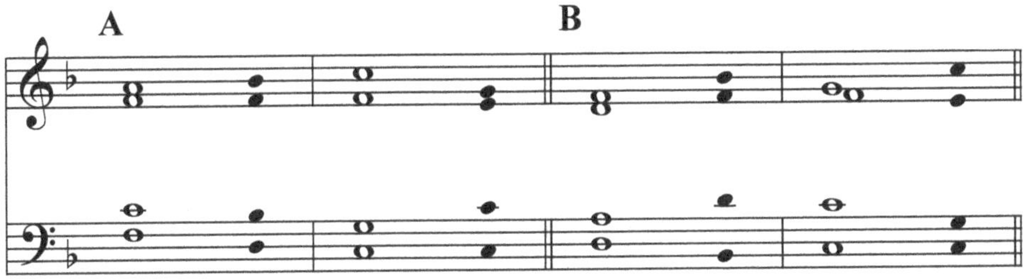

A 1 The LORD is King;
let the people tremble; *
he is enthroned upon the cherubim;
let the earth shake.
A 2 The LORD is great in Zion; *
he is high above all peoples.
B 3 Let them confess his Name, which is great and awesome; *
he is the Holy One. [ANT.]

4 "O mighty King, lover of justice,
you have established equity; *
you have executed justice and righteousness in Jacob."
5 Proclaim the greatness of the LORD our God
and fall down before his footstool; *
he is the Holy One. [ANT.]

6 Moses and Aaron among his priests,
and Samuel among those who call upon his Name, *
they called upon the LORD, and he answered them.
7 He spoke to them out of the pillar of cloud; *
they kept his testimonies and the decree that he gave them. [ANT.]

8 "O LORD our God, you answered them indeed; *
you were a God who forgave them,
yet punished them for their evil deeds."
9 Proclaim the greatness of the LORD our God
and worship him upon his holy hill; *
for the LORD our God is the Holy One. [ANT.]

RCL Proper 14A (C Track) Psalm 105: 1–6, 16–22, 45b

based on "Hanover" (H82–388)

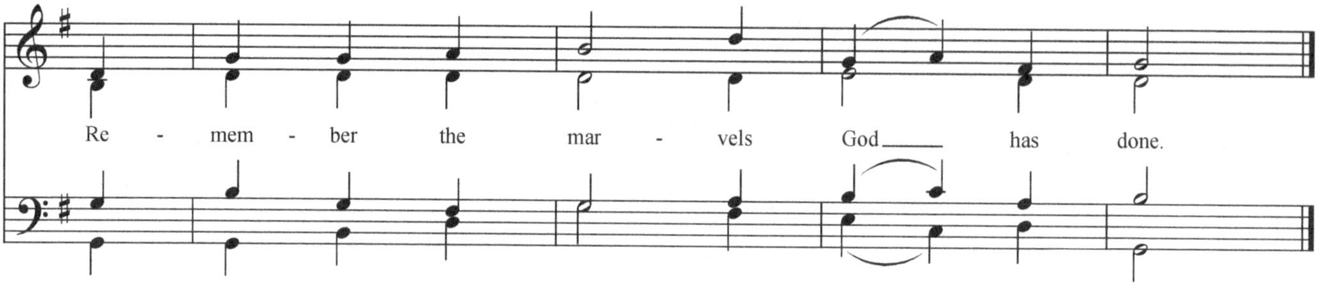

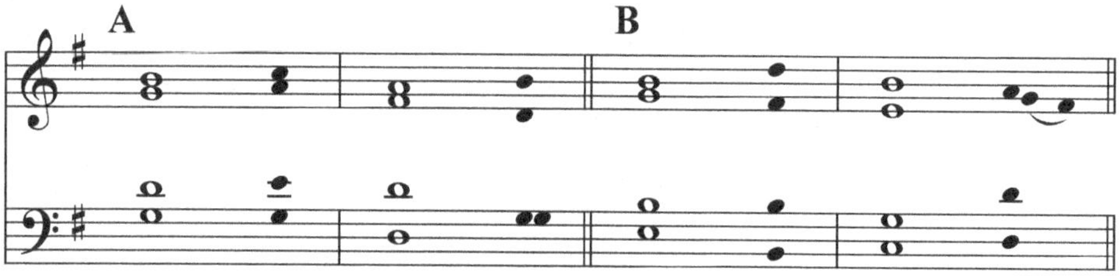

A 1 Give thanks to the LORD and call upon his Name; *
make known his deeds among the peoples.
A 2 Sing to him, sing praises to him, *
and speak of all his marvelous works.
B 3 Glory in his holy Name; *
let the hearts of those who seek the Lord rejoice. [ANT.]

A 4 Search for the LORD and his strength; *
continually seek his face.
A 5 Remember the marvels he has done, *
his wonders and the judgments of his mouth,
B 6 O offspring of Abraham his servant, *
O children of Jacob his chosen. [ANT.]

A 16 Then he called for a famine in the land *
and destroyed the supply of bread.
B 17 He sent a man before them, *
Joseph, who was sold as a slave.
A 18 They bruised his feet in fetters; *
his neck they put in an iron collar.
B 19 Until his prediction came to pass, *
the word of the LORD tested him. [ANT.]

A 20 The king sent and released him; *
the ruler of the peoples set him free.
A 21 He set him as a master over his household,
as a ruler over all his possessions,
B 22 To instruct his princes according to his will
and to teach his elders wisdom.
[45b.] Hallelujah! [ANT.]

RCL Proper 14A (G Track) **Psalm 85: 7–13**

based on "Aus tiefer Not" (H82–151)

8 I will listen to what the Lord God is saying, *
for he is speaking peace to his faithful people
and to those who turn their hearts to him.
9 Truly, his salvation is very near to those who fear him, *
that his glory may dwell in our land. [ANT.]

10 Mercy and truth have met together; *
righteousness and peace have kissed each other.
11 Truth shall spring up from the earth, *
and righteousness shall look down from heaven. [ANT.]

12 The Lord will indeed grant prosperity, *
and our land will yield its increase.
13 Righteousness shall go before him, *
and peace shall be a pathway for his feet. [ANT.]

RCL Proper 15A (C Track) Psalm 133

based on "Nyland" (H82–655)

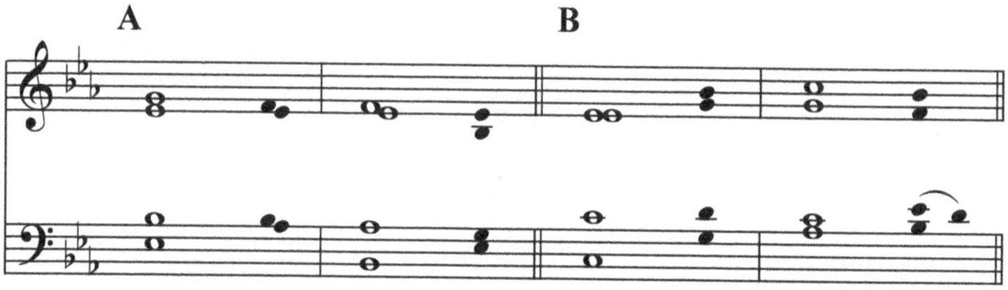

A 1 Oh, how good and pleasant it is, *
when brethren live together in unity!
A 2 It is like fine oil upon the head *
that runs down upon the beard,
B 3 Upon the beard of Aaron, *
and runs down upon the collar of his robe. [ANT.]

4 It is like the dew of Hermon *
that falls upon the hills of Zion.
5 For there the LORD has ordained the blessing: *
life for evermore. [ANT.]

RCL Proper 15A (G Track) Psalm 67

based on "Allein Gott in der Höh" (H82–421)

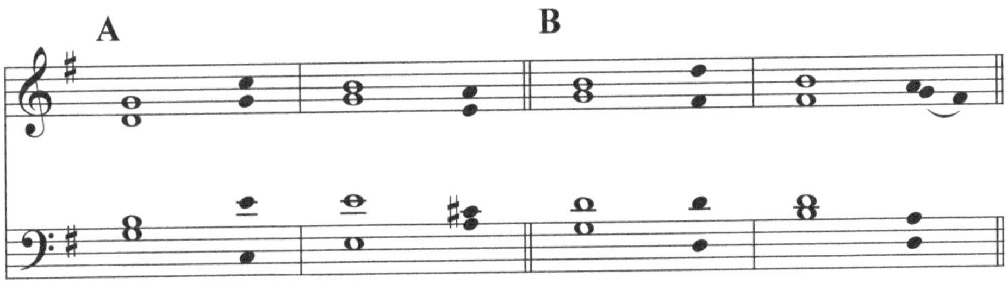

1 May God be merciful to us and bless us, *
show us the light of his countenance and come to us.
2 Let your ways be known upon earth, *
your saving health among all nations. [ANT.]

4 Let the nations be glad and sing for joy, *
for you judge the peoples with equity
and guide all the nations upon earth.
5 Let the peoples praise you, O God; *
let all the peoples praise you. [ANT.]

6 The earth has brought forth her increase; *
may God, our own God, give us his blessing.
7 May God give us his blessing, *
and may all the ends of the earth stand in awe of him. [ANT.]

RCL Proper 16A (C Track) Psalm 124

based on "Old 124th" (H82–149)

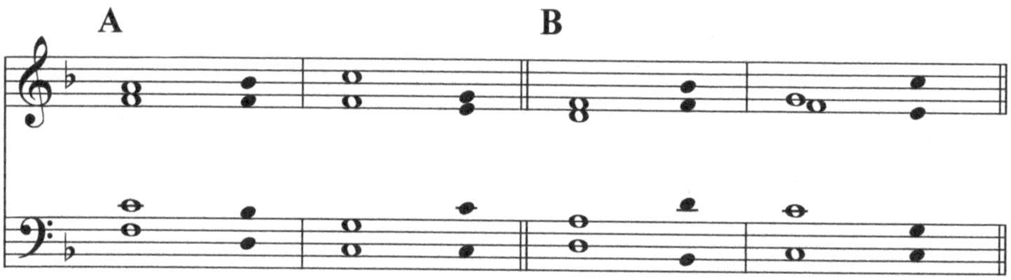

A 1 If the LORD had not been on our side, *
let Israel now say;
B 2 If the LORD had not been on our side, *
when enemies rose up against us;
A 3 Then would they have swallowed us up alive *
in their fierce anger toward us; [ANT.]

4 Then would the waters have overwhelmed us *
and the torrent gone over us;
5 Then would the raging waters *
have gone right over us. [ANT.]

A 6 Blessed be the LORD! *
he has not given us over to be a prey for their teeth.
A 7 We have escaped like a bird from the snare of the fowler; *
the snare is broken, and we have escaped.
B 8 Our help is in the Name of the LORD, *
the maker of heaven and earth. [ANT.]

RCL Proper 16A (G Track) **Psalm 138**

based on "Ton-y-Botel" (H82–381)

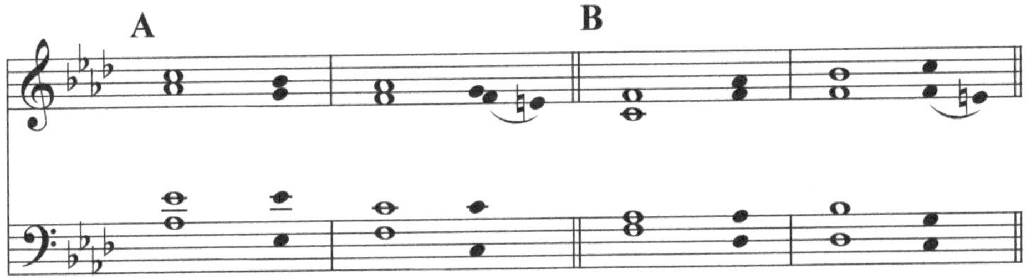

A 1 I will give thanks to you, O LORD, with my whole heart; *
before the gods I will sing your praise.
A 2 I will bow down toward your holy temple
and praise your Name, *
because of your love and faithfulness;
B 3 For you have glorified your Name *
and your word above all things. [ANT.]

A 4 When I called, you answered me; *
you increased my strength within me.
A 5 All the kings of the earth will praise you, O LORD, *
when they have heard the words of your mouth.
B 6 They will sing of the ways of the LORD, *
that great is the glory of the LORD. [ANT.]

A 7 Though the LORD be high, he cares for the lowly; *
he perceives the haughty from afar.
A 8 Though I walk in the midst of trouble, you keep me safe; *
you stretch forth your hand against the fury of my enemies;
your right hand shall save me.
B 9 The LORD will make good his purpose for me; *
O LORD, your love endures for ever;
do not abandon the works of your hands. [ANT.]

RCL Proper 17A (C Track) Psalm 105: 1–6, 23–26, 45b

based on "Hanover" (H82–388)

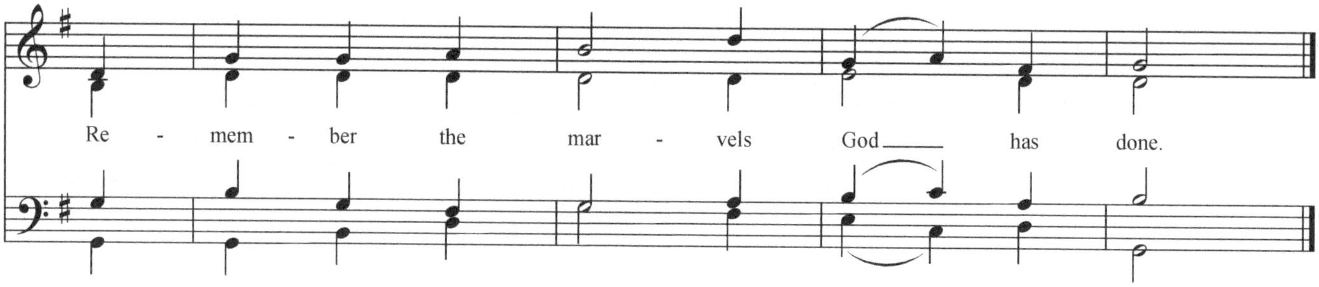

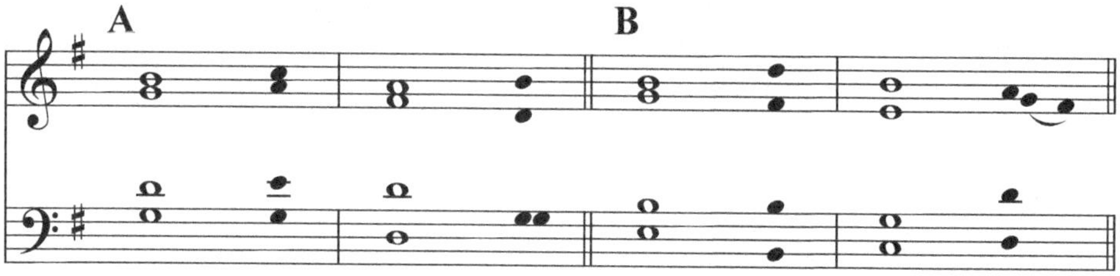

A 1 Give thanks to the LORD and call upon his Name; *
make known his deeds among the peoples.
A 2 Sing to him, sing praises to him, *
and speak of all his marvelous works.
B 3 Glory in his holy Name; *
let the hearts of those who seek the Lord rejoice. [ANT.]

A 4 Search for the LORD and his strength; *
continually seek his face.
A 5 Remember the marvels he has done, *
his wonders and the judgments of his mouth,
B 6 O offspring of Abraham his servant, *
O children of Jacob his chosen. [ANT.]

A 23 Israel came into Egypt, *
and Jacob became a sojourner in the land of Ham.
B 24 The Lord made his people exceedingly fruitful; *
he made them stronger than their enemies;
A 25 Whose heart he turned, so that they hated his people, *
and dealt unjustly with his servants.
B 26 He sent Moses his servant, *
and Aaron whom he had chosen.
[45b.] Hallelujah! [ANT.]

RCL Proper 17A (G Track) Psalm 26: 1–8

based on "Repton" (H82–653)

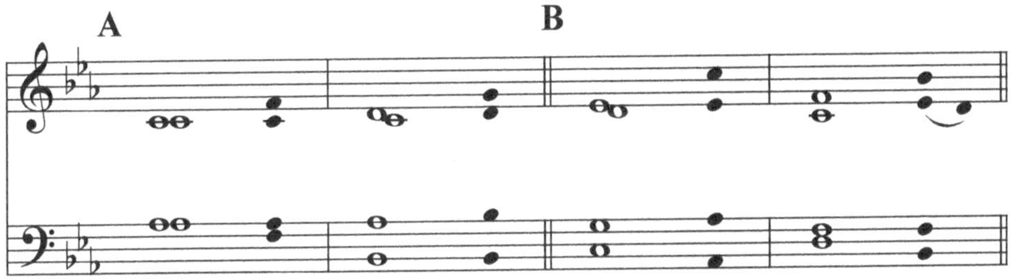

1 Give judgment for me, O LORD,
for I have lived with integrity; *
I have trusted in the Lord and have not faltered.
2 Test me, O LORD, and try me; *
examine my heart and my mind. [ANT.]

A 3 For your love is before my eyes; *
I have walked faithfully with you.
A 4 I have not sat with the worthless, *
nor do I consort with the deceitful.
B 5 I have hated the company of evildoers; *
I will not sit down with the wicked. [ANT.]

A 6 I will wash my hands in innocence, O LORD, *
that I may go in procession round your altar,
A 7 Singing aloud a song of thanksgiving *
and recounting all your wonderful deeds.
B 8 LORD, I love the house in which you dwell *
and the place where your glory abides. [ANT.]

RCL Proper 18A (C Track) Psalm 149

based on "Mit Freuden zart" (H82–408)

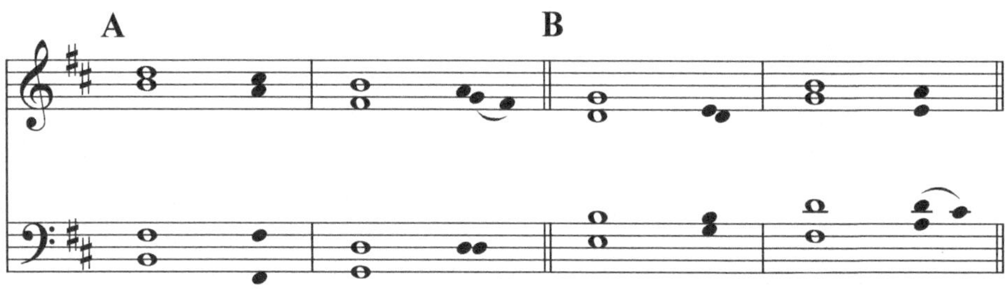

A 1 Hallelujah!
Sing to the LORD a new song; *
sing his praise in the congregation of the faithful.
A 2 Let Israel rejoice in his Maker; *
let the children of Zion be joyful in their King.
B 3 Let them praise his Name in the dance; *
let them sing praise to him with timbrel and harp. [ANT.]

4 For the LORD takes pleasure in his people *
and adorns the poor with victory.
5 Let the faithful rejoice in triumph; *
let them be joyful on their beds. [ANT.]

6 Let the praises of God be in their throat *
and a two-edged sword in their hand;
7 To wreak vengeance on the nations *
and punishment on the peoples; [ANT.]

8 To bind their kings in chains *
and their nobles with links of iron;
9 To inflict on them the judgment decreed; *
this is glory for all his faithful people.
Hallelujah! [ANT.]

RCL Proper 18A (G Track) Psalm 119: 33–40

based on "Cwm Rhondda" (H82–690)

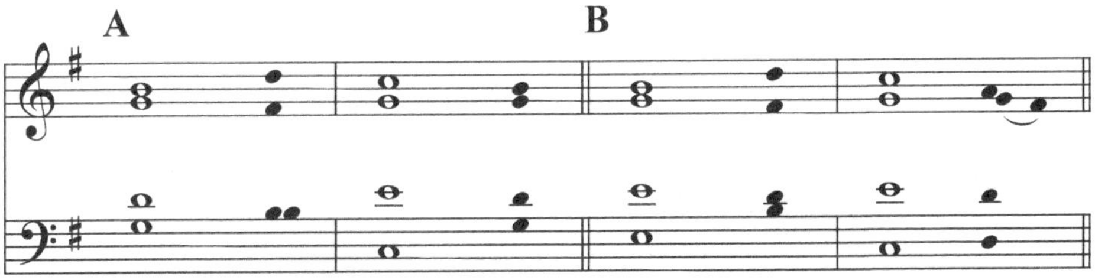

33 Teach me, O LORD, the way of your statutes, *
and I shall keep it to the end.
34 Give me understanding, and I shall keep your law; *
I shall keep it with all my heart. [ANT.]

35 Make me go in the path of your commandments, *
for that is my desire.
36 Incline my heart to your decrees *
and not to unjust gain. [ANT.]

37 Turn my eyes from watching what is worthless; *
give me life in your ways.
38 Fulfill your promise to your servant, *
which you make to those who fear you. [ANT.]

39 Turn away the reproach which I dread, *
because your judgments are good.
40 Behold, I long for your commandments; *
in your righteousness preserve my life. [ANT.]

RCL Proper 19A (C Track) Psalm 114

based on "Ton-y-Botel" (H82–381, 527)

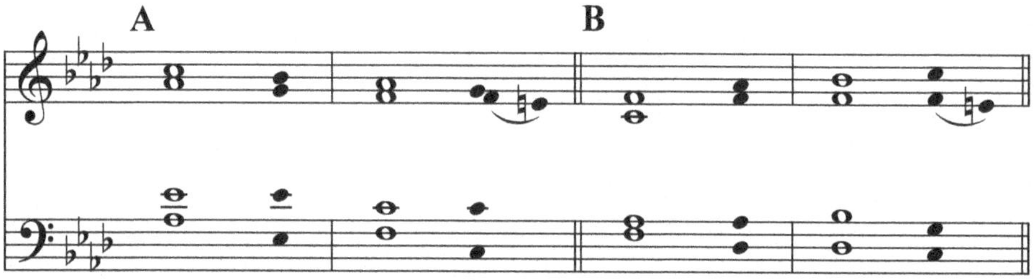

1 Hallelujah!
When Israel came out of Egypt, *
the house of Jacob from a people of strange speech,
2 Judah became God's sanctuary *
and Israel his dominion. [ANT.]

3 The sea beheld it and fled; *
Jordan turned and went back.
4 The mountains skipped like rams, *
and the little hills like young sheep. [ANT.]

5 What ailed you, O sea, that you fled? *
O Jordan, that you turned back?
6 You mountains, that you skipped like rams? *
you little hills like young sheep? [ANT.]

7 Tremble, O earth, at the presence of the LORD, *
at the presence of the God of Jacob,
8 Who turned the hard rock into a pool of water *
and flint-stone into a flowing spring. [ANT.]

This page intentionally left blank

RCL Proper 19A (C Track, alt.) **The Songs of Moses and Miriam** (Exodus 15: 1b–11, 20–21)

based on "Go down, Moses" (H82–636)

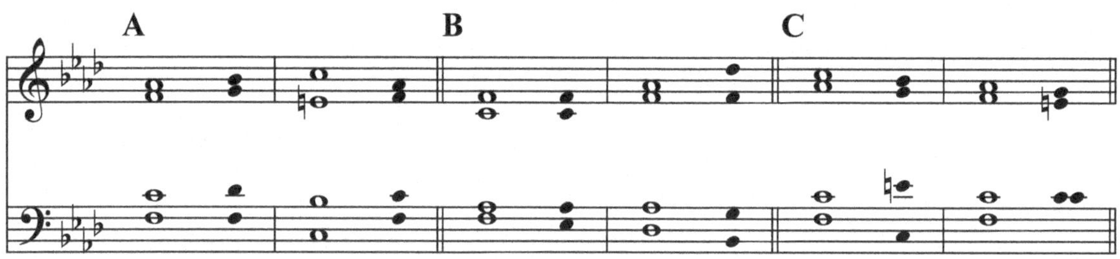

The text is found on the following page.

A God is my strength and my song *
and has become my salvation.
B Let me glorify this God of mine! *
Let me magnify this God of my ancestors!
C For valiant in battle is the God *
whose holy name is The LORD. [ANT.]

A The chariots and troops of Pharoah *
were thrown into the sea;
B even the handpicked commanders *
went down in the Red Sea waves.
C The flood covered them over, *
and they sank into the depths like a stone. [ANT.]

A Your right hand, so glorious in battle, *
your right hand, O LORD, shattered the foe.
C In triumph you tumbled your adversaries; *
your fire consumed them like stubble.
A The blast of your breath piled up the waters: *
the floods stood up like a towering wall;
C in the very heart of the sea, *
the murky depths congealed. [ANT.]

A "I will chase and catch them!" crowed the enemy; *
"I will plunder and fulfill my lust;
C I will unsheath my sharpened sword *
and destroy them by my own hand."
A Then you blew forth a mighty tempest *
and the sea swallowed them up
B so that they plummeted like lead *
in the billows that brought you glory.
C Who among the gods is mighty like you, O LORD? *
Who is sovereign and awesome like you,
a powerful worker of wonders? [ANT.]

A Then Miriam the prophet, the sister of Aaron, *
raised a tambourine in her hand,
B and all the women danced after her with their tambourines *
while Miriam led the song:
C "Sing to the LORD, the Exalted One, *
who hurled horse and rider into the sea." [ANT.]

RCL Proper 19A (G Track) Psalm 103: (1–7), 8–13

based on "Wondrous Love" (H82–439)

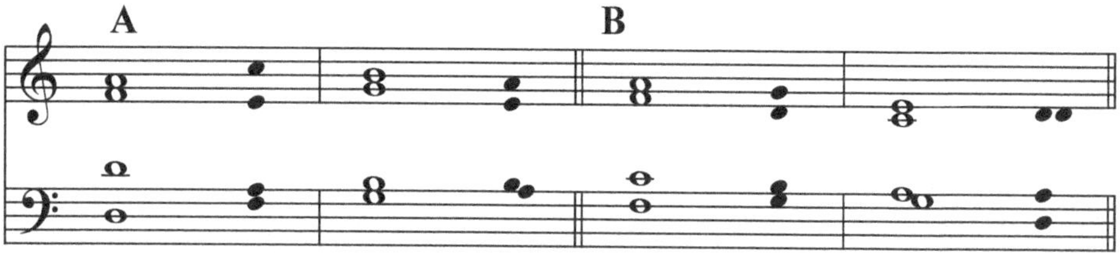

(1 Bless the LORD, O my soul, *
and all that is within me, bless his holy Name.
2 Bless the LORD, O my soul, *
and forget not all his benefits. [ANT.]

3 He forgives all your sins *
and heals all your infirmities;
4 He redeems your life from the grave *
and crowns you with mercy and loving-kindness; [ANT.]

A 5 He satisfies you with good things, *
and your youth is renewed like an eagle's.
A 6 The LORD executes righteousness *
and judgment for all who are oppressed.
B 7 He made his ways known to Moses *
and his works to the children of Israel. [ANT.])

9 He will not always accuse us, *
nor will he keep his anger for ever.
10 He has not dealt with us according to our sins, *
nor rewarded us according to our wickedness. [ANT.]

A 11 For as the heavens are high above the earth, *
so is his mercy great upon those who fear him.
A 12 As far as the east is from the west, *
so far has he removed our sins from us.
B 13 As a father cares for his children, *
so does the LORD care for those who fear him. [ANT.]

RCL Proper 20A (C Track) Psalm 105: 1–6, 37–45

based on "Hanover" (H82–388)

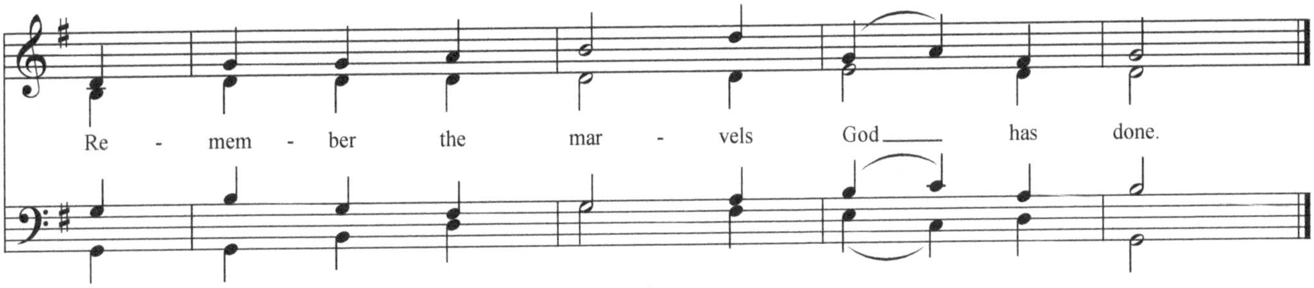

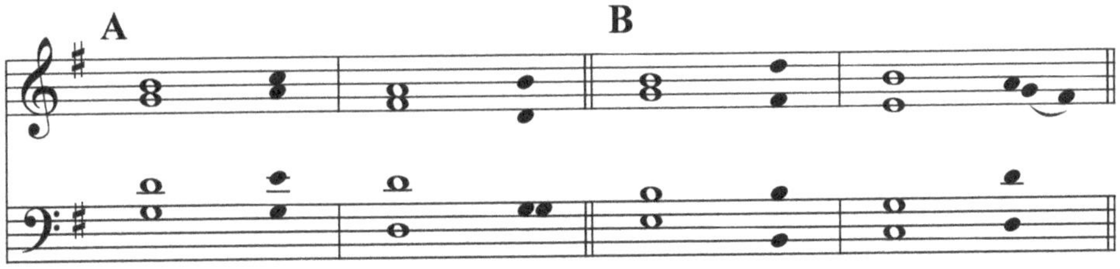

A 1 Give thanks to the LORD and call upon his Name; *
make known his deeds among the peoples.
A 2 Sing to him, sing praises to him, *
and speak of all his marvelous works.
B 3 Glory in his holy Name; *
let the hearts of those who seek the Lord rejoice. [ANT.]

A 4 Search for the LORD and his strength; *
continually seek his face.
A 5 Remember the marvels he has done, *
his wonders and the judgments of his mouth,
B 6 O offspring of Abraham his servant, *
O children of Jacob his chosen. [ANT.]

37 He led out his people with silver and gold; *
in all their tribes there was not one that stumbled.
38 Egypt was glad of their going, *
because they were afraid of them. [ANT.]

A 39 He spread out a cloud for a covering *
and a fire to give light in the night season.
A 40 They asked, and quails appeared, *
and he satisfied them with bread from heaven.
B 41 He opened the rock, and water flowed, *
so the river ran in the dry places. [ANT.]

A 42 For God remembered his holy word *
and Abraham his servant.
B 43 So he led forth his people with gladness, *
his chosen with shouts of joy.
A 44 He gave his people the lands of the nations, *
and they took the fruit of others' toil,
B 45 That they might keep his statutes *
and observe his laws.
Hallelujah! [ANT.]

RCL Proper 20A (G Track) Psalm 145: 1–8

based on "Foundation" (H82–636)

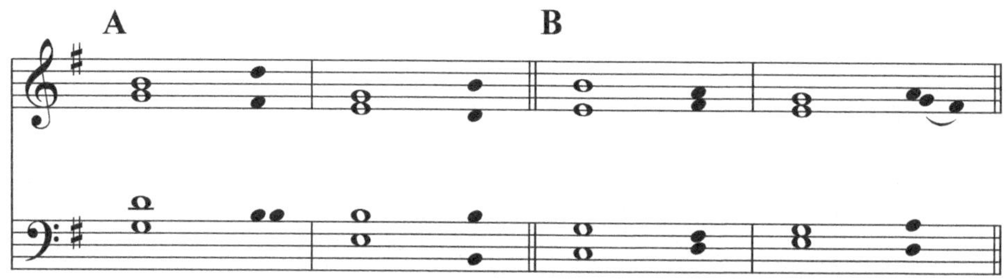

1 I will exalt you, O God my King, *
and bless your Name for ever and ever.
2 Every day will I bless you *
and praise your Name for ever and ever. [ANT.]

3 Great is the LORD and greatly to be praised; *
there is no end to his greatness.
4 One generation shall praise your works to another *
and shall declare your power. [ANT.]

5 I will ponder the glorious splendor of your majesty *
and all your marvelous works.
6 They shall speak of the might of your wondrous acts, *
and I will tell of your greatness. [ANT.]

7 They shall publish the remembrance of your great goodness; *
they shall sing of your righteous deeds.
8 The LORD is gracious and full of compassion, *
slow to anger and of great kindness. [ANT.]

RCL Proper 21A (C Track) Psalm 78: 1–4, 12–16

based on "Song 1" (H82–499)

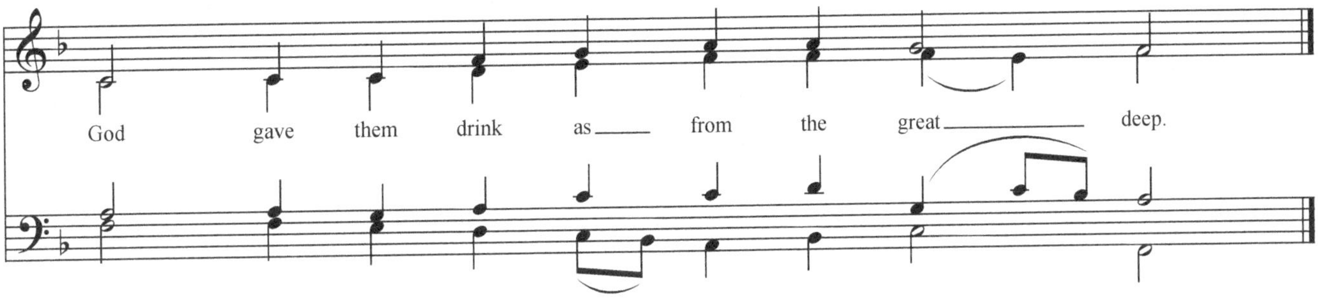

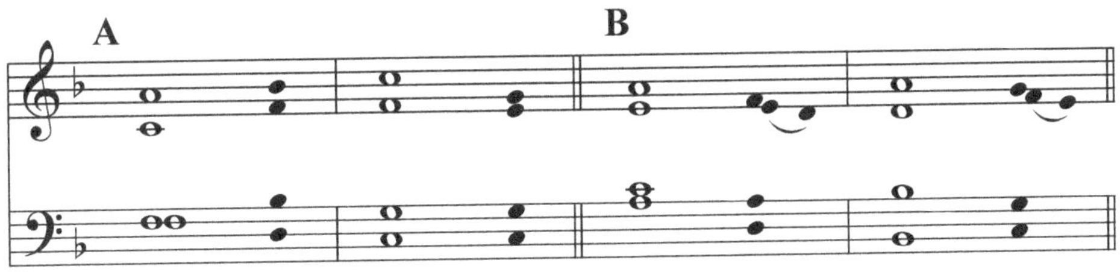

1 Hear my teaching, O my people; *
incline your ears to the words of my mouth.
2 I will open my mouth in a parable; *
I will declare the mysteries of ancient times. [ANT.]

3 That which we have heard and known,
and what our forefathers have told us, *
we will not hide from their children.
4 We will recount to generations to come
the praiseworthy deeds and the power of the LORD, *
and the wonderful works he has done. [ANT.]

12 He worked marvels in the sight of their forefathers, *
in the land of Egypt, in the field of Zoan.
13 He split open the sea and let them pass through; *
he made the waters stand up like walls. [ANT.]

A 14 He led them with a cloud by day, *
and all the night through with a glow of fire.
A 15 He split the hard rocks in the wilderness *
and gave them drink as from the great deep.
B 16 He brought streams out of the cliff, *
and the waters gushed out like rivers. [ANT.]

RCL Proper 21A (G Track) Psalm 25: 1–8

based on "Leoni" (H82–401)

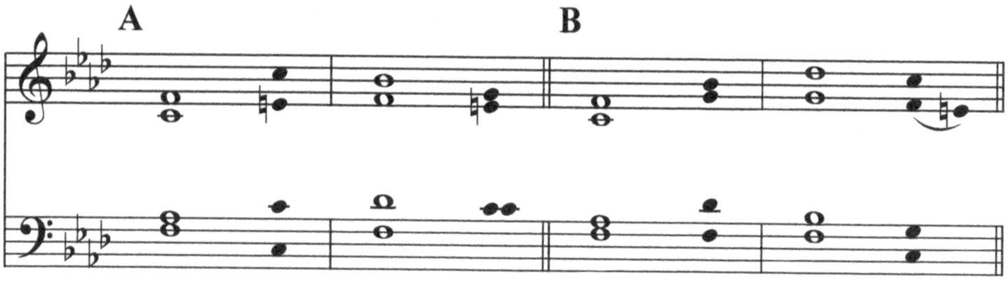

1 To you, O LORD, I lift up my soul;
my God, I put my trust in you; *
let me not be humiliated,
nor let my enemies triumph over me.
2 Let none who look to you be put to shame; *
let the treacherous be disappointed in their schemes. [ANT.]

3 Show me your ways, O LORD, *
and teach me your paths.
4 Lead me in your truth and teach me, *
for you are the God of my salvation;
in you have I trusted all the day long. [ANT.]

5 Remember, O LORD, your compassion and love, *
for they are from everlasting.
6 Remember not the sins of my youth and my transgressions; *
remember me according to your love
and for the sake of your goodness, O LORD. [ANT.]

7 Gracious and upright is the LORD; *
therefore he teaches sinners in his way.
8 He guides the humble in doing right *
and teaches his way to the lowly. [ANT.]

RCL Proper 22A (C Track) Psalm 19

based on "Song 1" (H82–499)

A 1 The heavens declare the glory of God, *
and the firmament shows his handiwork.
B 2 One day tells its tale to another, *
and one night imparts knowledge to another.
A 3 Although they have no words or language, *
and their voices are not heard,
B 4 Their sound has gone out into all lands, *
and their message to the ends of the world. [ANT.]

5 In the deep has he set a pavilion for the sun; *
it comes forth like a bridegroom out of his chamber;
it rejoices like a champion to run its course.
6 It goes forth from the uttermost edge of the heavens
and runs about to the end of it again; *
nothing is hidden from its burning heat. [ANT.]

7 The law of the LORD is perfect
and revives the soul; *
the testimony of the LORD is sure
and gives wisdom to the innocent.
8 The statutes of the LORD are just
and rejoice the heart; *
the commandment of the LORD is clear
and gives light to the eyes. [ANT.]

9 The fear of the LORD is clean
and endures for ever; *
the judgments of the LORD are true
and righteous altogether.
10 More to be desired are they than gold,
more than much fine gold, *
sweeter far than honey,
than honey in the comb. [ANT.]

11 By them also is your servant enlightened, *
and in keeping them there is great reward.
12 Who can tell how often he offends? *
cleanse me from my secret faults. [ANT.]

13 Above all, keep your servant from presumptuous sins;
let them not get dominion over me; *
then shall I be whole and sound,
and innocent of a great offense.
14 Let the words of my mouth and the meditation of my
heart be acceptable in your sight, *
O LORD, my strength and my redeemer. [ANT.]

RCL Proper 22A (G Track) Psalm 80: 7–14

based on "Picardy" (H82–324)

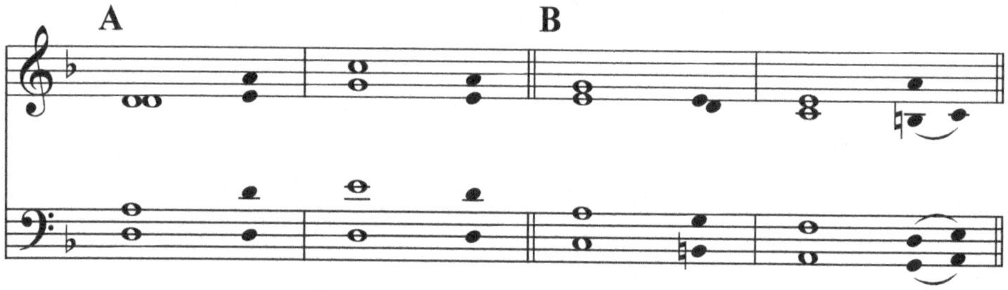

7 Restore us, O God of hosts; *
show the light of your countenance, and we shall be saved.
8 You have brought a vine out of Egypt; *
you cast out the nations and planted it. [ANT.]

A 9 You prepared the ground for it; *
it took root and filled the land.
A 10 The mountains were covered by its shadow *
and the towering cedar trees by its boughs.
B 11 You stretched out its tendrils to the Sea *
and its branches to the River. [ANT.]

A 12 Why have you broken down its wall, *
so that all who pass by pluck off its grapes?
A 13 The wild boar of the forest has ravaged it, *
and the beasts of the field have grazed upon it.
B 14 Turn now, O God of hosts, look down from heaven;
behold and tend this vine; *
preserve what your right hand has planted. [ANT.]

RCL Proper 23A (C Track) Psalm 106: 1–6, 19–23

based on "Rouen" (H82–360)

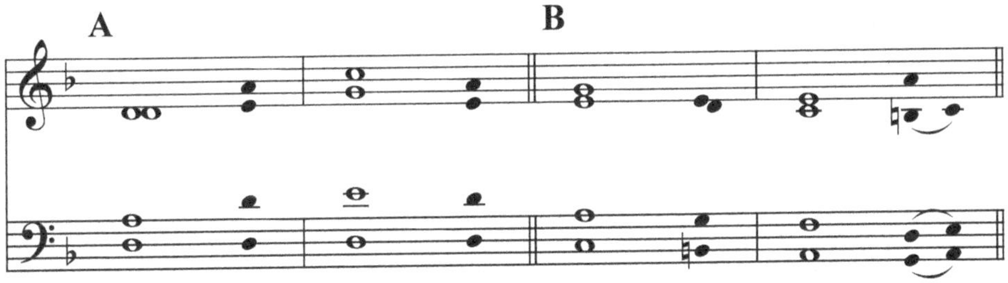

A 1 Hallelujah!
Give thanks to the LORD, for he is good, *
for his mercy endures for ever.
A 2 Who can declare the mighty acts of the LORD *
or show forth all his praise?
3 Happy are those who act with justice *
B and always do what is right! [ANT.]

4 Remember me, O LORD, with the favor you have
for your people, *
and visit me with your saving help;
5 That I may see the prosperity of your elect
and be glad with the gladness of your people, *
that I may glory with your inheritance. [ANT.]

A 6 We have sinned as our forebears did; *
we have done wrong and dealt wickedly.
A 19 Israel made a bull-calf at Horeb *
and worshiped a molten image;
B 20 And so they exchanged their Glory *
for the image of an ox that feeds on grass. [ANT.]

A 21 They forgot God their Savior, *
who had done great things in Egypt,
A 22 Wonderful deeds in the land of Ham, *
and fearful things at the Red Sea.
B 23 So he would have destroyed them,
had not Moses his chosen stood before him in the breach, *
to turn away his wrath from consuming them. [ANT.]

RCL Proper 23A (G Track) Psalm 23

based on "St. Columba" (H82–645)

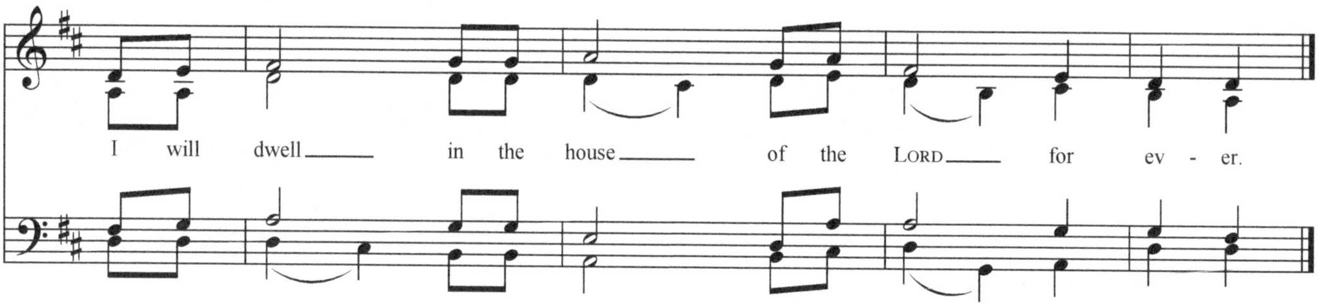

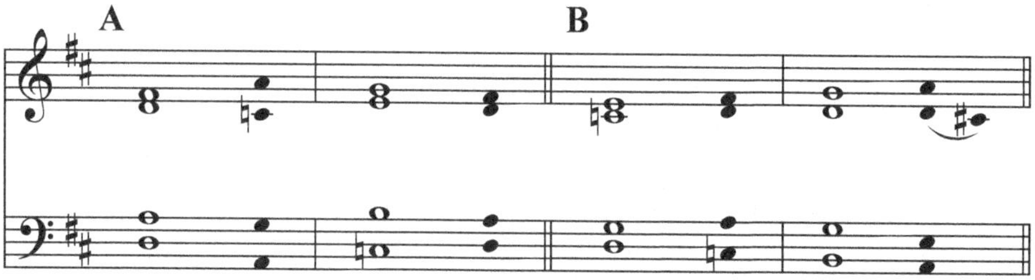

1 The LORD is my shepherd; *
  I shall not be in want.
2 He makes me lie down in green pastures *
  and leads me beside still waters. [ANT.]

3 He revives my soul *
  and guides me along right pathways for his Name's sake.
4 Though I walk through the valley of the shadow of death,
  I shall fear no evil; *
  for you are with me;
  your rod and your staff, they comfort me. [ANT.]

5 You spread a table before me in the presence of those who trouble me; *
  you have anointed my head with oil,
  and my cup is running over.
6 Surely your goodness and mercy shall follow me all the days of my life, *
  and I will dwell in the house of the LORD for ever. [ANT.]

RCL Proper 24A (C Track) Psalm 99

based on "Old 124th" (H82–149)

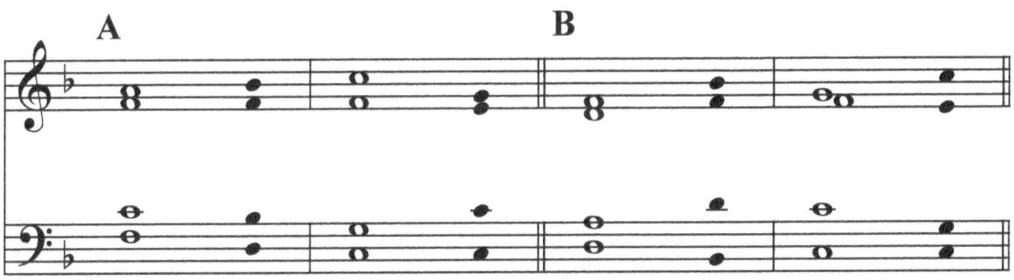

A 1 The LORD is King;
let the people tremble; *
he is enthroned upon the cherubim;
let the earth shake.
A 2 The LORD is great in Zion; *
he is high above all peoples.
B 3 Let them confess his Name, which is great and awesome; *
he is the Holy One. [ANT.]

4 "O mighty King, lover of justice,
you have established equity; *
you have executed justice and righteousness in Jacob."
5 Proclaim the greatness of the LORD our God
and fall down before his footstool; *
he is the Holy One. [ANT.]

6 Moses and Aaron among his priests,
and Samuel among those who call upon his Name, *
they called upon the LORD, and he answered them.
7 He spoke to them out of the pillar of cloud; *
they kept his testimonies and the decree that he gave them. [ANT.]

8 "O LORD our God, you answered them indeed; *
you were a God who forgave them,
yet punished them for their evil deeds."
9 Proclaim the greatness of the LORD our God
and worship him upon his holy hill; *
for the LORD our God is the Holy One. [ANT.]

RCL Proper 24A (G Track) Psalm 96: 1–9, (10–13)

based on "Old 104th" (H82–532)

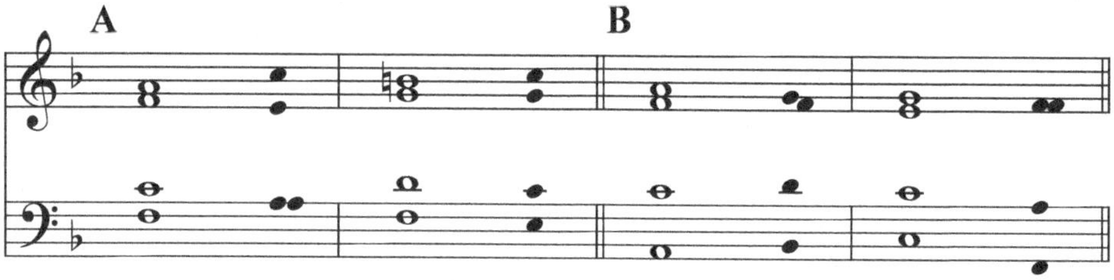

1 Sing to the LORD a new song; *
sing to the LORD, all the whole earth.
2 Sing to the LORD and bless his Name; *
proclaim the good news of his salvation from day to day. [ANT.]

3 Declare his glory among the nations *
and his wonders among all peoples.
4 For great is the LORD and greatly to be praised; *
he is more to be feared than all gods. [ANT.]

5 As for all the gods of the nations, they are but idols; *
but it is the LORD who made the heavens.
6 Oh, the majesty and magnificence of his presence! *
Oh, the power and the splendor of his sanctuary! [ANT.]

A 7 Ascribe to the LORD, you families of the peoples; *
ascribe to the LORD honor and power.
A 8 Ascribe to the LORD the honor due his Name; *
bring offerings and come into his courts.
B 9 Worship the LORD in the beauty of holiness; *
let the whole earth tremble before him. [ANT.]

(10 Tell it out among the nations: "The LORD is King! *
he has made the world so firm that it cannot be moved;
he will judge the peoples with equity."
11 Let the heavens rejoice, and let the earth be glad;
let the sea thunder and all that is in it; *
let the field be joyful and all that is therein. [ANT.]

12 Then shall all the trees of the wood shout for joy
before the LORD when he comes, *
when he comes to judge the earth.
13 He will judge the world with righteousness *
and the peoples with his truth. [ANT.])

RCL Proper 25A (C Track) Psalm 90: 1–6, 13–17

based on "O quanta qualia" (H82–623)

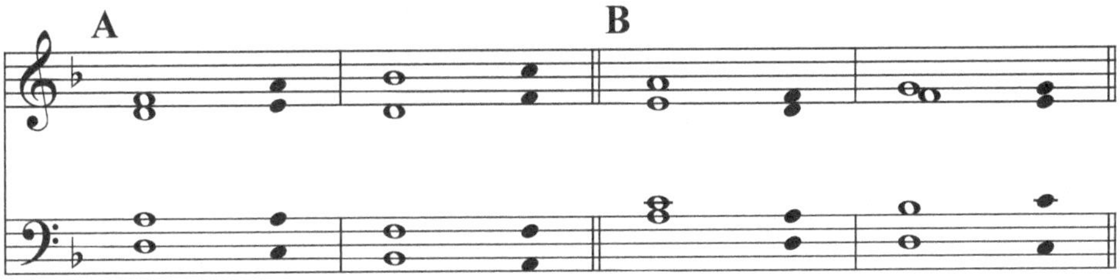

1 Lord, you have been our refuge *
from one generation to another.
2 Before the mountains were brought forth,
or the land and the earth were born, *
from age to age you are God. [ANT.]

3 You turn us back to the dust and say, *
"Go back, O child of earth."
4 For a thousand years in your sight are like yesterday
when it is past *
and like a watch in the night. [ANT.]

5 You sweep us away like a dream; *
we fade away suddenly like the grass.
6 In the morning it is green and flourishes; *
in the evening it is dried up and withered. [ANT.]

13 Return, O Lord; how long will you tarry? *
be gracious to your servants.
14 Satisfy us by your loving-kindness in the morning; *
so shall we rejoice and be glad all the days of our life. [ANT.]

A 15 Make us glad by the measure of the days that you afflicted us *
and the years in which we suffered adversity.
B 16 Show your servants your works *
and your splendor to their children.
B 17 May the graciousness of the Lord our God be upon us; *
prosper the work of our hands;
prosper our handiwork. [ANT.]

RCL Proper 25A (G Track) Psalm 1

based on "Hymn to Joy" (H82–376)

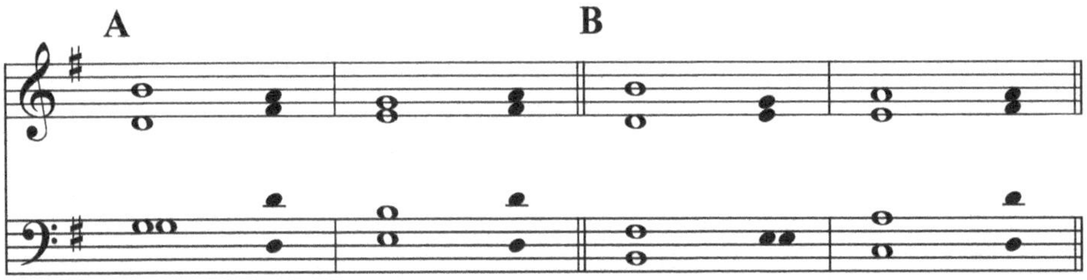

1 Happy are they who have not walked in the counsel of
the wicked, *
nor lingered in the way of sinners,
nor sat in the seats of the scornful!
2 Their delight is in the law of the LORD, *
and they meditate on his law day and night. [ANT.]

3 They are like trees planted by streams of water,
bearing fruit in due season, with leaves that do not wither; *
everything they do shall prosper.
4 It is not so with the wicked; *
they are like chaff which the wind blows away. [ANT.]

5 Therefore the wicked shall not stand upright when
judgment comes, *
nor the sinner in the council of the righteous.
6 For the LORD knows the way of the righteous, *
but the way of the wicked is doomed. [ANT.]

RCL All Saints' Day A   Psalm 34: 1–10, 22

based on "Martyrdom" (H82–658)

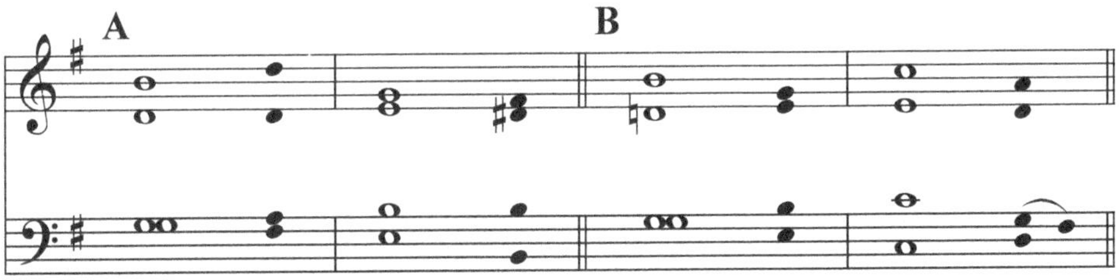

1 I will bless the LORD at all times; *
his praise shall ever be in my mouth.
2 I will glory in the LORD; *
let the humble hear and rejoice. [ANT.]

3 Proclaim with me the greatness of the LORD;
let us exalt his Name together.
4 I sought the LORD, and he answered me *
and delivered me out of all my terror. [ANT.]

5 Look upon him and be radiant, *
and let not your faces be ashamed.
6 I called in my affliction and the LORD heard me *
and saved me from all my troubles. [ANT.]

7 The angel of the LORD encompasses those who fear him, *
and he will deliver them.
8 Taste and see that the LORD is good; *
happy are they who trust in him! [ANT.]

A 9 Fear the LORD, you that are his saints, *
for those who fear him lack nothing *
A 10 The young lions lack and suffer hunger, *
but those who seek the LORD lack nothing that is good.
B 22 The LORD ransoms the life of his servants, *
and none will be punished who trust in him. [ANT.]

RCL Proper 26A (C Track) Psalm 107: 1–7, 33–37

based on "Darwall's 148th" (H82–625)

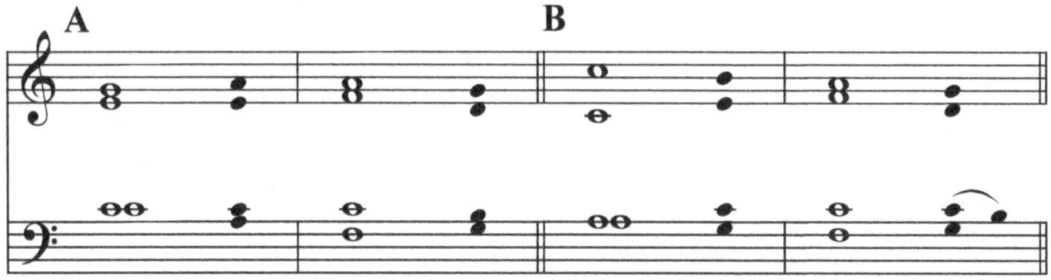

1 Give thanks to the LORD, for he is good, *
and his mercy endures for ever.
2 Let all those whom the LORD has redeemed proclaim *
that he redeemed them from the hand of the foe. [ANT.]

3 He gathered them out of the lands; *
from the east and from the west,
from the north and from the south.
4 Some wandered in desert wastes; *
they found no way to a city where they might dwell. [ANT.]

A 5 They were hungry and thirsty; *
their spirits languished within them.
A 6 Then they cried to the LORD in their trouble, *
and he delivered them from their distress.
B 7 He put their feet on a straight path *
to go to a city where they might dwell. [ANT.]

A 33 The LORD changed rivers into deserts, *
and water-springs into thirsty ground,
A 34 A fruitful land into salt flats, *
because of the wickedness of those who dwell there.
B 35 He changed deserts into pools of water *
and dry land into water-springs. [ANT.]

36 He settled the hungry there, *
and they founded a city to dwell in.
37 They sowed fields, and planted vineyards, *
and brought in a fruitful harvest. [ANT.]

RCL Proper 26A (G Track) Psalm 43

based on "St. Thomas (Williams)" (H82–411)

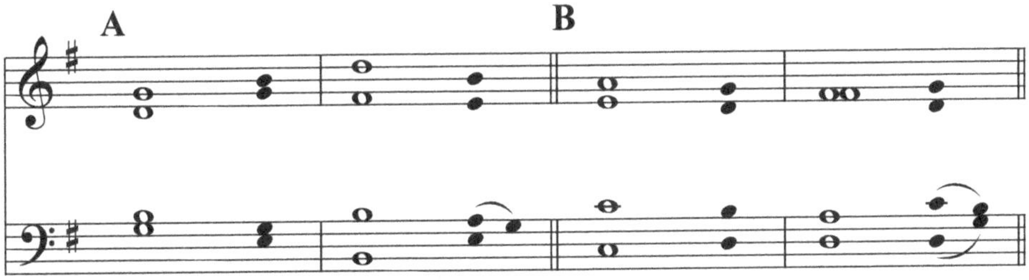

1 Give judgment for me, O God,
and defend my cause against an ungodly people; *
deliver me from the deceitful and the wicked.
2 For you are the God of my strength;
why have you put me from you? *
and why do I go so heavily while the enemy
oppresses me? [ANT.]

3 Send out your light and your truth, that they may lead me, *
and bring me to your holy hill
and to your dwelling;
4 That I may go to the altar of God,
to the God of my joy and gladness; *
and on the harp I will give thanks to you,
O God my God. [ANT.]

5 Why are you so full of heaviness, O my soul? *
and why are you so disquieted within me?
6 Put your trust in God; *
for I will yet give thanks to him,
who is the help of my countenance, and my God. [ANT.]

RCL Proper 27A (C Track) Psalm 78: 1–7

based on "Song 1" (H82–499)

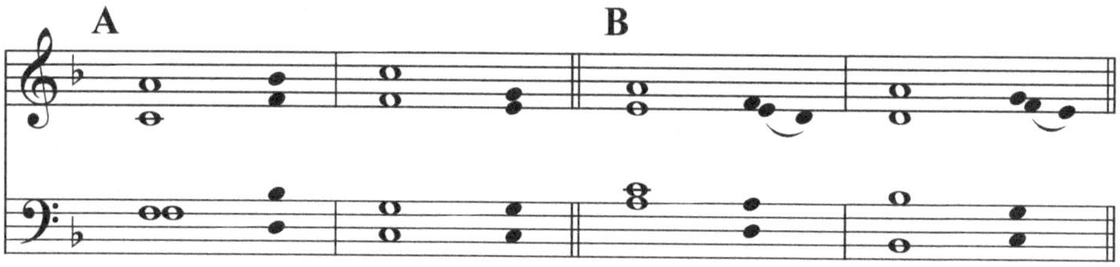

1 Hear my teaching, O my people; *
incline your ears to the words of my mouth.
2 I will open my mouth in a parable; *
I will declare the mysteries of ancient times. [ANT.]

3 That which we have heard and known,
and what our forefathers have told us, *
we will not hide from their children.
4 We will recount to generations to come
the praiseworthy deeds and the power of the LORD, *
and the wonderful works he has done. [ANT.]

A 5 He gave his decrees to Jacob
and established a law for Israel, *
which he commanded them to teach their children;
A 6 That the generations to come might know,
and the children yet unborn; *
that they in their turn might tell it to their children;
B 7 So that they might put their trust in God, *
and not forget the deeds of God,
but keep his commandments. [ANT.]

RCL Proper 27A (C Track, alt.)

A Song of the Love of Wisdom (Wisdom of Solomon 6: 17–20)

based on "Adoro devote" (H82–314)

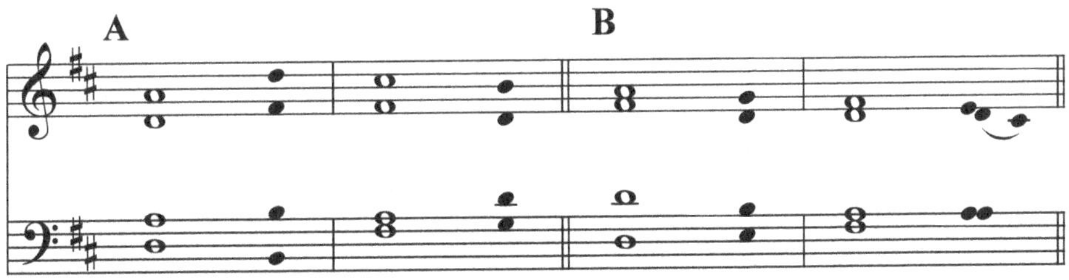

The beginning of wisdom is the true desire to receive teaching,
 and a longing to be taught comes from a love of her;
the one who loves her
 will keep her laws. [ANT.]

Observing the laws of wisdom assures immortality,
 and immortality brings one nearer still to God;
so the desire for wisdom
 leads to the authority of one who rules. [ANT.]

RCL Proper 27A (G Track) Psalm 70

based on "Balm in Gilead" (H82–676)

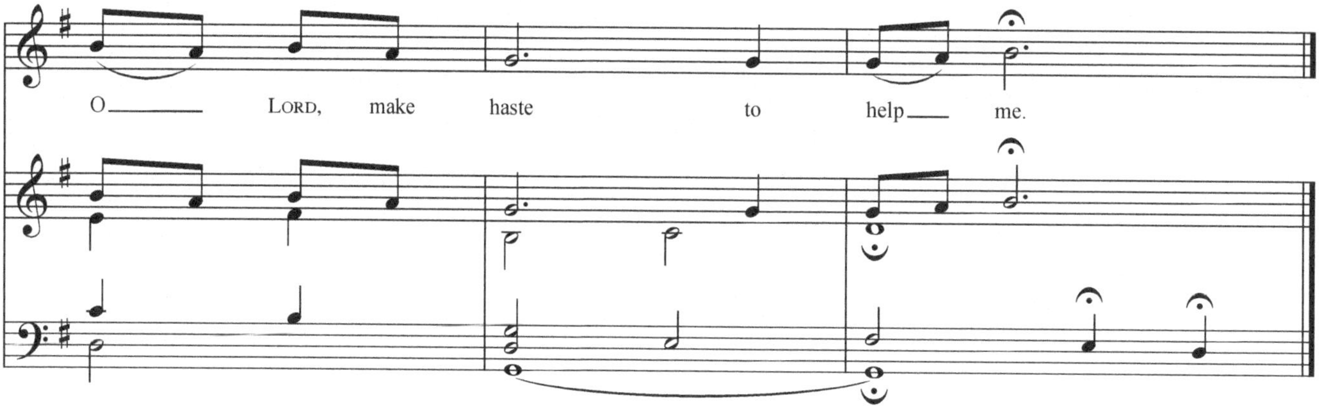

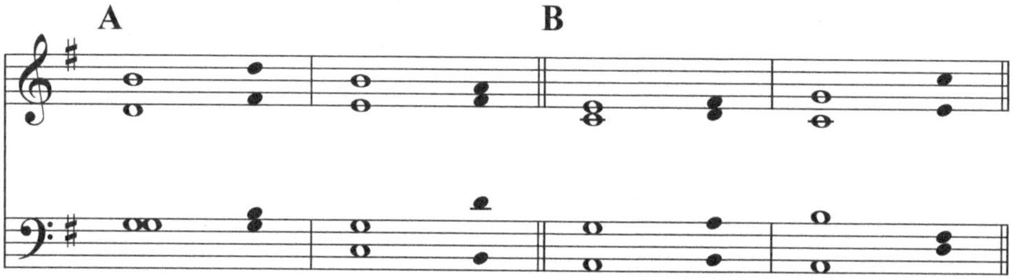

1 Be pleased, O God, to deliver me; *
O Lord, make haste to help me.
2 Let those who seek my life be ashamed
and altogether dismayed; *
let those who take pleasure in my misfortune
draw back and be disgraced. [ANT.]

3 Let those who say to me "Aha!" and gloat over me turn back, *
because they are ashamed.
4 Let all who seek you rejoice and be glad in you; *
let those who love your salvation say for ever,
"Great is the Lord!" [ANT.]

5 But as for me, I am poor and needy; *
come to me speedily, O God.
6 You are my helper and my deliverer; *
O Lord, do not tarry. [ANT.]

RCL Proper 28A (C Track) Psalm 123

based on "Pleading Savior" (H82–586)

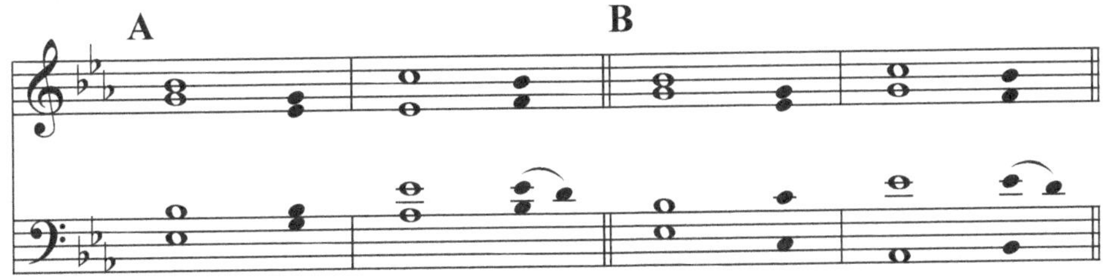

A 1 To you I lift up my eyes, *
to you enthroned in the heavens.

A 2 As the eyes of servants look to the hand of their masters, *
and the eyes of a maid to the hand of her mistress,

B 3 So our eyes look to the LORD our God, *
until he show us his mercy. [ANT.]

4 Have mercy upon us, O LORD, have mercy, *
for we have had more than enough of contempt,

5 Too much of the scorn of the indolent rich, *
and of the derision of the proud. [ANT.]

RCL Proper 28A (G Track) Psalm 90: 1–12

based on "O quanta qualia" (H82–623)

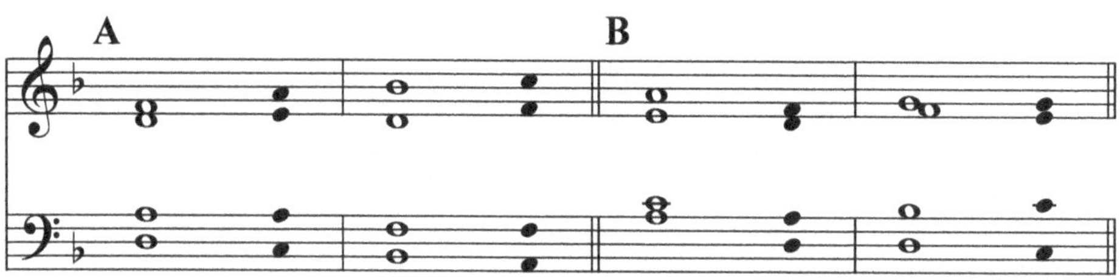

1 LORD, you have been our refuge *
from one generation to another.
2 Before the mountains were brought forth,
or the land and the earth were born, *
from age to age you are God. [ANT.]

3 You turn us back to the dust and say, *
"Go back, O child of earth."
4 For a thousand years in your sight are like yesterday
when it is past *
and like a watch in the night. [ANT.]

5 You sweep us away like a dream; *
we fade away suddenly like the grass.
6 In the morning it is green and flourishes; *
in the evening it is dried up and withered. [ANT.]

A 7 For we consume away in your displeasure; *
we are afraid because of your wrathful indignation.
A 8 Our iniquities you have set before you, *
and our secret sins in the light of your countenance.
B 9 When you are angry, all our days are gone; *
we bring our years to an end like a sigh. [ANT.]

A 10 The span of our life is seventy years,
perhaps in strength even eighty; *
yet the sum of them is but labor and sorrow,
for they pass away quickly and we are gone.
A 11 Who regards the power of your wrath? *
who rightly fears your indignation?
B 12 So teach us to number our days *
that we may apply our hearts to wisdom. [ANT.]

RCL Proper 29A (C Track) Psalm 100

based on "Old 100th" (H82–377)

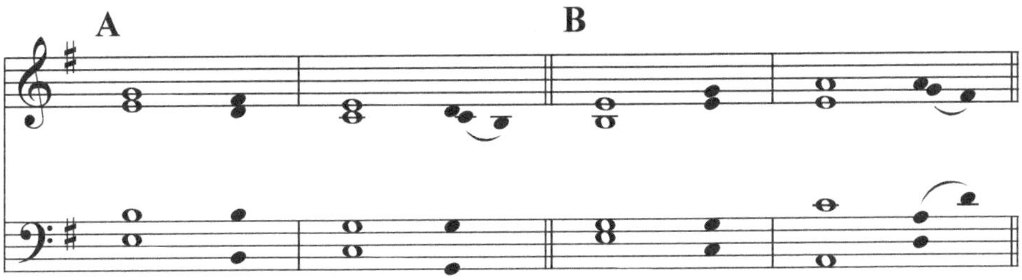

1 Be joyful in the LORD, all you lands; *
serve the LORD with gladness
and come before his presence with a song.
2 Know this: The LORD himself is God; *
he himself has made us, and we are his;
we are his people and the sheep of his pasture. [ANT.]

3 Enter his gates with thanksgiving;
go into his courts with praise; *
give thanks to him and call upon his Name.
4 For the LORD is good;
his mercy is everlasting; *
and his faithfulness endures from age to age. [ANT.]

RCL Proper 29A (G Track) Psalm 95: 1–7a

based on "Old 124th" (H82–149)

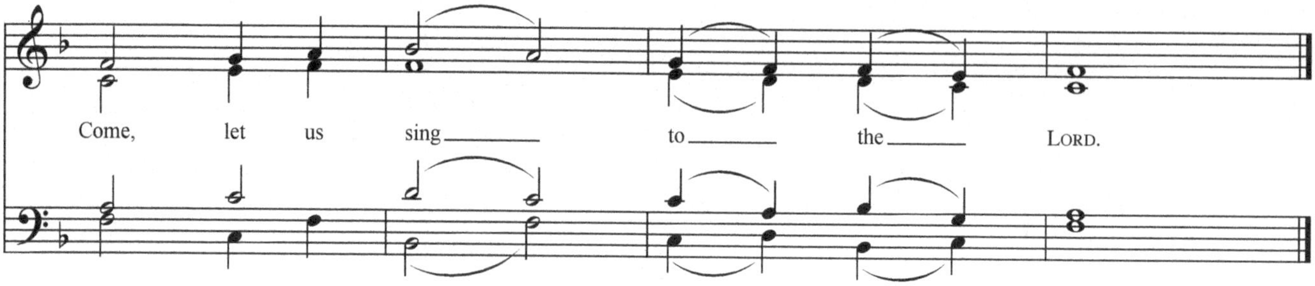

1 Come, let us sing to the LORD; *
let us shout for joy to the Rock of our salvation.
2 Let us come before his presence with thanksgiving *
and raise a loud shout to him with psalms. [ANT.]

A 3 For the LORD is a great God, *
and a great King above all gods.
A 4 In his hand are the caverns of the earth, *
and the heights of the hills are his also.
B 5 The sea is his, for he made it, *
and his hands have molded the dry land. [ANT.]

6 Come, let us bow down, and bend the knee, *
and kneel before the LORD our Maker.
7a For he is our God,
and we are the people of his pasture
and the sheep of his hand. [ANT.]

RCL Year B

Trinity Sunday
through
Proper 29

RCL Trinity Sunday B Psalm 29

based on "Ratisbon" (H82–7)

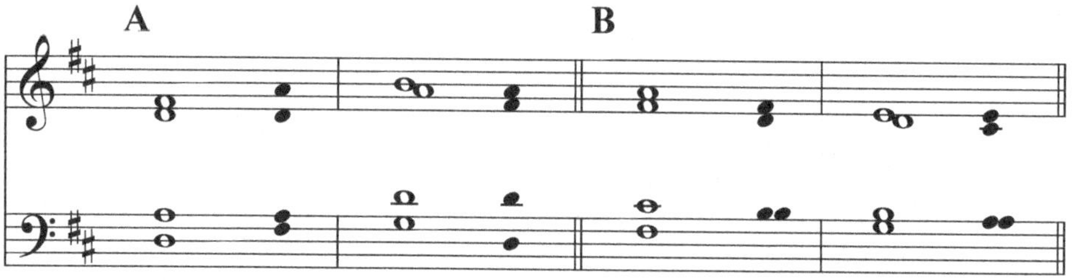

1 Ascribe to the LORD, you gods, *
ascribe to the LORD glory and strength.
2 Ascribe to the LORD the glory due his Name; *
worship the LORD in the beauty of holiness. [ANT.]

A 3 The voice of the LORD is upon the waters;
the God of glory thunders; *
the LORD is upon the mighty waters.
A 4 The voice of the LORD is a powerful voice; *
the voice of the LORD is a voice of splendor.
B 5 The voice of the LORD breaks the cedar trees; *
the LORD breaks the cedars of Lebanon; [ANT.]

6 He makes Lebanon skip like a calf, *
and Mount Hermon like a young wild ox.
7 The voice of the LORD splits the flames of fire;
the voice of the LORD shakes the wilderness; *
the LORD shakes the wilderness of Kadesh. [ANT.]

8 The voice of the LORD makes the oak trees writhe *
and strips the forests bare.
9 And in the temple of the LORD *
all are crying, "Glory!" [ANT.]

10 The LORD sits enthroned above the flood; *
the LORD sits enthroned as King for evermore.
11 The LORD shall give strength to his people; *
the LORD shall give his people the blessing of peace. [ANT.]

RCL Trinity Sunday B Canticle 13

based on "Foundation" (H82–636)

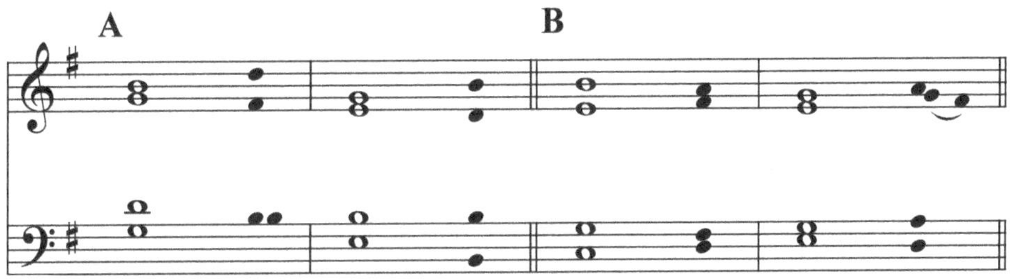

1 Glory to you, Lord God of our fathers; *
you are worthy of praise; glory to you.
2 Glory to you for the radiance of your holy Name; *
we will praise you and highly exalt you for ever. [ANT.]

3 Glory to you in the splendor of your temple; *
on the throne of your majesty, glory to you.
4 Glory to you, seated between the Cherubim; *
we will praise you and highly exalt you for ever. [ANT.]

5 Glory to you, beholding the depths; *
in the high vault of heaven, glory to you.
6 Glory to you, Father, Son, and Holy Spirit; *
we will praise you and highly exalt you for ever. [ANT.]

RCL Proper 1B Psalm 30

based on "Wer nur den lieben Gott" (H82–635)

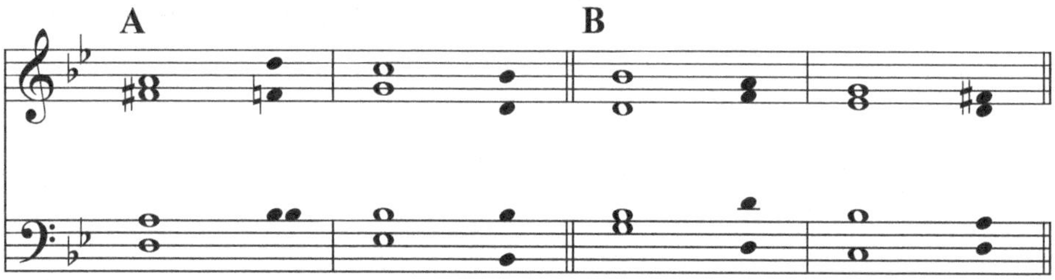

A 1 I will exalt you, O LORD,
because you have lifted me up *
and have not let my enemies triumph over me.
A 2 O LORD my God, I cried out to you, *
and you restored me to health.
B 3 You brought me up, O LORD, from the dead; *
you restored my life as I was going down to the grave. [ANT.]

A 4 Sing to the LORD, you servants of his; *
give thanks for the remembrance of his holiness.
A 5 For his wrath endures but the twinkling of an eye, *
his favor for a lifetime.
B 6 Weeping may spend the night, *
but joy comes in the morning. [ANT.]

7 While I felt secure, I said,
"I shall never be disturbed. *
You, LORD, with your favor, made me as strong as the mountains."
8 Then you hid your face, *
and I was filled with fear. [ANT.]

A 9 I cried to you, O LORD; *
I pleaded with the LORD, saying,
A 10 "What profit is there in my blood, if I go down to the Pit? *
will the dust praise you or declare your faithfulness?
B 11 Hear, O LORD, and have mercy upon me; *
O LORD, be my helper." [ANT.]

12 You have turned my wailing into dancing; *
you have put off my sack-cloth and clothed me with joy.
13 Therefore my heart sings to you without ceasing; *
O LORD my God, I will give you thanks for ever. [ANT.]

RCL Proper 2B Psalm 41

based on "St. Ethelwald" (H82–628)

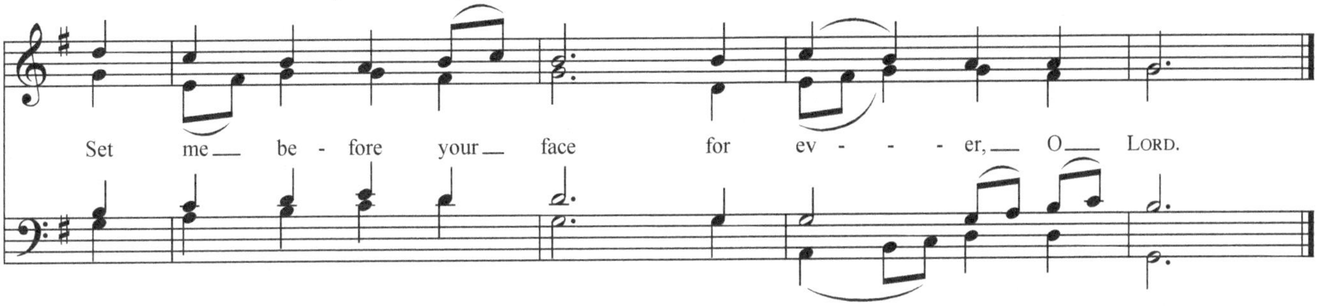

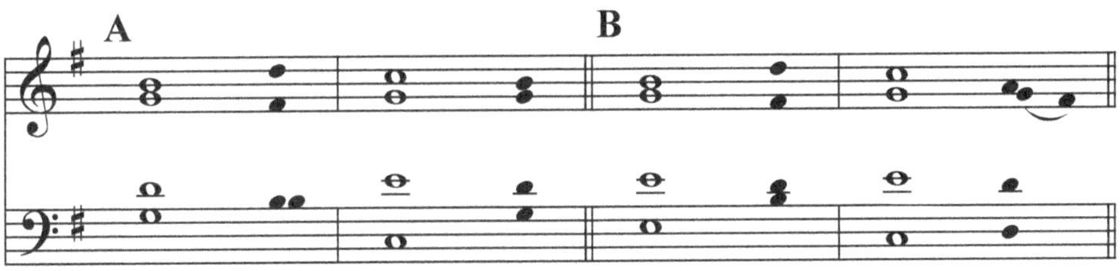

A 1 Happy are they who consider the poor and needy! *
the LORD will deliver them in the time of trouble.
A 2 The LORD preserves them and keeps them alive,
so that they may be happy in the land; *
he does not hand them over to the will of their enemies.
B 3 The LORD sustains them on their sickbed *
and ministers to them in their illness. [ANT.]

A 4 I said, "LORD, be merciful to me; *
heal me, for I have sinned against you."
A 5 My enemies are saying wicked things about me: *
"When will he die, and his name perish?"
B 6 Even if they come to see me, they speak empty words; *
their heart collects false rumors;
they go outside and spread them. [ANT.]

A 7 All my enemies whisper together about me *
and devise evil against me.
A 8 "A deadly thing," they say, "has fastened on him; *
he has taken to his bed and will never get up again."
B 9 Even my best friend, whom I trusted,
who broke bread with me, *
has lifted up his heel and turned against me. [ANT.]

A 10 But you, O LORD, be merciful to me and raise me up, *
and I shall repay them.
B 11 By this I know you are pleased with me, *
that my enemy does not triumph over me.
A 12 In my integrity you hold me fast, *
and shall set me before your face for ever.
B 13 Blessed be the LORD God of Israel, *
from age to age. Amen. Amen. [ANT.]

RCL Proper 3B Psalm 103: 1–13, 22

based on "Wondrous Love" (H82–439)

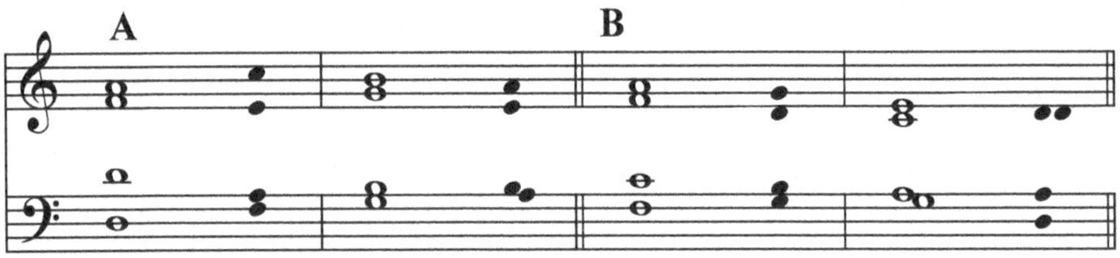

1 Bless the LORD, O my soul, *
and all that is within me, bless his holy Name.
2 Bless the LORD, O my soul, *
and forget not all his benefits. [ANT.]

3 He forgives all your sins *
and heals all your infirmities;
4 He redeems your life from the grave *
and crowns you with mercy and loving-kindness; [ANT.]

A 5 He satisfies you with good things, *
and your youth is renewed like an eagle's.
A 6 The LORD executes righteousness *
and judgment for all who are oppressed.
B 7 He made his ways known to Moses *
and his works to the children of Israel. [ANT.]

A 9 He will not always accuse us, *
nor will he keep his anger for ever.
B 10 He has not dealt with us according to our sins, *
nor rewarded us according to our wickedness.
A 11 For as the heavens are high above the earth, *
so is his mercy great upon those who fear him.
B 12 As far as the east is from the west, *
so far has he removed our sins from us. [ANT.]

13 As a father cares for his children, *
so does the LORD care for those who fear him.
22 Bless the LORD, all you works of his,
in all places of his dominion; *
bless the LORD, O my soul. [ANT.]

RCL Proper 4B (C Track) Psalm 139: 1–5, 12–17

based on "Tender Thought" (H82–702)

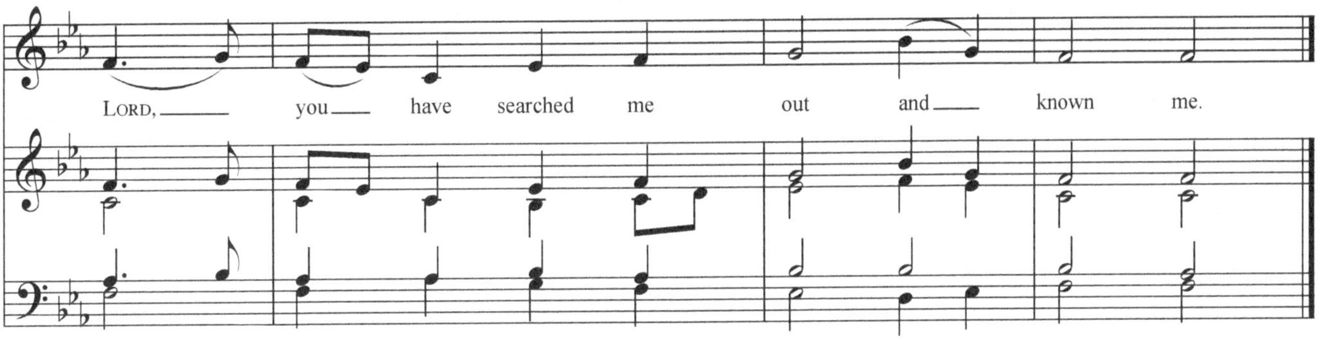

1 LORD, you have searched me out and known me; *
you know my sitting down and my rising up;
you discern my thoughts from afar.
2 You trace my journeys and my resting-places *
and are acquainted with all my ways. [ANT.]

A 3 Indeed, there is not a word on my lips, *
but you, O LORD, know it altogether.
A 4 You press upon me behind and before *
and lay your hand upon me.
B 5 Such knowledge is too wonderful for me; *
it is so high that I cannot attain to it. [ANT.]

12 For you yourself created my inmost parts; *
you knit me together in my mother's womb.
13 I will thank you because I am marvelously made; *
your works are wonderful, and I know it well. [ANT.]

A 14 My body was not hidden from you, *
while I was being made in secret
and woven in the depths of the earth.
A 15 Your eyes beheld my limbs, yet unfinished in the womb;
all of them were written in your book; *
B they were fashioned day by day,
when as yet there was none of them. [ANT.]

16 How deep I find your thoughts, O God! *
how great is the sum of them!
17 If I were to count them,
they would be more in number than the sand; *
to count them all,
my life span would need to be like yours. [ANT.]

RCL Proper 4B (G Track) **Psalm 81: 1–10**

based on "Gott sei Dank" (H82–47)

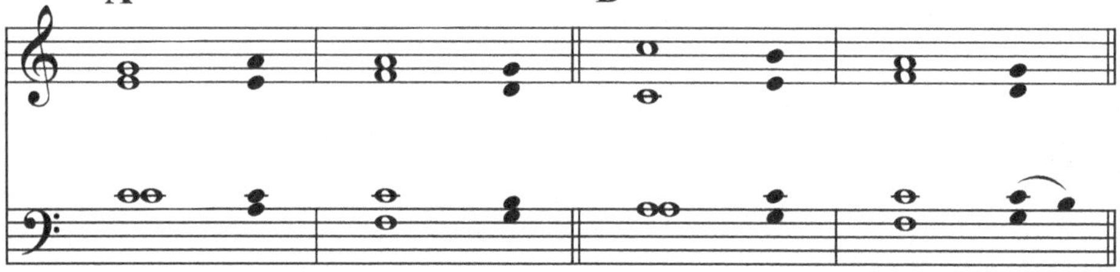

A 1 Sing with joy to God our strength *
and raise a loud shout to the God of Jacob.
A 2 Raise a song and sound the timbrel, *
the merry harp, and the lyre.
B 3 Blow the ram's-horn at the new moon, *
and at the full moon, the day of our feast. [ANT.]

4 For this is a statute for Israel, *
a law of the God of Jacob.
5 He laid it as a solemn charge upon Joseph, *
when he came out of the land of Egypt. [ANT.]

6 I heard an unfamiliar voice saying *
"I eased his shoulder from the burden;
his hands were set free from bearing the load."
7 You called on me in trouble, and I saved you; *
I answered you from the secret place of thunder
and tested you at the waters of Meribah. [ANT.]

A 8 Hear, O my people, and I will admonish you: *
O Israel, if you would but listen to me!
A 9 There shall be no strange god among you; *
you shall not worship a foreign god.
B 10 I am the LORD your God,
who brought you out of the land of Egypt and said, *
"Open your mouth wide, and I will fill it." [ANT.]

RCL Proper 5B (C Track) Psalm 138

based on "Ton-y-Botel" (H82–381)

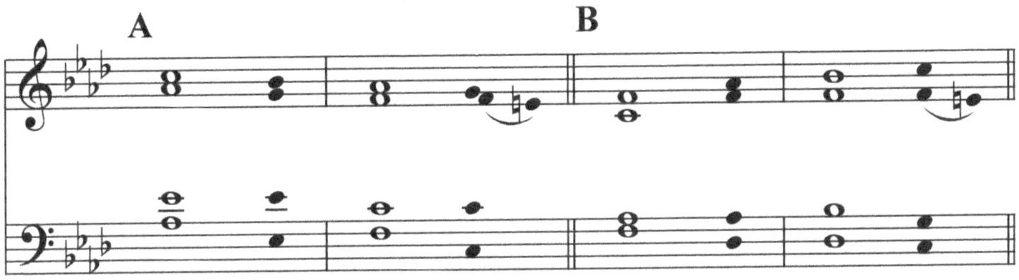

A 1 I will give thanks to you, O LORD, with my whole heart; *
before the gods I will sing your praise.
A 2 I will bow down toward your holy temple
and praise your Name, *
because of your love and faithfulness;
B 3 For you have glorified your Name *
and your word above all things. [ANT.]

A 4 When I called, you answered me; *
you increased my strength within me.
A 5 All the kings of the earth will praise you, O LORD, *
when they have heard the words of your mouth.
B 6 They will sing of the ways of the LORD, *
that great is the glory of the LORD. [ANT.]

A 7 Though the LORD be high, he cares for the lowly; *
he perceives the haughty from afar.
A 8 Though I walk in the midst of trouble, you keep me safe; *
you stretch forth your hand against the fury of my enemies;
your right hand shall save me.
B 9 The LORD will make good his purpose for me; *
O LORD, your love endures for ever;
do not abandon the works of your hands. [ANT.]

RCL Proper 5B (G Track) Psalm 130

based on "Foundation" (H82–636)

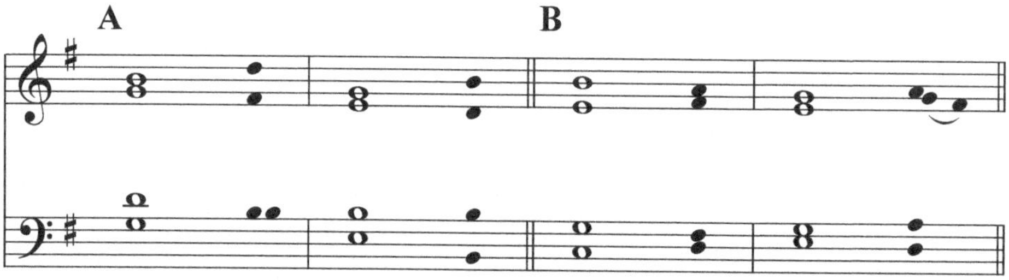

A 1 Out of the depths have I called to you, O LORD;
LORD, hear my voice; *
let your ears consider well the voice of my supplication.
A 2 If you, LORD, were to note what is done amiss, *
O LORD, who could stand?
B 3 For there is forgiveness with you; *
therefore you shall be feared. [ANT.]

4 I wait for the LORD; my soul waits for him; *
in his word is my hope.
5 My soul waits for the LORD,
more than watchmen for the morning, *
more than watchmen for the morning. [ANT.]

6 O Israel, wait for the LORD, *
for with the LORD there is mercy;
7 With him there is plenteous redemption, *
and he shall redeem Israel from all their sins. [ANT.]

RCL Proper 6B (C Track) Psalm 20

based on "Deo gratias" (H82–449)

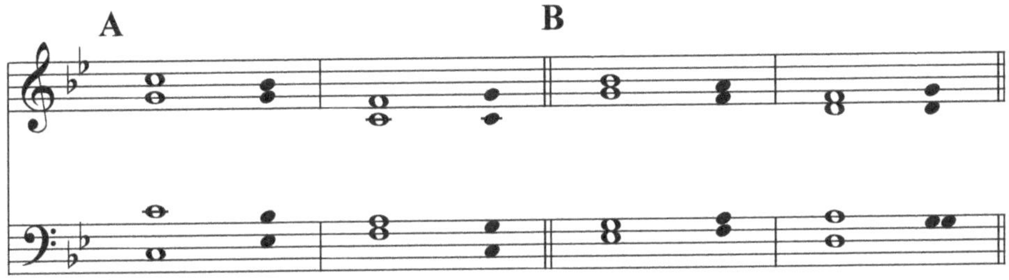

A 1 May the LORD answer you in the day of trouble, *
the Name of the God of Jacob defend you;
B 2 Send you help from his holy place *
and strengthen you out of Zion;
A 3 Remember all your offerings *
and accept your burnt sacrifice;
B 4 Grant you your heart's desire *
and prosper all your plans. [ANT.]

5 We will shout for joy at your victory
and triumph in the Name of our God; *
may the LORD grant all your requests.
6 Now I know that the LORD gives victory to his anointed; *
he will answer him out of his holy heaven,
with the victorious strength of his right hand. [ANT.]

A 7 Some put their trust in chariots and some in horses, *
but we will call upon the Name of the LORD our God.
A 8 They collapse and fall down, *
but we will arise and stand upright.
B 9 O LORD, give victory to the king *
and answer us when we call. [ANT.]

RCL Proper 6B (G Track) Psalm 92: 1–4, 11–14

based on "Paderborn" (H82–535)

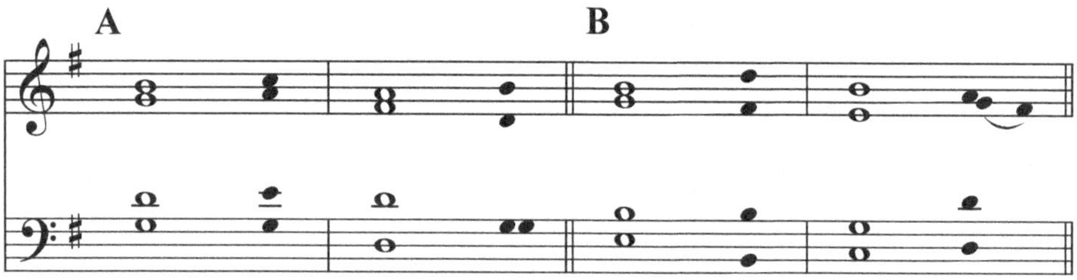

A 1 It is a good thing to give thanks to the LORD, *
and to sing praises to your Name, O Most High;
A 2 To tell of your loving-kindness early in the morning *
and of your faithfulness in the night season;
B 3 On the psaltery, and on the lyre, *
and to the melody of the harp. [ANT.]

4 For you have made me glad by your acts, O LORD; *
and I shout for joy because of the works of your hands.
11 The righteous shall flourish like a palm tree, *
and shall spread abroad like a cedar of Lebanon. [ANT.]

A 12 Those who are planted in the house of the LORD *
shall flourish in the courts of our God;
A 13 They shall still bear fruit in old age; *
they shall be green and succulent;
B 14 That they may show how upright the LORD is, *
my Rock, in whom there is no fault. [ANT.]

RCL Proper 7B (C Track)   Psalm 9: 9–20

based on "Paderborn" (H82–535)

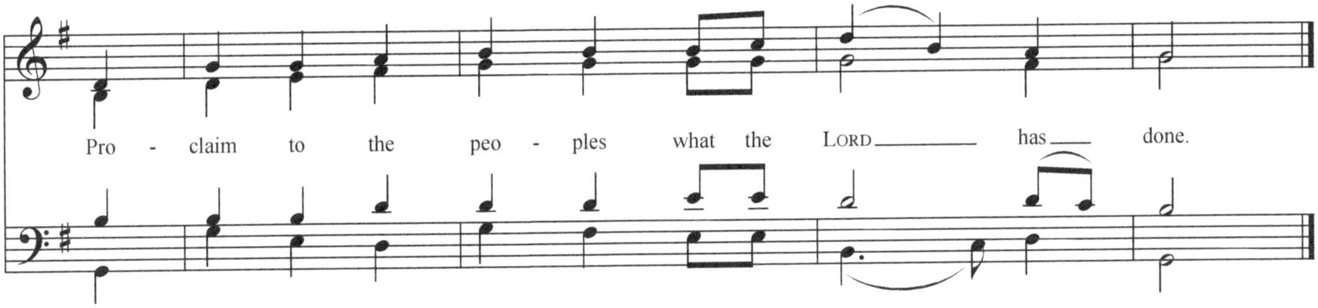

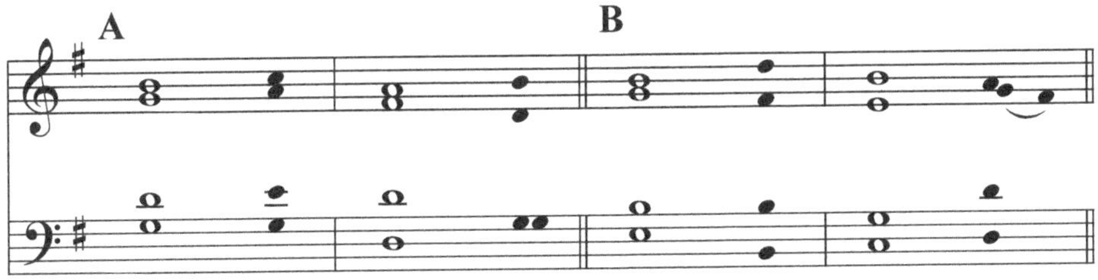

9 The LORD will be a refuge for the oppressed, *
a refuge in time of trouble.
10 Those who know your Name will put their trust in you, *
for you never forsake those who seek you, O LORD. [ANT.]

11 Sing praise to the LORD who dwells in Zion; *
proclaim to the peoples the things he has done.
12 The Avenger of blood will remember them; *
he will not forget the cry of the afflicted. [ANT.]

13 Have pity on me, O LORD; *
see the misery I suffer from those who hate me,
O you who lift me up from the gate of death;
14 So that I may tell of all your praises
and rejoice in your salvation *
in the gates of the city of Zion. [ANT.]

A 15 The ungodly have fallen into the pit they dug, *
and in the snare they set is their own foot caught.
A 16 The LORD is known by his acts of justice; *
the wicked are trapped in the works of their own hands.
B 17 The wicked shall be given over to the grave, *
and also all the peoples that forget God. [ANT.]

A 18 For the needy shall not always be forgotten, *
and the hope of the poor shall not perish for ever.
A 19 Rise up, O LORD, let not the ungodly have the upper hand; *
let them be judged before you.
B 20 Put fear upon them, O LORD; *
let the ungodly know they are but mortal. [ANT.]

RCL Proper 7B (C Track, alt.) Psalm 133

based on "Ellacombe" (H82–210)

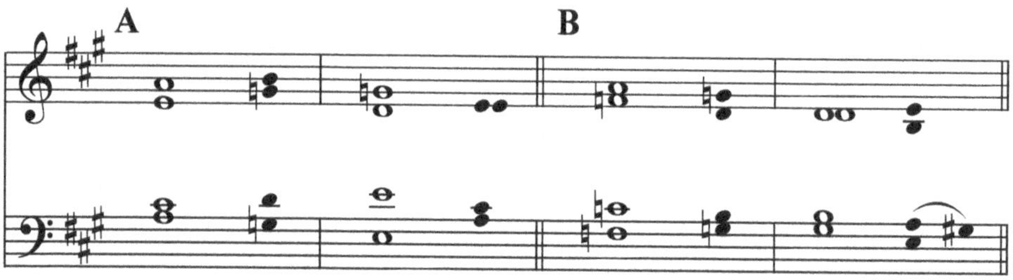

A 1 Oh, how good and pleasant it is, *
when brethren live together in unity!
A 2 It is like fine oil upon the head *
that runs down upon the beard,
B 3 Upon the beard of Aaron, *
and runs down upon the collar of his robe. [ANT.]

4 It is like the dew of Hermon *
that falls upon the hills of Zion.
5 For there the LORD has ordained the blessing: *
life for evermore. [ANT.]

RCL Proper 7B (G Track) Psalm 107: 1–3, 23–32

based on "Darwall's 148th" (H82–625)

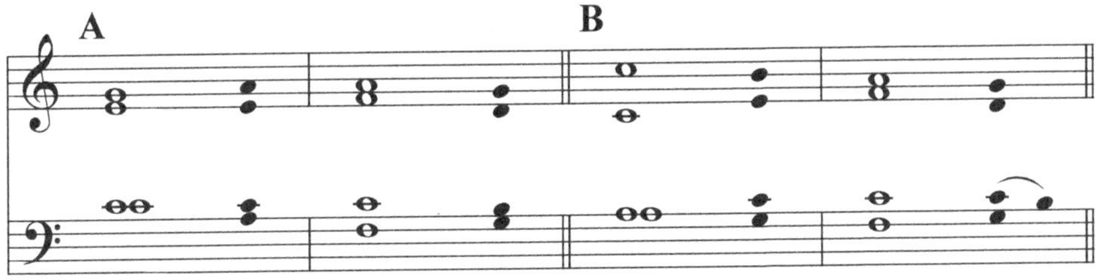

A 1 Give thanks to the LORD, for he is good, *
and his mercy endures for ever.
A 2 Let all those whom the LORD has redeemed proclaim *
that he redeemed them from the hand of the foe.
B 3 He gathered them out of the lands; *
from the east and from the west,
from the north and from the south. [ANT.]

A 23 Some went down to the sea in ships *
and plied their trade in deep waters;
A 24 They beheld the works of the LORD *
and his wonders in the deep.
B 25 Then he spoke, and a stormy wind arose, *
which tossed high the waves of the sea. [ANT.]

A 26 They mounted up to the heavens and fell back to the depths; *
their hearts melted because of their peril.
A 27 They reeled and staggered like drunkards *
and were at their wits' end.
B 28 Then they cried to the LORD in their trouble,
and he delivered them from their distress. [ANT.]

29 He stilled the storm to a whisper *
and quieted the waves of the sea.
30 Then were they glad because of the calm, *
and he brought them to the harbor they were bound for. [ANT.]

31 Let them give thanks to the LORD for his mercy *
and the wonders he does for his children.
32 Let them exalt him in the congregation of the people *
and praise him in the council of the elders. [ANT.]

RCL Proper 8B (C Track) Psalm 130

based on "Foundation" (H82–636)

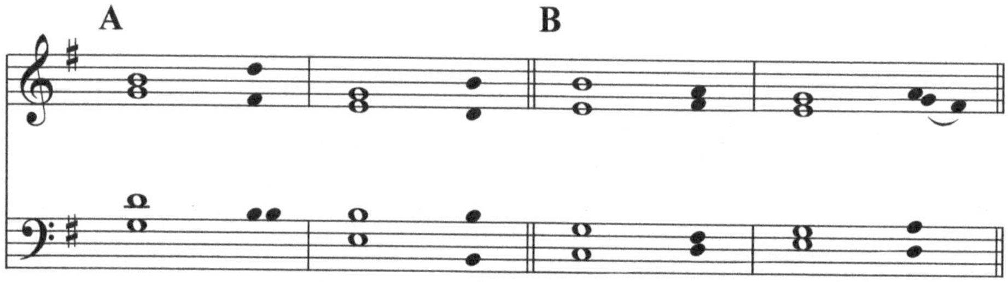

A 1 Out of the depths have I called to you, O LORD;
LORD, hear my voice; *
let your ears consider well the voice of my supplication.
A 2 If you, LORD, were to note what is done amiss, *
O LORD, who could stand?
B 3 For there is forgiveness with you; *
therefore you shall be feared. [ANT.]

4 I wait for the LORD; my soul waits for him; *
in his word is my hope.
5 My soul waits for the LORD,
more than watchmen for the morning, *
more than watchmen for the morning. [ANT.]

6 O Israel, wait for the LORD, *
for with the LORD there is mercy;
7 With him there is plenteous redemption, *
and he shall redeem Israel from all their sins. [ANT.]

RCL Proper 8B (C Track, alt.) A Song of God's Mercy

based on "Hyfrydol" (H82–657)

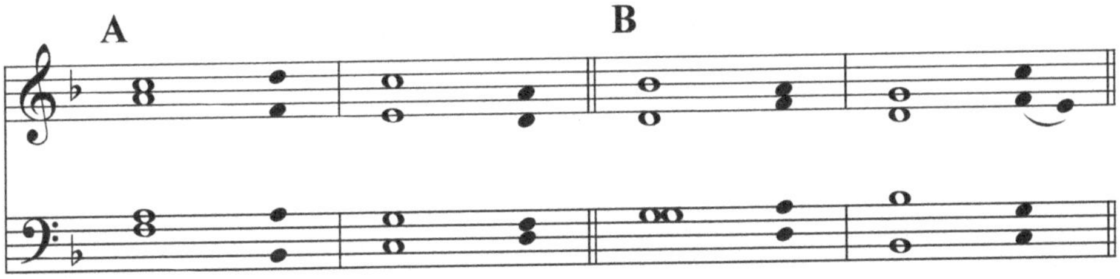

When I remember this, I have hope:
    by God's kindness, we are not destroyed;
for God's mercies are never-ending
    and are new every morning. [ANT.]

How great is your faithfulness, O God!
    "You are my portion," says my soul, "therefore I hope in you."
You are good to those who wait with patience,
    to every soul that seeks you. [ANT.]

A It is good to wait, even in silence,
    for the salvation of the LORD.
B It is good to bear in youth
    the yoke that God imposes,
A to sit silent and alone,
    clinging to hope even when tasting the dust.
B It is good to turn one's cheek to those who hit it
    and to bear up under insults. [ANT.]

The LORD does not reject us for ever,
    but after sending grief, relents
in compassion and loving-kindness,
    not desiring to torment anyone. [ANT.]

RCL Proper 8B (G Track) Psalm 30

based on "Wer nur den lieben Gott" (H82–635)

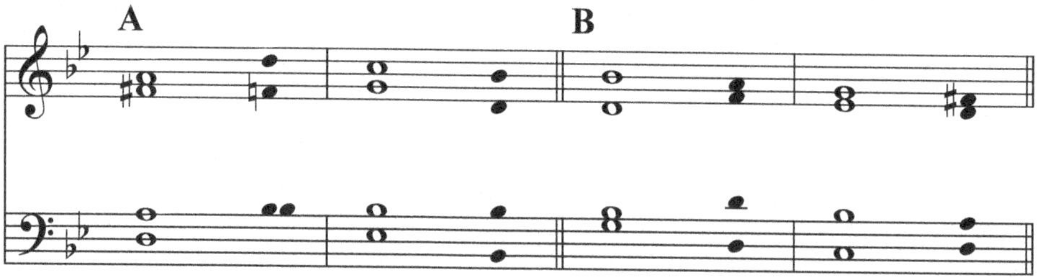

A 1 I will exalt you, O LORD,
because you have lifted me up *
and have not let my enemies triumph over me.
A 2 O LORD my God, I cried out to you, *
and you restored me to health.
B 3 You brought me up, O LORD, from the dead; *
you restored my life as I was going down to the grave. [ANT.]

A 4 Sing to the LORD, you servants of his; *
give thanks for the remembrance of his holiness.
A 5 For his wrath endures but the twinkling of an eye, *
his favor for a lifetime.
B 6 Weeping may spend the night, *
but joy comes in the morning. [ANT.]

7 While I felt secure, I said,
"I shall never be disturbed. *
You, LORD, with your favor, made me as strong as
the mountains."
8 Then you hid your face, *
and I was filled with fear. [ANT.]

A 9 I cried to you, O LORD; *
I pleaded with the LORD, saying,
A 10 "What profit is there in my blood, if I go down to the Pit? *
will the dust praise you or declare your faithfulness?
B 11 Hear, O LORD, and have mercy upon me; *
O LORD, be my helper." [ANT.]

12 You have turned my wailing into dancing; *
you have put off my sack-cloth and clothed me with joy.
13 Therefore my heart sings to you without ceasing; *
O LORD my God, I will give you thanks for ever. [ANT.]

RCL Proper 9B (C Track) Psalm 48

based on "Song 1" (H82–499)

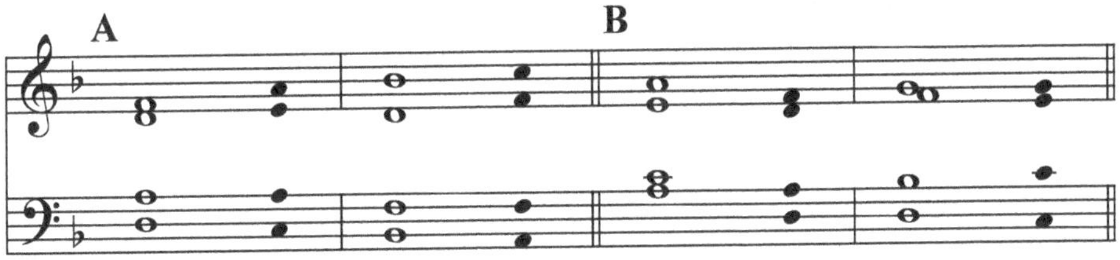

A 1 Great is the LORD, and highly to be praised; *
in the city of our God is his holy hill.
A 2 Beautiful and lofty, the joy of all the earth, is the hill of Zion, *
the very center of the world and the city of the great King.
B 3 God is in her citadels; *
he is known to be her sure refuge. [ANT.]

A 4 Behold, the kings of the earth assembled *
and marched forward together.
A 5 They looked and were astounded; *
they retreated and fled in terror.
B 6 Trembling seized them there; *
they writhed like a woman in childbirth,
like ships of the sea when the east wind shatters them. [ANT.]

A 7 As we have heard, so have we seen,
in the city of the LORD of hosts, in the city of our God; *
God has established her for ever.
A 8 We have waited in silence on your loving-kindness, O God, *
in the midst of your temple.
B 9 Your praise, like your Name, O God, reaches to the world's end; *
your right hand is full of justice. [ANT.]

10 Let Mount Zion be glad
and the cities of Judah rejoice, *
because of your judgments.
11 Make the circuit of Zion;
walk round about her; *
count the number of her towers. [ANT.]

12 Consider well her bulwarks; examine her strongholds; *
that you may tell those who come after.
13 This God is our God for ever and ever; *
he shall be our guide for evermore. [ANT.]

RCL Proper 9B (G Track) Psalm 123

based on "Pleading Savior" (H82–586)

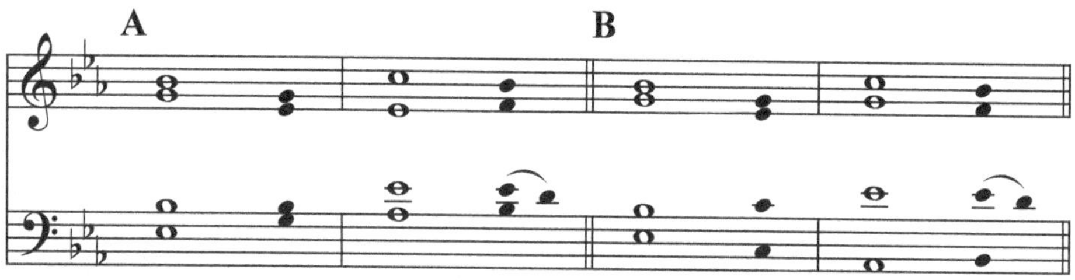

A 1 To you I lift up my eyes, *
to you enthroned in the heavens.
A 2 As the eyes of servants look to the hand of their masters, *
and the eyes of a maid to the hand of her mistress,
B 3 So our eyes look to the LORD our God, *
until he show us his mercy. [ANT.]

4 Have mercy upon us, O LORD, have mercy, *
for we have had more than enough of contempt,
5 Too much of the scorn of the indolent rich, *
and of the derision of the proud. [ANT.]

RCL Proper 10B (C Track) **Psalm 24**

based on "Truro" (H82–436)

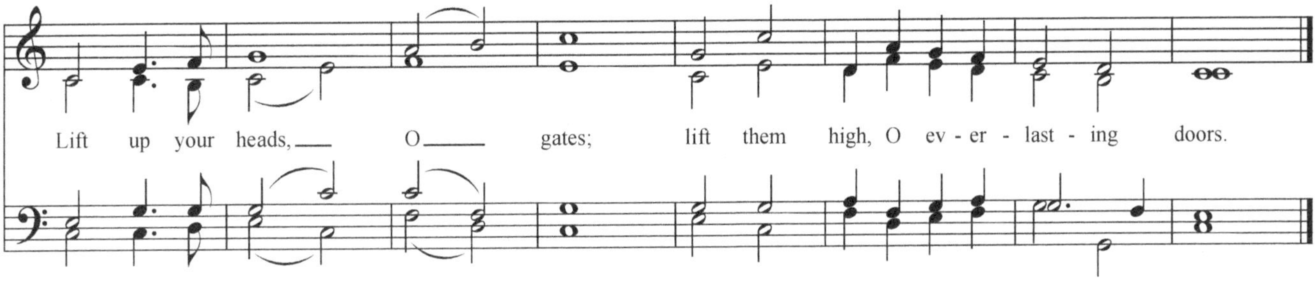

1 The earth is the LORD's and all that is in it, *
the world and all who dwell therein.
2 For it is he who founded it upon the seas *
and made it firm upon the rivers of the deep. [ANT.]

3 "Who can ascend the hill of the LORD? *
and who can stand in his holy place?"
4 "Those who have clean hands and a pure heart, *
who have not pledged themselves to falsehood,
nor sworn by what is a fraud. [ANT.]

5 They shall receive a blessing from the LORD *
and a just reward from the God of their salvation."
6 Such is the generation of those who seek him, *
of those who seek your face, O God of Jacob. [ANT.]

7 Lift up your heads, O gates;
lift them high, O everlasting doors; *
and the King of glory shall come in.
8 "Who is this King of glory?" *
"The LORD, strong and mighty,
the LORD, mighty in battle." [ANT.]

9 Lift up your heads, O gates;
lift them high, O everlasting doors; *
and the King of glory shall come in.
10 "Who is he, this King of glory?" *
"The LORD of hosts,
he is the King of glory." [ANT.]

RCL Proper 10B (G Track) Psalm 85: 7–13

based on "Aus tiefer Not" (H82–151)

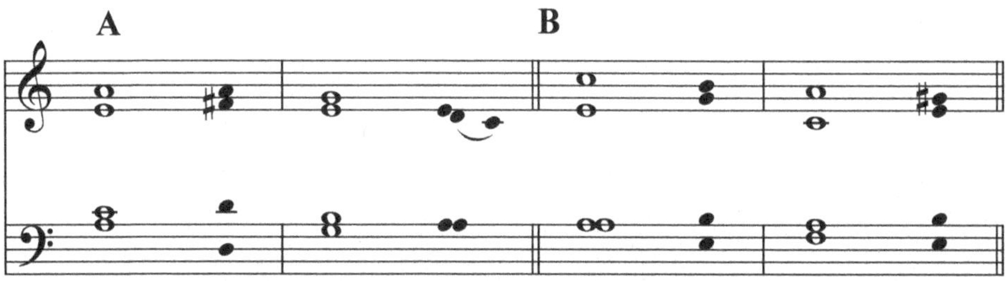

8 I will listen to what the LORD God is saying, *
for he is speaking peace to his faithful people
and to those who turn their hearts to him.
9 Truly, his salvation is very near to those who fear him, *
that his glory may dwell in our land. [ANT.]

10 Mercy and truth have met together; *
righteousness and peace have kissed each other.
11 Truth shall spring up from the earth, *
and righteousness shall look down from heaven. [ANT.]

12 The LORD will indeed grant prosperity, *
and our land will yield its increase.
13 Righteousness shall go before him, *
and peace shall be a pathway for his feet. [ANT.]

RCL Proper 11B (C Track) Psalm 89: 20–37

based on "St. Denio" (H82–423)

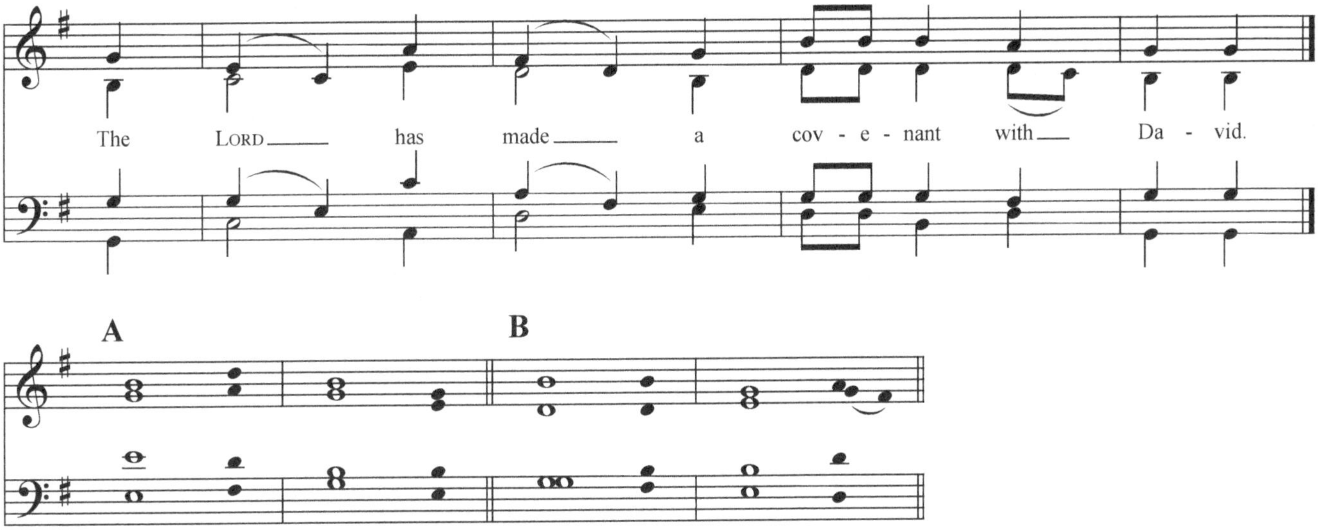

A 20 "I have found David my servant; *
with my holy oil have I anointed him.
B 21 My hand will hold him fast *
and my arm will make him strong.
A 22 No enemy shall deceive him, *
nor any wicked man bring him down.
B 23 I will crush his foes before him *
and strike down those who hate him. [ANT.]

A 24 My faithfulness and love shall be with him, *
and he shall be victorious through my Name.
A 25 I shall make his dominion extend *
from the Great Sea to the River.
B 26 He will say to me, 'You are my Father, *
my God, and the rock of my salvation.' [ANT.]

A 27 I will make him my firstborn *
and higher than the kings of the earth.
A 28 I will keep my love for him for ever, *
and my covenant will stand firm for him.
B 29 I will establish his line for ever *
and his throne as the days of heaven." [ANT.]

A 30 "If his children forsake my law *
and do not walk according to my judgments;
A 31 If they break my statutes *
and do not keep my commandments;
B 32 I will punish their transgressions with a rod *
and their iniquities with the lash;
A 33 But I will not take my love from him, *
nor let my faithfulness prove false.
B 34 I will not break my covenant, *
nor change what has gone out of my lips. [ANT.]

A 35 Once for all I have sworn by my holiness: *
'I will not lie to David.
A 36 His line shall endure for ever *
and his throne as the sun before me;
B 37 It shall stand fast for evermore like the moon, *
the abiding witness in the sky.'" [ANT.]

RCL Proper 11B (G Track) Psalm 23

based on "St. Columba" (H82–645)

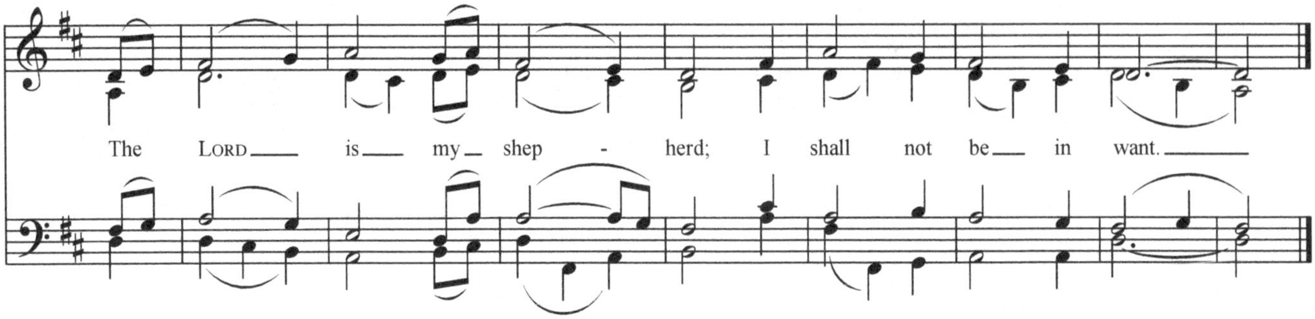

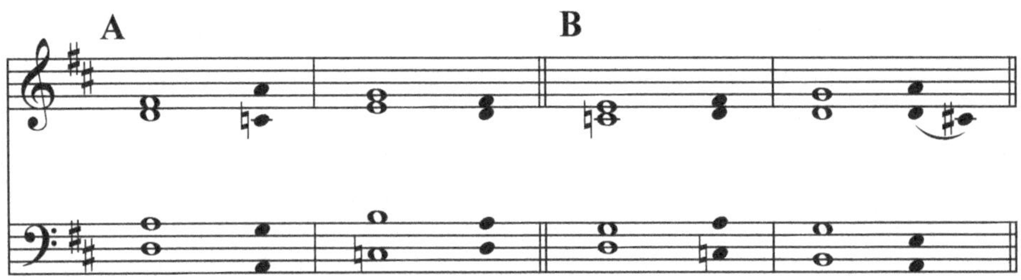

1 The LORD is my shepherd; *
I shall not be in want.
2 He makes me lie down in green pastures *
and leads me beside still waters. [ANT.]

3 He revives my soul *
and guides me along right pathways for his Name's sake.
4 Though I walk through the valley of the shadow of death,
I shall fear no evil; *
for you are with me;
your rod and your staff, they comfort me. [ANT.]

5 You spread a table before me in the presence of those who trouble me; *
you have anointed my head with oil,
and my cup is running over.
6 Surely your goodness and mercy shall follow me all the days of my life, *
and I will dwell in the house of the LORD for ever. [ANT.]

RCL Proper 12B (C Track) Psalm 14

based on "Martyrdom" (H82–658)

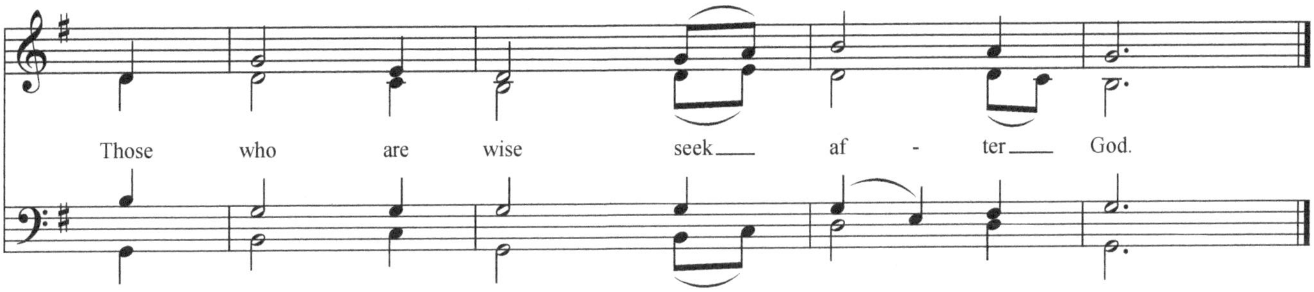

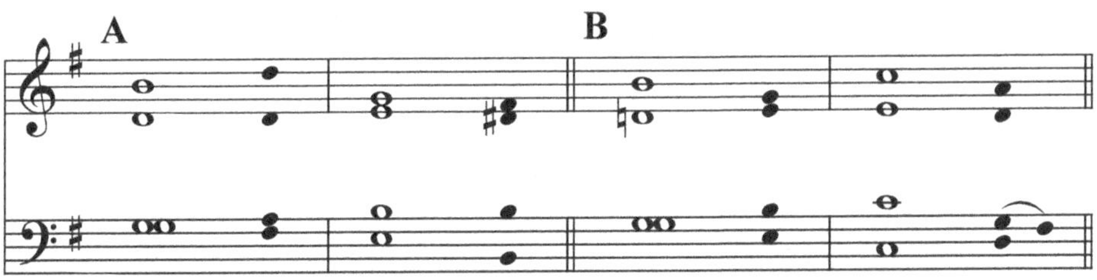

A 1 The fool has said in his heart, "There is no God." *
All are corrupt and commit abominable acts;
there is none who does any good.
B 2 The Lord looks down from heaven upon us all, *
to see if there is any who is wise,
if there is one who seeks after God.
B 3 Every one has proved faithless;
all alike have turned bad; *
there is none who does good; no, not one. [ANT.]

4 Have they no knowledge, all those evildoers *
who eat up my people like bread
and do not call upon the Lord?
5 See how they tremble with fear, *
because God is in the company of the righteous. [ANT.]

6 Their aim is to confound the plans of the afflicted, *
but the Lord is their refuge.
7 Oh, that Israel's deliverance would come out of Zion! *
when the Lord restores the fortunes of his people,
Jacob will rejoice and Israel be glad. [ANT.]

RCL Proper 12B (G Track) Psalm 145: 10–19

based on "Old 124th" (H82–404)

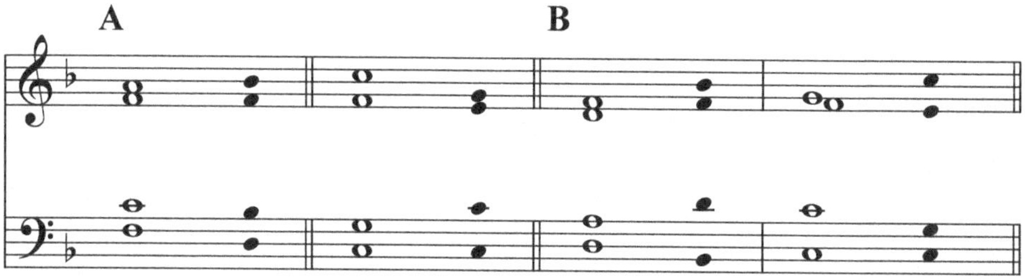

A 10 All your works praise you, O LORD, *
and your faithful servants bless you.
A 11 They make known the glory of your kingdom *
speak of your power;
B 12 That the peoples may know of your power *
and the glorious splendor of your kingdom. [ANT.]

A 13 Your kingdom is an everlasting kingdom; *
your dominion endures throughout all ages.
A 14 The LORD is faithful in all his words *
and merciful in all his deeds.
B 15 The LORD upholds all those who fall; *
he lifts up those who are bowed down. [ANT.]

16 The eyes of all wait upon you, O LORD, *
and you give them their food in due season.
17 You open wide your hand *
and satisfy the needs of every living creature. [ANT.]

18 The Lord is righteous in all his ways *
and loving in all his works.
19 The Lord is near to those who call upon him, *
to all who call upon him faithfully. [ANT.]

RCL Proper 13B (C Track) Psalm 51: 1–13

based on "Wer nur den lieben Gott" (H82–635)

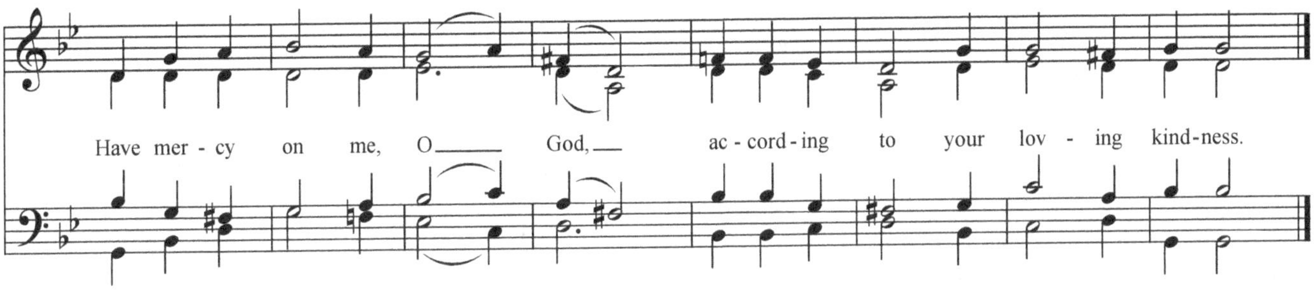

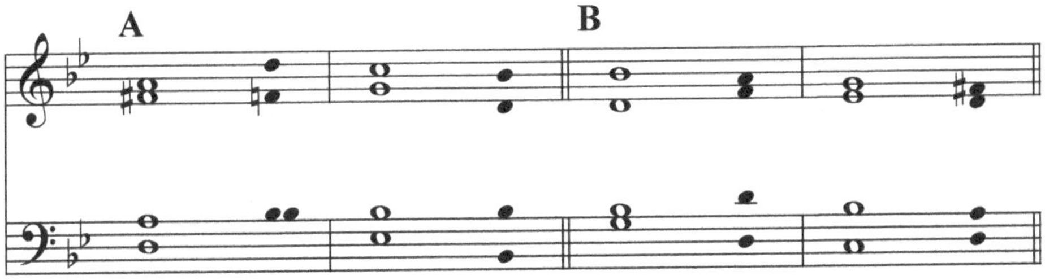

A 1 Have mercy on me, O God, according to your
loving-kindness; *
in your great compassion blot out my offenses.
A 2 Wash me through and through from my wickedness *
and cleanse me from my sin.
B 3 For I know my transgressions, *
and my sin is ever before me. [ANT.]

4 Against you only have I sinned *
and done what is evil in your sight.
5 And so you are justified when you speak *
and upright in your judgment. [ANT.]

A 6 Indeed, I have been wicked from my birth, *
a sinner from my mother's womb.
B 7 For behold, you look for truth deep within me, *
and will make me understand wisdom secretly.
A 8 Purge me from my sin, and I shall be pure; *
wash me, and I shall be clean indeed.
B 9 Make me hear of joy and gladness, *
that the body you have broken may rejoice. [ANT.]

A 10 Hide your face from my sins *
and blot out all my iniquities.
B 11 Create in me a clean heart, O God, *
and renew a right spirit within me.
A 12 Cast me not away from your presence *
and take not your holy Spirit from me.
B 13 Give me the joy of your saving help again *
and sustain me with your bountiful Spirit. [ANT.]

RCL Proper 13B (G Track) Psalm 78: 23–29

based on "Let Us Break Bread Together" (H82–325)

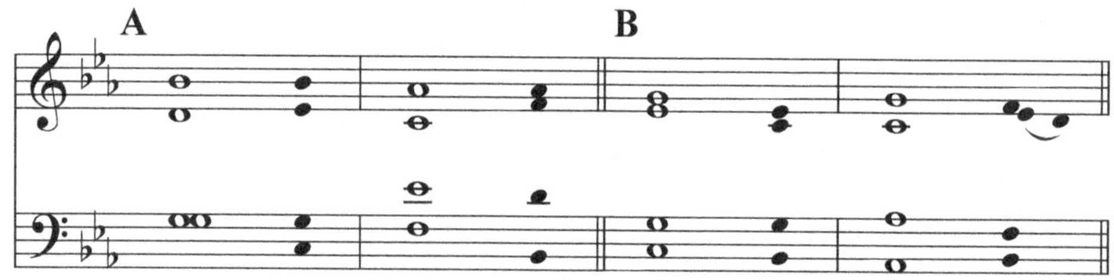

A 23 So he commanded the clouds above *
and opened the doors of heaven.
A 24 He rained down manna upon them to eat *
and gave them grain from heaven.
B 25 So mortals ate the bread of angels; *
he provided for them food enough. [ANT.]

26 He caused the east wind to blow in the heavens *
and led out the south wind by his might.
27 He rained down flesh upon them like dust *
and wingèd birds like the sand of the sea. [ANT.]

28 He let it fall in the midst of their camp *
and round about their dwellings.
29 So they ate and were well filled, *
for he gave them what they craved. [ANT.]

RCL Transfiguration ABC August 6 Psalm 99

based on "Old 124th" (H82–404)

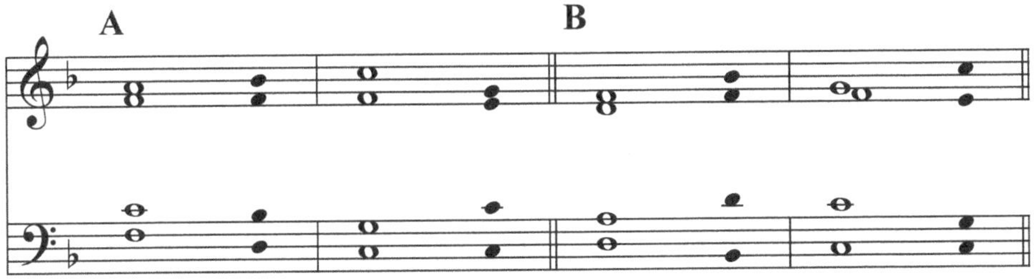

A 1 The LORD is King;
let the people tremble; *
he is enthroned upon the cherubim;
let the earth shake.
A 2 The LORD is great in Zion; *
he is high above all peoples.
B 3 Let them confess his Name, which is great and awesome; *
he is the Holy One. [ANT.]

4 "O mighty King, lover of justice,
you have established equity; *
you have executed justice and righteousness in Jacob."
5 Proclaim the greatness of the LORD our God
and fall down before his footstool; *
he is the Holy One. [ANT.]

6 Moses and Aaron among his priests,
and Samuel among those who call upon his Name, *
they called upon the LORD, and he answered them.
7 He spoke to them out of the pillar of cloud; *
they kept his testimonies and the decree that he gave them. [ANT.]

8 "O LORD our God, you answered them indeed; *
you were a God who forgave them,
yet punished them for their evil deeds."
9 Proclaim the greatness of the LORD our God
and worship him upon his holy hill; *
for the LORD our God is the Holy One. [ANT.]

RCL Proper 14B (C Track) Psalm 130

based on "Foundation" (H82–636)

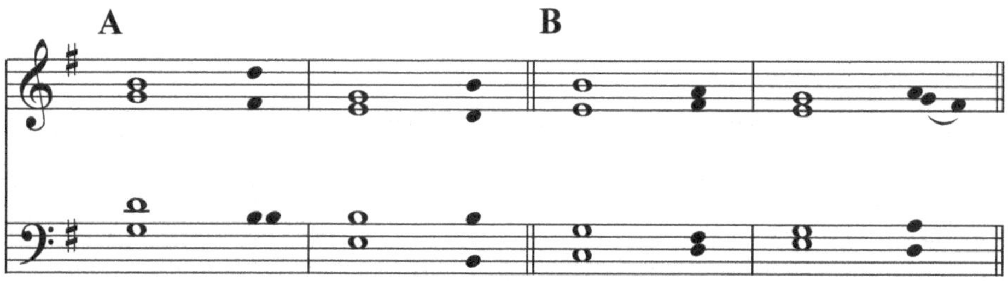

A 1 Out of the depths have I called to you, O LORD;
LORD, hear my voice; *
let your ears consider well the voice of my supplication.
A 2 If you, LORD, were to note what is done amiss, *
O LORD, who could stand?
B 3 For there is forgiveness with you; *
therefore you shall be feared. [ANT.]

4 I wait for the LORD; my soul waits for him; *
in his word is my hope.
5 My soul waits for the LORD,
more than watchmen for the morning, *
more than watchmen for the morning. [ANT.]

6 O Israel, wait for the LORD, *
for with the LORD there is mercy;
7 With him there is plenteous redemption, *
and he shall redeem Israel from all their sins. [ANT.]

RCL Proper 14B (G Track) Psalm 34: 1–8

based on "Martyrdom" (H82–658)

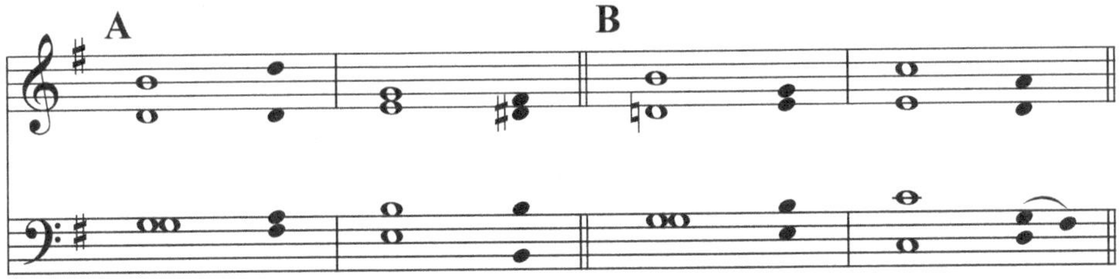

1 I will bless the LORD at all times; *
his praise shall ever be in my mouth.
2 I will glory in the LORD; *
let the humble hear and rejoice. [ANT.]

3 Proclaim with me the greatness of the LORD;
let us exalt his Name together.
4 I sought the LORD, and he answered me *
and delivered me out of all my terror. [ANT.]

5 Look upon him and be radiant, *
and let not your faces be ashamed.
6 I called in my affliction and the LORD heard me *
and saved me from all my troubles. [ANT.]

7 The angel of the LORD encompasses those who fear him, *
and he will deliver them.
8 Taste and see that the LORD is good; *
happy are they who trust in him! [ANT.]

RCL Proper 15B (C Track) Psalm 111

based on "Picardy" (H82–324)

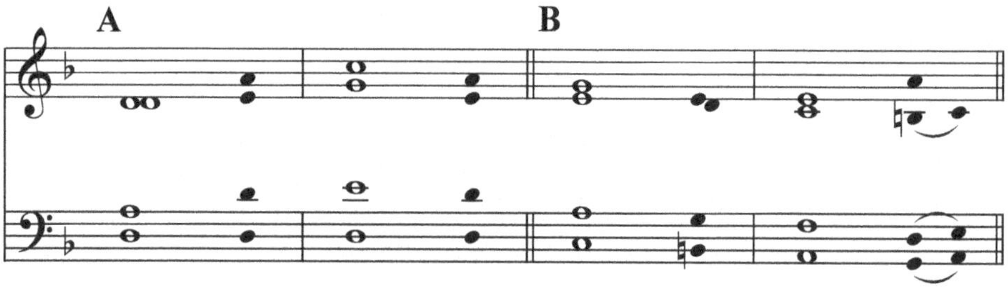

1 Hallelujah!
I will give thanks to the LORD with my whole heart, *
in the assembly of the upright, in the congregation.
2 Great are the deeds of the LORD! *
they are studied by all who delight in them. [ANT.]

3 His work is full of majesty and splendor, *
and his righteousness endures for ever.
4 He makes his marvelous works to be remembered; *
the LORD is gracious and full of compassion. [ANT.]

5 He gives food to those who fear him; *
he is ever mindful of his covenant.
6 He has shown his people the power of his works *
in giving them the lands of the nations. [ANT.]

7 The works of his hands are faithfulness and justice; *
all his commandments are sure.
8 They stand fast for ever and ever, *
because they are done in truth and equity. [ANT.]

9 He sent redemption to his people;
he commanded his covenant for ever; *
holy and awesome is his Name.
10 The fear of the LORD is the beginning of wisdom; *
those who act accordingly have a good understanding;
his praise endures for ever. [ANT.]

RCL Proper 15B (G Track) Psalm 34: 9–14

based on "Martyrdom" (H82–658)

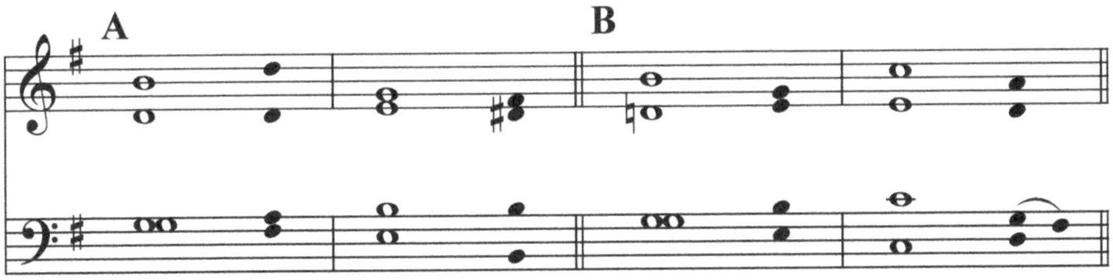

9 Fear the Lord, you that are his saints, *
for those who fear him lack nothing.
10 The young lions lack and suffer hunger, *
but those who seek the LORD lack nothing that is good. [ANT.]

11 Come, children, and listen to me; *
I will teach you the fear of the LORD.
12 Who among you loves life *
and desires long life to enjoy prosperity? [ANT.]

13 Keep your tongue from evil-speaking *
and your lips from lying words.
14 Turn from evil and do good; *
seek peace and pursue it. [ANT.]

RCL Proper 16B (C Track) Psalm 84

based on "Brother James' Air" (H82–517)

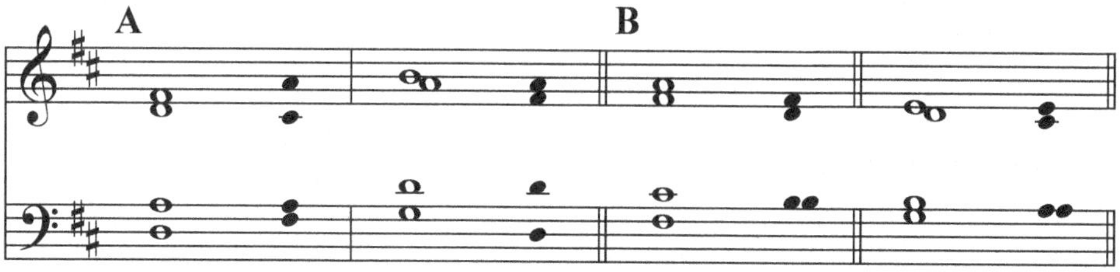

1 My soul has a desire and longing for the courts of the LORD; *
my heart and my flesh rejoice in the living God.
2 The sparrow has found her a house
and the swallow a nest where she may lay her young; *
by the side of your altars, O LORD of hosts,
my King and my God. [ANT.]

3 Happy are they who dwell in your house! *
they will always be praising you.
4 Happy are the people whose strength is in you! *
whose hearts are set on the pilgrims' way. [ANT.]

A 5 Those who go through the desolate valley will find
it a place of springs, *
for the early rains have covered it with pools of water.
A 6 They will climb from height to height, *
and the God of gods will reveal himself in Zion.
B 7 LORD God of hosts, hear my prayer; *
hearken, O God of Jacob. [ANT.]

8 Behold our defender, O God; *
and look upon the face of your Anointed.
9 For one day in your courts is better than
a thousand in my own room, *
and to stand at the threshold of the house of my God
than to dwell in the tents of the wicked. [ANT.]

A 10 For the LORD God is both sun and shield; *
he will give grace and glory;
A 11 No good thing will the LORD withhold *
from those who walk with integrity.
B 12 O LORD of hosts, *
happy are they who put their trust in you! [ANT.]

RCL Proper 16B (G Track) Psalm 34: 15–22

based on "Martyrdom" (H82–658)

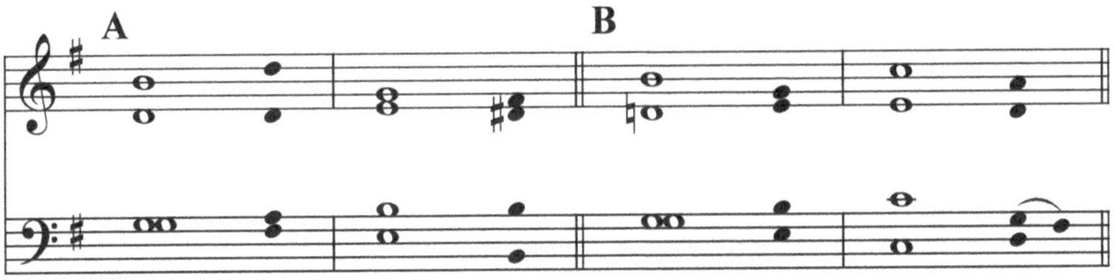

15 The eyes of the LORD are upon the righteous, *
and his ears are open to their cry.
16 The face of the LORD is against those who do evil, *
to root out the remembrance of them from the earth. [ANT.]

17 The righteous cry, and the LORD hears them *
and delivers them from all their troubles.
18 The LORD is near to the brokenhearted *
and will save those whose spirits are crushed. [ANT.]

19 Many are the troubles of the righteous, *
but the LORD will deliver him out of them all.
20 He will keep safe all his bones; *
not one of them shall be broken. [ANT.]

RCL Proper 17B (C Track) Psalm 45: 1–2, 7–10

based on "Nun danket alle Gott" (H82–397)

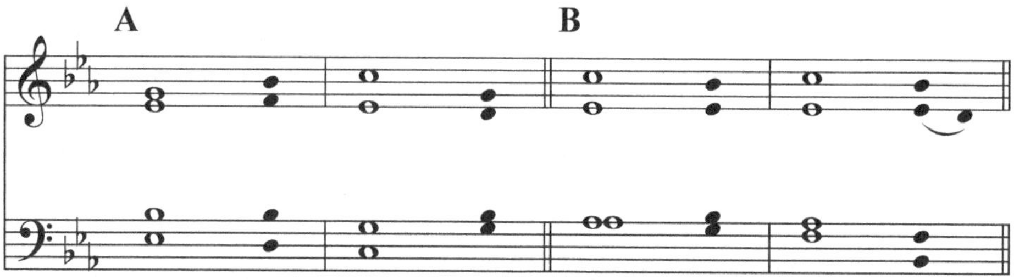

1 My heart is stirring with a noble song;
let me recite what I have fashioned for the king; *
my tongue shall be the pen of a skilled writer.
2 You are the fairest of men; *
grace flows from your lips,
because God has blessed you for ever. [ANT.]

7 Your throne, O God, endures for ever and ever, *
a scepter of righteousness is the scepter of your kingdom;
you love righteousness and hate iniquity.
8 Therefore God, your God, has anointed you *
with the oil of gladness above your fellows. [ANT.]

9 All your garments are fragrant with myrrh, aloes, and cassia, *
and the music of strings from ivory palaces makes you glad.
10 Kings' daughters stand among the ladies of the court; *
on your right hand is the queen,
adorned with the gold of Ophir. [ANT.]

RCL Proper 17B (G Track) Psalm 15

based on "Festal Song" (H82–551)

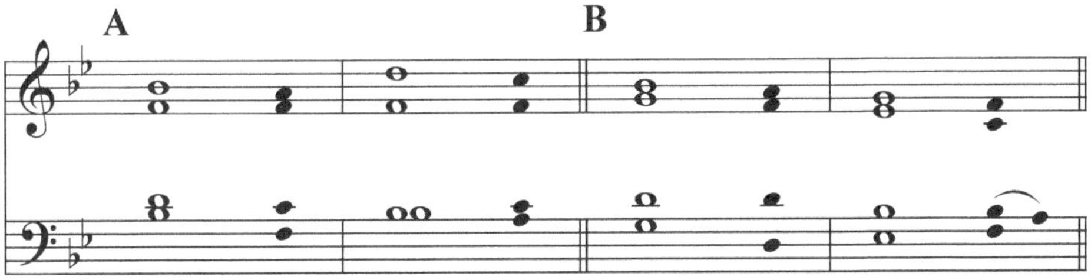

1 Lord, who may dwell in your tabernacle? *
who may abide upon your holy hill?
2 Whoever leads a blameless life and does what is right, *
who speaks the truth from his heart. [ANT.]

3 There is no guile upon his tongue;
he does no evil to his friend; *
he does not heap contempt upon his neighbor.
4 In his sight the wicked is rejected, *
but he honors those who fear the Lord. [ANT.]

A 5 He has sworn to do no wrong *
and does not take back his word.
A 6 He does not give his money in hope of gain, *
nor does he take a bribe against the innocent.
B 7 Whoever does these things *
shall never be overthrown. [ANT.]

RCL Proper 18B (C Track) Psalm 125

based on "Adoro devote" (H82–314)

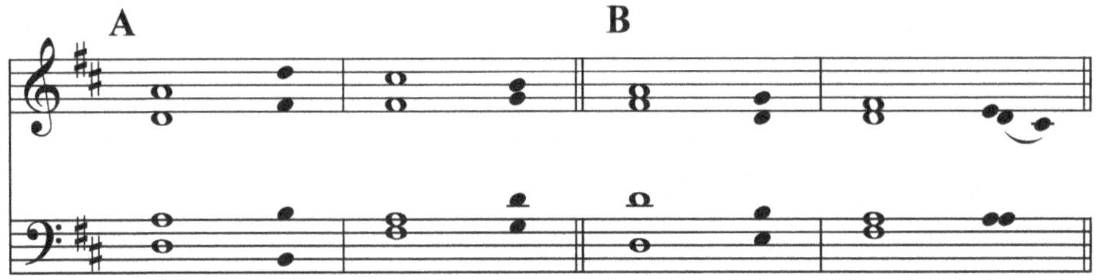

1 Those who trust in the LORD are like Mount Zion, *
which cannot be moved, but stands fast for ever.
2 The hills stand about Jerusalem; *
so does the LORD stand round about his people,
from this time forth for evermore. [ANT.]

A 3 The scepter of the wicked shall not hold sway over the land allotted to the just, *
so that the just shall not put their hands to evil.
A 4 Show your goodness, O LORD, to those who are good *
and to those who are true of heart.
B 5 As for those who turn aside to crooked ways,
the LORD will lead them away with the evildoers; *
but peace be upon Israel. [ANT.]

RCL Proper 18B (G Track) Psalm 146

based on "Old 124th" (H82–404)

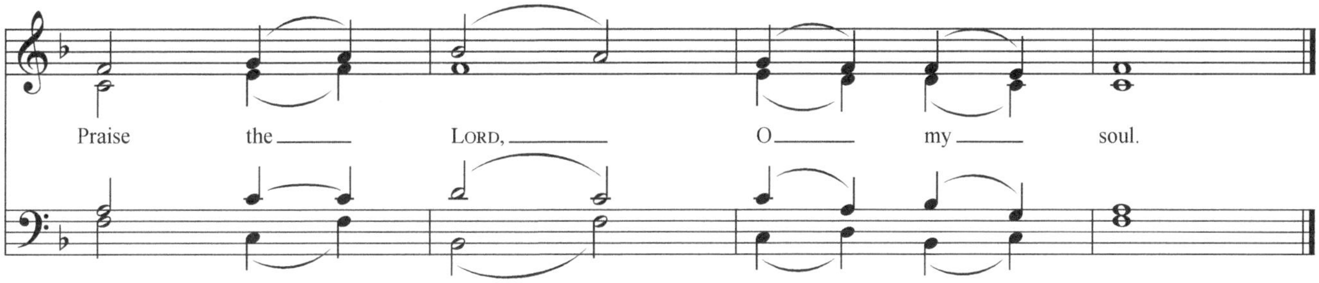

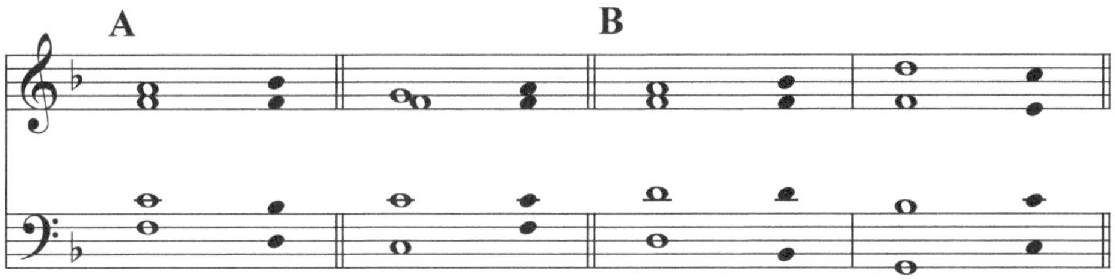

A 1 Hallelujah!
Praise the LORD, O my soul! *
I will praise the LORD as long as I live;
I will sing praises to my God while I have my being.
A 2 Put not your trust in rulers, nor in any child of earth, *
for there is no help in them.
B 3 When they breathe their last, they return to earth, *
and in that day their thoughts perish. [ANT.]

A 4 Happy are they who have the God of Jacob for their help! *
whose hope is in the LORD their God;
A 5 Who made heaven and earth, the seas, and all that is in them; *
who keeps his promise for ever;
B 6 Who gives justice to those who are oppressed, *
and food to those who hunger. [ANT.]

A 7 The LORD sets the prisoners free;
the LORD opens the eyes of the blind; *
the LORD lifts up those who are bowed down;
A 8 The LORD loves the righteous;
the LORD cares for the stranger; *
he sustains the orphan and widow,
but frustrates the way of the wicked.
B 9 The LORD shall reign for ever, *
your God, O Zion, throughout all generations.
Hallelujah! [ANT.]

RCL Proper 19B (C Track) Psalm 19

based on "Song 1" (H82–499)

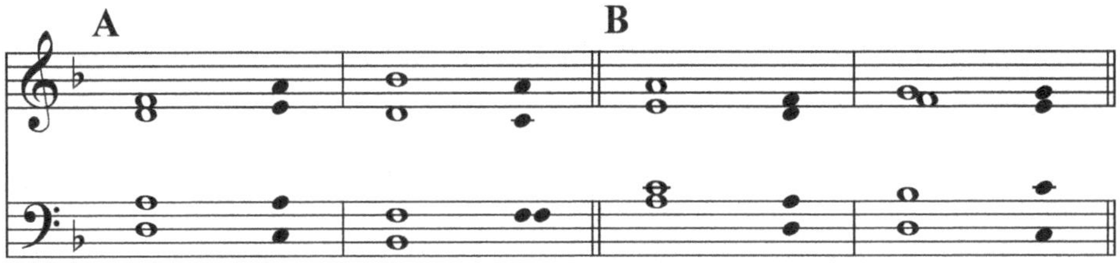

A 1 The heavens declare the glory of God, *
and the firmament shows his handiwork.
B 2 One day tells its tale to another, *
and one night imparts knowledge to another.
A 3 Although they have no words or language, *
and their voices are not heard,
B 4 Their sound has gone out into all lands, *
and their message to the ends of the world. [ANT.]

5 In the deep has he set a pavilion for the sun; *
it comes forth like a bridegroom out of his chamber;
it rejoices like a champion to run its course.
6 It goes forth from the uttermost edge of the heavens
and runs about to the end of it again; *
nothing is hidden from its burning heat. [ANT.]

7 The law of the LORD is perfect
and revives the soul; *
the testimony of the LORD is sure
and gives wisdom to the innocent.
8 The statutes of the LORD are just
and rejoice the heart; *
the commandment of the LORD is clear
and gives light to the eyes. [ANT.]

9 The fear of the LORD is clean
and endures for ever; *
the judgments of the LORD are true
and righteous altogether.
10 More to be desired are they than gold,
more than much fine gold, *
sweeter far than honey,
than honey in the comb. [ANT.]

11 By them also is your servant enlightened, *
and in keeping them there is great reward.
12 Who can tell how often he offends? *
cleanse me from my secret faults. [ANT.]

13 Above all, keep your servant from presumptuous sins;
let them not get dominion over me; *
then shall I be whole and sound,
and innocent of a great offense.
14 Let the words of my mouth and the meditation of my
heart be acceptable in your sight, *
O LORD, my strength and my redeemer. [ANT.]

RCL Proper 19B (C Track, alt.) A Song in Praise of Wisdom

based on "Picardy" (H82–324)

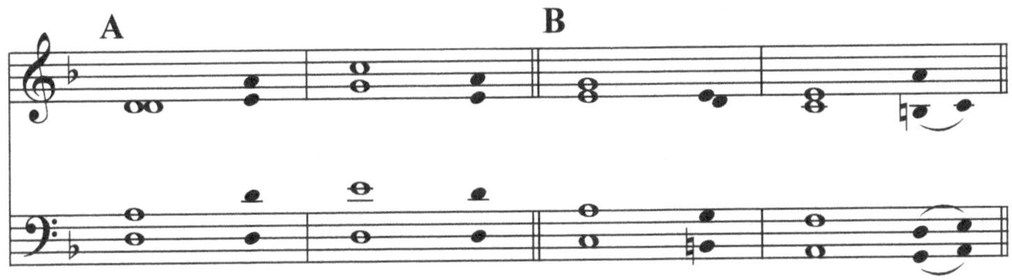

A Wisdom is a reflection of eternal light, *
  a flawless mirror of God's activity,
  an image of divine goodness.
A Through Wisdom is only one, *
  she accomplishes everything;
B remaining self-contained, *
  she transforms all around her. [ANT.]

A In every generation *
  Wisdom enlightens holy souls,
A making them friends of God, *
  making them prophets.
B For God love nothing so much *
  as the person who loves Wisdom. [ANT.]

A She is more radiant than the sun, *
  and outshines every constellation.
A She excels daylight by far, for day is eclipsed by night; *
  but evil does not overshadow Wisdom.
B She spans the earth from pole to pole *
  and orders all things well. [ANT.]

RCL Proper 19B (G Track) Psalm 116: 1–8

based on "Holy Manna" (H82–238, 580)

Alternate harmonization for accompaniment

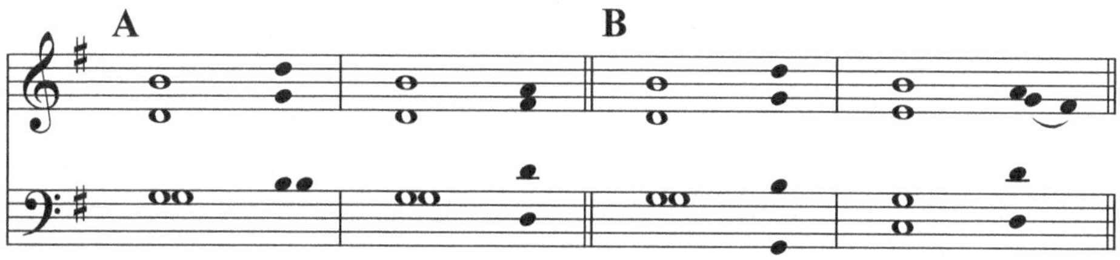

A 1 I love the LORD, because he has heard the voice of
my supplication, *
because he has inclined his ear to me whenever
I called upon him.
A 2 The cords of death entangled me;
the grip of the grave took hold of me; *
I came to grief and sorrow.
B 3 Then I called upon the Name of the LORD: *
"O LORD, I pray you, save my life." [ANT.]

4 Gracious is the LORD and righteous; *
our God is full of compassion.
5 The LORD watches over the innocent; *
I was brought very low, and he helped me. [ANT.]

6 Turn again to your rest, O my soul, *
for the LORD has treated you well.
7 For you have rescued my life from death, *
my eyes from tears, and my feet from stumbling. [ANT.]

RCL Proper 20B (C Track) Psalm 1

based on "Old 100th" (H82–377)

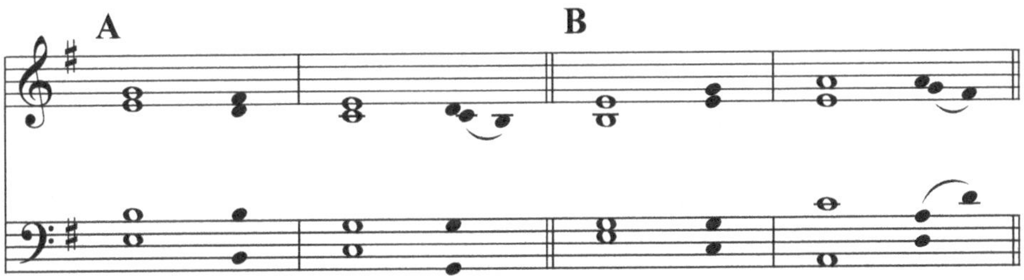

1 Happy are they who have not walked in the counsel of the wicked, *
nor lingered in the way of sinners,
nor sat in the seats of the scornful!
2 Their delight is in the law of the LORD, *
and they meditate on his law day and night. [ANT.]

3 They are like trees planted by streams of water,
bearing fruit in due season, with leaves that do not wither; *
everything they do shall prosper.
4 It is not so with the wicked; *
they are like chaff which the wind blows away. [ANT.]

5 Therefore the wicked shall not stand upright when judgment comes, *
nor the sinner in the council of the righteous.
6 For the LORD knows the way of the righteous, *
but the way of the wicked is doomed. [ANT.]

RCL Proper 20B (G Track) **Psalm 54**

based on "Dundee" (H82–526, 709)

Alternate harmonization for choir

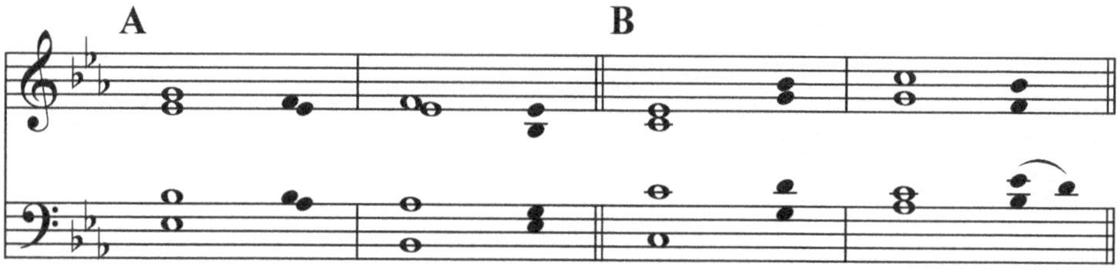

A 1 Save me, O God, by your Name; *
in your might, defend my cause.
A 2 Hear my prayer, O God; *
give ear to the words of my mouth.
B 3 For the arrogant have risen up against me,
and the ruthless have sought my life, *
those who have no regard for God. [ANT.]

4 Behold, God is my helper; *
it is the LORD who sustains my life.
5 Render evil to those who spy on me; *
in your faithfulness, destroy them. [ANT.]

6 I will offer you a freewill sacrifice *
and praise your Name, O LORD, for it is good.
7 For you have rescued me from every trouble, *
and my eye has seen the ruin of my foes. [ANT.]

RCL Proper 21B (C Track) Psalm 124

based on "Old 124th" (H82–149)

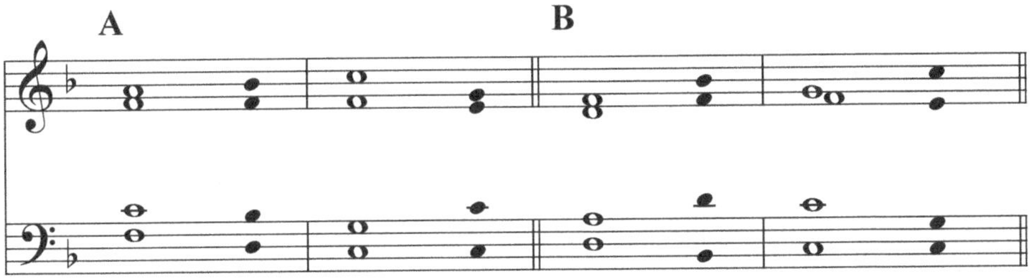

A 1 If the LORD had not been on our side, *
let Israel now say;
A 2 If the LORD had not been on our side, *
when enemies rose up against us;
B 3 Then would they have swallowed us up alive *
in their fierce anger toward us; [ANT.]

4 Then would the waters have overwhelmed us *
and the torrent gone over us;
5 Then would the raging waters *
have gone right over us. [ANT.]

A 6 Blessed be the LORD! *
he has not given us over to be a prey for their teeth.
A 7 We have escaped like a bird from the snare of the fowler; *
the snare is broken, and we have escaped.
B 8 Our help is in the Name of the LORD, *
the maker of heaven and earth. [ANT.]

RCL Proper 21B (G Track) Psalm 19: 7–14

based on "Song 1" (H82–499)

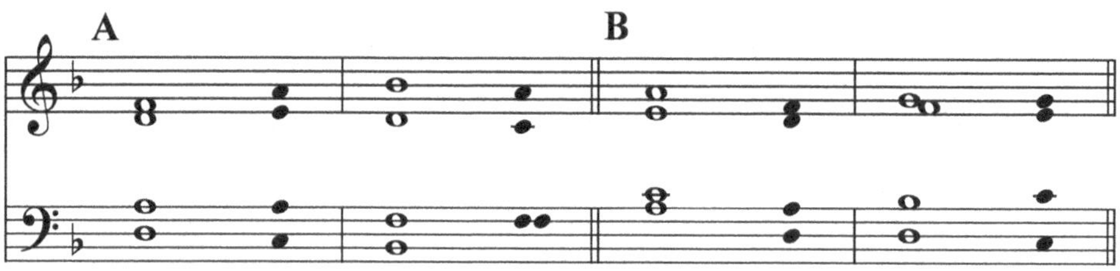

7 The law of the Lord is perfect
and revives the soul; *
the testimony of the Lord is sure
and gives wisdom to the innocent.
8 The statutes of the Lord are just
and rejoice the heart; *
the commandment of the Lord is clear
and gives light to the eyes. [ANT.]

9 The fear of the Lord is clean
and endures for ever; *
the judgments of the Lord are true
and righteous altogether.
10 More to be desired are they than gold,
more than much fine gold, *
sweeter far than honey,
than honey in the comb. [ANT.]

11 By them also is your servant enlightened, *
and in keeping them there is great reward.
12 Who can tell how often he offends? *
cleanse me from my secret faults. [ANT.]

13 Above all, keep your servant from presumptuous sins;
let them not get dominion over me; *
then shall I be whole and sound,
and innocent of a great offense.
14 Let the words of my mouth and the meditation of my
heart be acceptable in your sight, *
O Lord, my strength and my redeemer. [ANT.]

RCL Proper 22B (C Track) Psalm 26

based on "Repton" (H82–653)

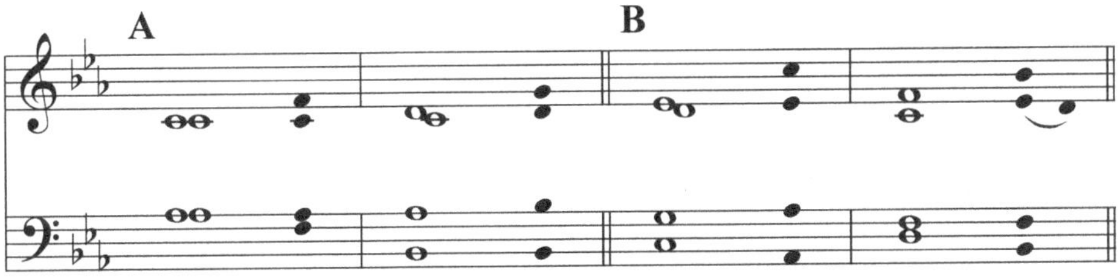

1 Give judgment for me, O Lord,
for I have lived with integrity; *
I have trusted in the Lord and have not faltered.
2 Test me, O Lord, and try me; *
examine my heart and my mind. [ANT.]

A 3 For your love is before my eyes; *
I have walked faithfully with you.
A 4 I have not sat with the worthless, *
nor do I consort with the deceitful.
B 5 I have hated the company of evildoers; *
I will not sit down with the wicked. [ANT.]

A 6 I will wash my hands in innocence, O Lord, *
that I may go in procession round your altar,
A 7 Singing aloud a song of thanksgiving *
and recounting all your wonderful deeds.
B 8 Lord, I love the house in which you dwell *
and the place where your glory abides. [ANT.]

9 Do not sweep me away with sinners, *
nor my life with those who thirst for blood,
10 Whose hands are full of evil plots, *
and their right hand full of bribes. [ANT.]

11 As for me, I will live with integrity; *
redeem me, O Lord, and have pity on me.
12 My foot stands on level ground; *
in the full assembly I will bless the Lord. [ANT.]

RCL Proper 22B (G Track) Psalm 8

based on "Leoni" (H82–372)

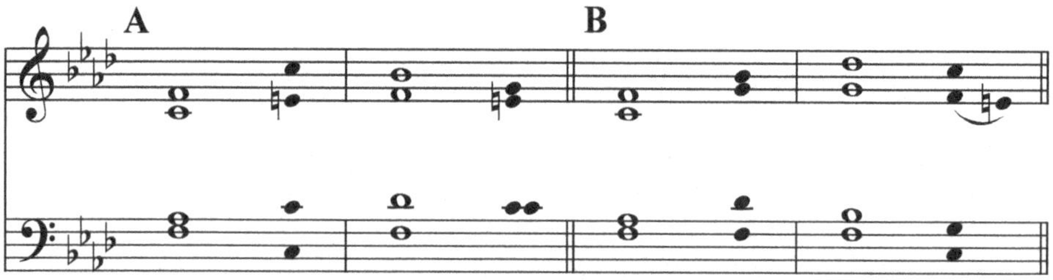

2 Out of the mouths of infants and children *
your majesty is praised above the heavens.
3 You have set up a stronghold against your adversaries, *
to quell the enemy and the avenger. [ANT.]

4 When I consider your heavens, the work of your fingers, *
the moon and the stars you have set in their courses,
5 What is man that you should be mindful of him? *
the son of man that you should seek him out? [ANT.]

A 6 You have made him but little lower than the angels; *
you adorn him with glory and honor;
B 7 You give him mastery over the works of your hands; *
you put all things under his feet:
A 8 All sheep and oxen, *
even the wild beasts of the field,
B 9 The birds of the air, the fish of the sea, *
and whatsoever walks in the paths of the sea. [ANT.]

RCL Proper 23B (C Track) Psalm 22: 1–15

based on "Picardy" (H82–324)

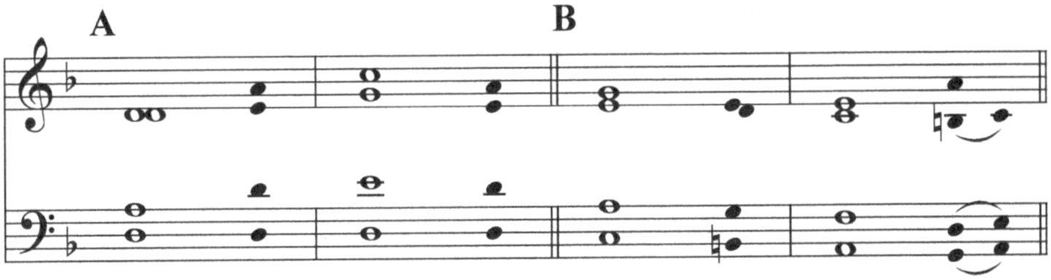

1 My God, my God, why have you forsaken me? *
and are so far from my cry
and from the words of my distress?
2 O my God, I cry in the daytime, but you do not answer; *
by night as well, but I find no rest. [ANT.]

A 3 Yet you are the Holy One, *
enthroned upon the praises of Israel.
A 4 Our forefathers put their trust in you; *
they trusted, and you delivered them.
B 5 They cried out to you and were delivered; *
they trusted in you and were not put to shame. [ANT.]

A 6 But as for me, I am a worm and no man, *
scorned by all and despised by the people.
A 7 All who see me laugh me to scorn; *
they curl their lips and wag their heads, saying,
B 8 "He trusted in the LORD; let him deliver him; *
let him rescue him, if he delights in him." [ANT.]

A 9 Yet you are he who took me out of the womb, *
and kept me safe upon my mother's breast.
A 10 I have been entrusted to you ever since I was born; *
you were my God when I was still in my
mother's womb.
B 11 Be not far from me, for trouble is near, *
and there is none to help. [ANT.]

A 12 Many young bulls encircle me; *
strong bulls of Bashan surround me.
B 13 They open wide their jaws at me, *
like a ravening and a roaring lion.
A 14 I am poured out like water;
all my bones are out of joint; *
my heart within my breast is melting wax.
B 15 My mouth is dried out like a pot-sherd;
my tongue sticks to the roof of my mouth; *
and you have laid me
in the dust of the grave. [ANT.]

RCL Proper 23B (G Track) Psalm 90: 12–17

based on "St. Anne" (H82–680)

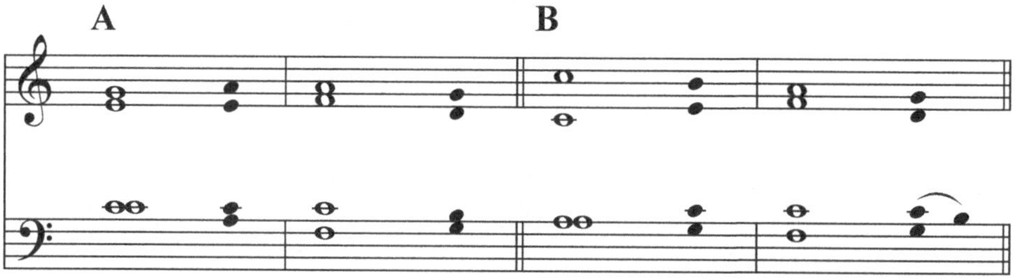

12 So teach us to number our days *
that we may apply our hearts to wisdom.
13 Return, O LORD; how long will you tarry? *
be gracious to your servants. [ANT.]

14 Satisfy us by your loving-kindness in the morning; *
so shall we rejoice and be glad all the days of our life.
15 Make us glad by the measure of the days that you afflicted us *
and the years in which we suffered adversity. [ANT.]

16 Show your servants your works *
and your splendor to their children.
17 May the graciousness of the LORD our God be upon us; *
prosper the work of our hands;
prosper our handiwork. [ANT.]

RCL Proper 24B (C Track) Psalm 104: 1–9, 25, 37b

based on "Paderborn" (H82–535)

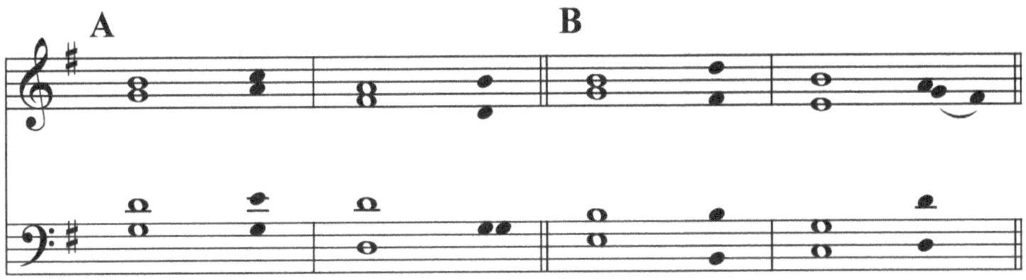

1 Bless the LORD, O my soul; *
O LORD my God, how excellent is your greatness!
you are clothed with majesty and splendor.
2 You wrap yourself with light as with a cloak *
and spread out the heavens like a curtain. [ANT.]

A 3 You lay the beams of your chambers in the waters above; *
you make the clouds your chariot;
you ride on the wings of the wind.
A 4 You make the winds your messengers *
and flames of fire your servants.
B 5 You have set the earth upon its foundations, *
so that it never shall move at any time. [ANT.]

A 6 You covered it with the Deep as with a mantle; *
the waters stood higher than the mountains.
B 7 At your rebuke they fled; *
at the voice of your thunder they hastened away.
A 8 They went up into the hills and down to the valleys beneath, *
to the places you had appointed for them.
B 9 You set the limits that they should not pass; *
they shall not again cover the earth. [ANT.]

A 25 O LORD, how manifold are your works! *
in wisdom you have made them all;
the earth is full of your creatures.
B 37b Hallelujah! [ANT.]

RCL Proper 24B (G Track) Psalm 91: 9–16

based on "Tender Thought" (H82–702)

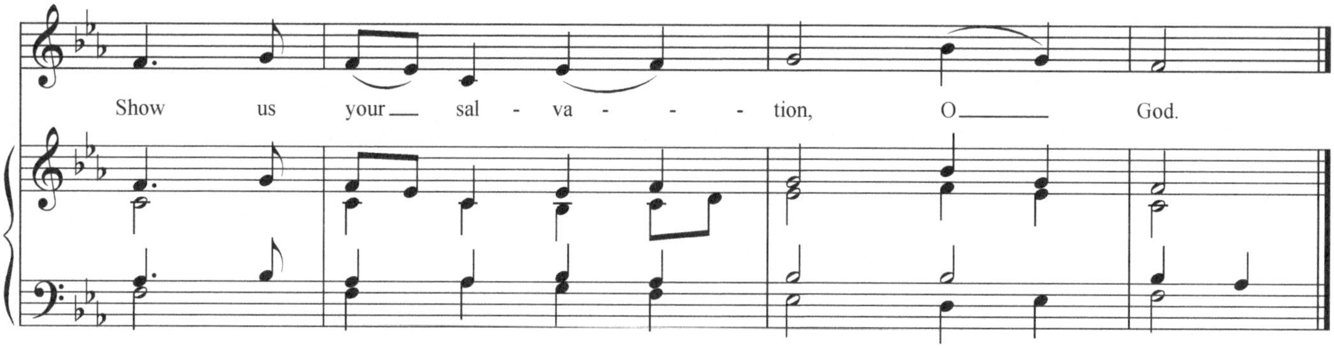

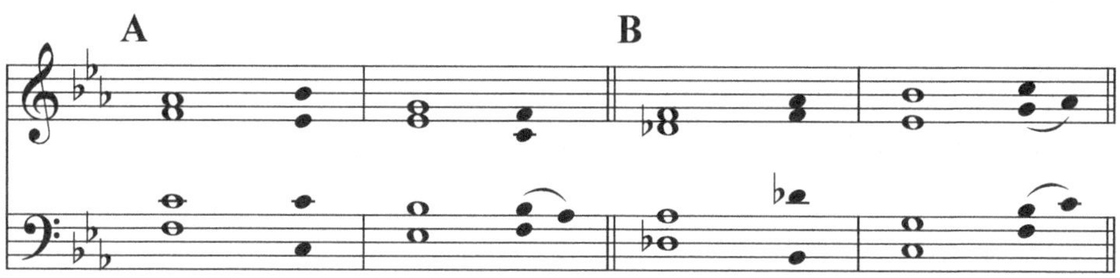

9 Because you have made the LORD your refuge, *
and the Most High your habitation,
10 There shall no evil happen to you, *
neither shall any plague come near your dwelling. [ANT.]

A 11 For he shall give his angels charge over you, *
to keep you in all your ways.
A 12 They shall bear you in their hands, *
lest you dash your foot against a stone.
B 13 You shall tread upon the lion and adder; *
you shall trample the young lion and the serpent
under your feet. [ANT.]

A 14 Because he is bound to me in love,
therefore will I deliver him; *
I will protect him, because he knows my Name.
A 15 He shall call upon me, and I will answer him; *
I am with him in trouble;
I will rescue him and bring him to honor.
B 16 With long life will I satisfy him, *
and show him my salvation. [ANT.]

RCL Proper 25B (C Track) Psalm 34: 1–8, 19–22

based on "Martyrdom" (H82–658)

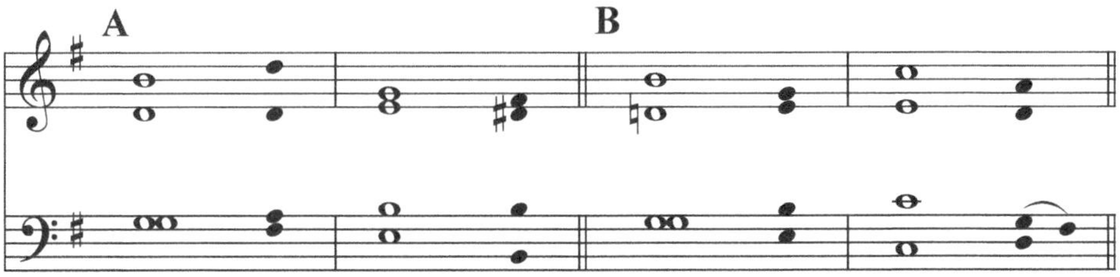

1 I will bless the LORD at all times; *
his praise shall ever be in my mouth.
2 I will glory in the LORD; *
let the humble hear and rejoice. [ANT.]

3 Proclaim with me the greatness of the LORD;
let us exalt his Name together.
4 I sought the LORD, and he answered me *
and delivered me out of all my terror. [ANT.]

5 Look upon him and be radiant, *
and let not your faces be ashamed.
6 I called in my affliction and the LORD heard me *
and saved me from all my troubles. [ANT.]

7 The angel of the LORD encompasses those who fear him, *
and he will deliver them.
8 Taste and see that the LORD is good; *
happy are they who trust in him! [ANT.]

19 Many are the troubles of the righteous, *
but the LORD will deliver him out of them all.
20 He will keep safe all his bones; *
not one of them shall be broken. [ANT.]

21 Evil shall slay the wicked, *
and those who hate the righteous will be punished.
22 The LORD ransoms the life of his servants, *
and none will be punished who trust in him. [ANT.]

RCL Proper 25B (G Track) Psalm 126

based on "New Britain" (H82–671)

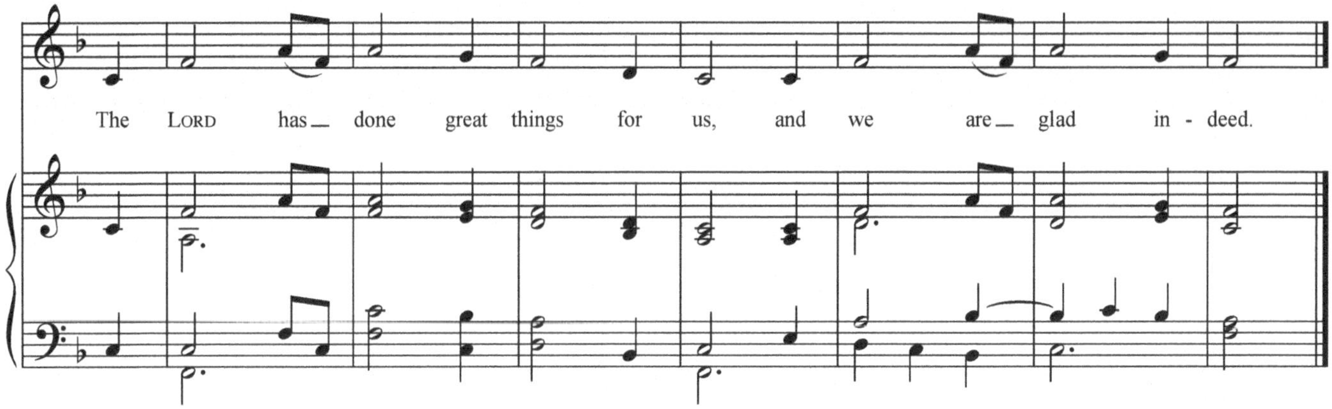

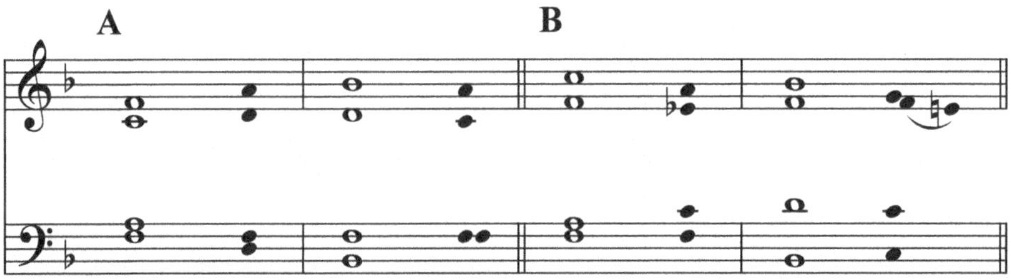

1 When the LORD restored the fortunes of Zion, *
then were we like those who dream.
2 Then was our mouth filled with laughter, *
and our tongue with shouts of joy. [ANT.]

3 Then they said among the nations, *
"The LORD has done great things for them."
5 Restore our fortunes, O LORD, *
like the watercourses of the Negev. [ANT.]

6 Those who sowed with tears *
will reap with songs of joy.
7 Those who go out weeping, carrying the seed, *
will come again with joy, shouldering their sheaves. [ANT.]

RCL All Saints' Day B Psalm 24

based on "Truro" (H82–436)

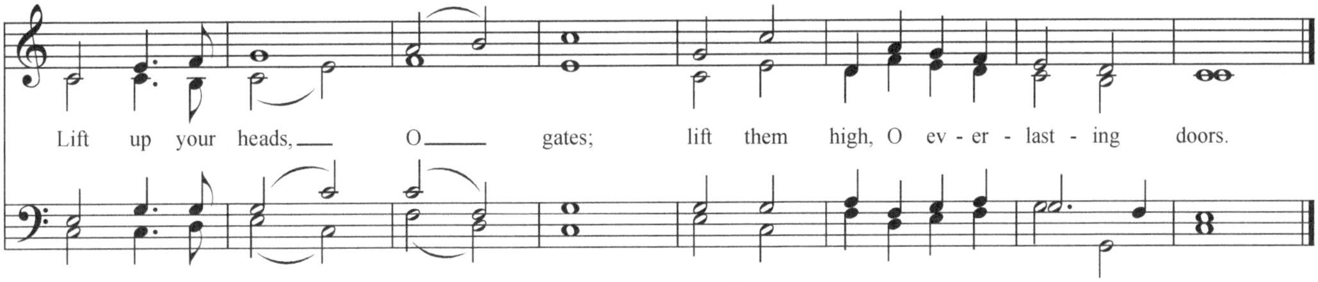

1 The earth is the LORD's and all that is in it, *
the world and all who dwell therein.
2 For it is he who founded it upon the seas *
and made it firm upon the rivers of the deep. [ANT.]

3 "Who can ascend the hill of the LORD? *
and who can stand in his holy place?"
4 "Those who have clean hands and a pure heart, *
who have not pledged themselves to falsehood,
nor sworn by what is a fraud. [ANT.]

5 They shall receive a blessing from the LORD *
and a just reward from the God of their salvation."
6 Such is the generation of those who seek him, *
of those who seek your face, O God of Jacob. [ANT.]

7 Lift up your heads, O gates;
lift them high, O everlasting doors; *
and the King of glory shall come in.
8 "Who is this King of glory?" *
"The LORD, strong and mighty,
the LORD, mighty in battle." [ANT.]

9 Lift up your heads, O gates;
lift them high, O everlasting doors; *
and the King of glory shall come in.
10 "Who is he, this King of glory?"
"The LORD of hosts,
he is the King of glory." [ANT.]

RCL Proper 26B (C Track) Psalm 146

based on "Old 124th" (H82–404)

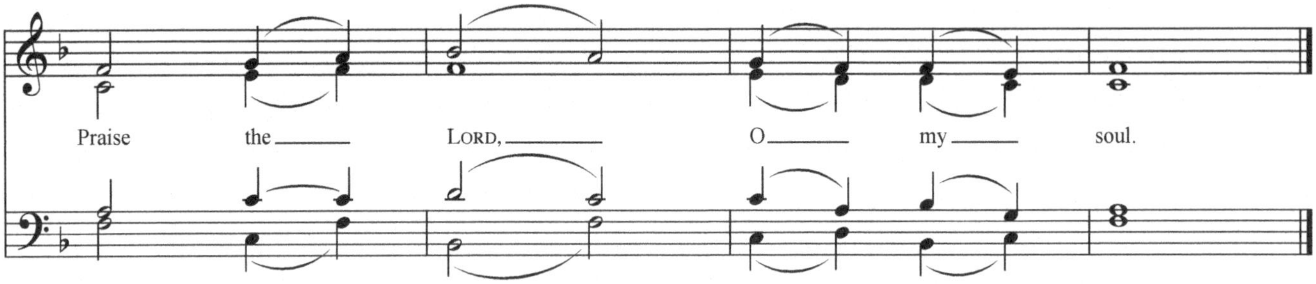

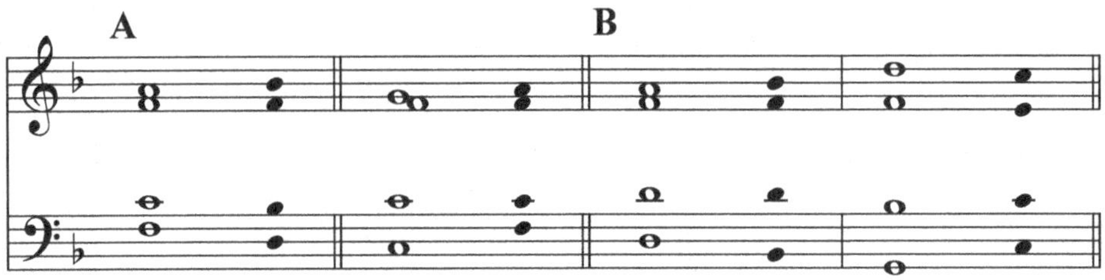

A 1 Hallelujah!
Praise the LORD, O my soul! *
I will praise the LORD as long as I live;
I will sing praises to my God while I have my being.
A 2 Put not your trust in rulers, nor in any child of earth, *
for there is no help in them.
B 3 When they breathe their last, they return to earth, *
and in that day their thoughts perish. [ANT.]

A 4 Happy are they who have the God of Jacob for their help! *
whose hope is in the LORD their God;
A 5 Who made heaven and earth, the seas, and all that is in them; *
who keeps his promise for ever;
B 6 Who gives justice to those who are oppressed, *
and food to those who hunger. [ANT.]

A 7 The LORD sets the prisoners free;
the LORD opens the eyes of the blind; *
the LORD lifts up those who are bowed down;
A 8 The LORD loves the righteous;
the LORD cares for the stranger; *
he sustains the orphan and widow,
but frustrates the way of the wicked.
B 9 The LORD shall reign for ever, *
your God, O Zion, throughout all generations.
Hallelujah! [ANT.]

RCL Proper 26B (G Track) Psalm 119: 1–8

based on "Balm in Gilead" (H82–676)

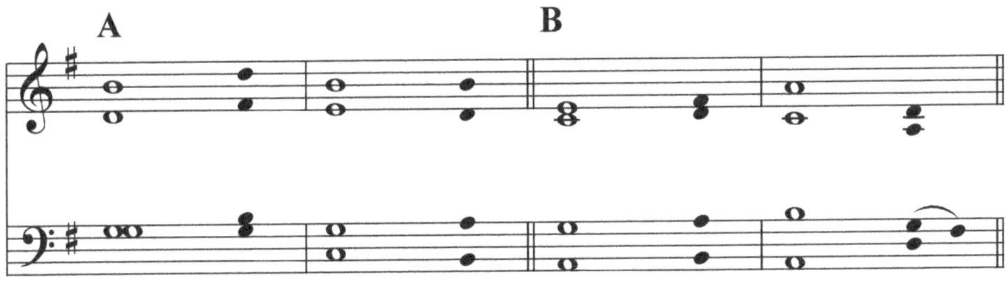

A 1 Happy are they whose way is blameless, *
who walk in the law of the LORD!

A 2 Happy are they who observe his decrees *
and seek him with all their hearts!

B 3 Who never do any wrong, *
but always walk in his ways. [ANT.]

A 4 You laid down your commandments, *
that we should fully keep them.

A 5 Oh, that my ways were made so direct *
that I might keep your statutes!

B 6 Then I should not be put to shame, *
when I regard all your commandments. [ANT.]

7 I will thank you with an unfeigned heart, *
when I have learned your righteous judgments.

8 I will keep your statutes; *
do not utterly forsake me. [ANT.]

RCL Proper 27B (C Track) Psalm 127

based on "Moscow" (H82–365)

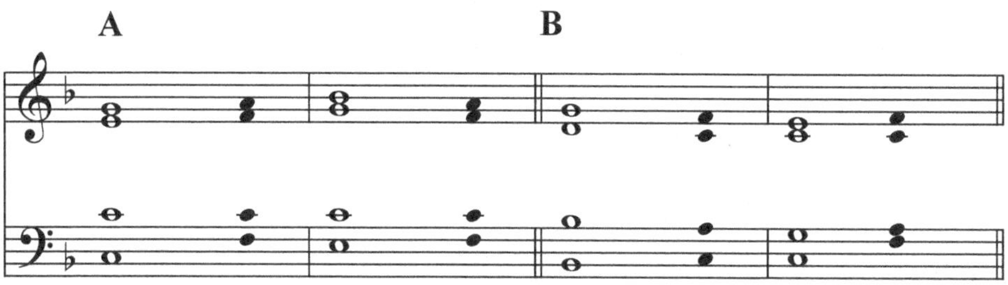

1 Unless the LORD builds the house, *
their labor is in vain who build it.
2 Unless the LORD watches over the city, *
in vain the watchman keeps his vigil. [ANT.]

A 3 It is in vain that you rise so early
and go to bed so late; *
B vain, too, to eat the bread of toil,
for he gives to his beloved sleep. [ANT.]

A 4 Children are a heritage from the LORD, *
and the fruit of the womb is a gift.
A 5 Like arrows in the hand of a warrior *
are the children of one's youth.
B 6 Happy is the man who has his quiver full of them! *
he shall not be put to shame
when he contends with his enemies in the gate. [ANT.]

RCL Proper 27B (G Track) Psalm 146

based on "Old 124th" (H82–404)

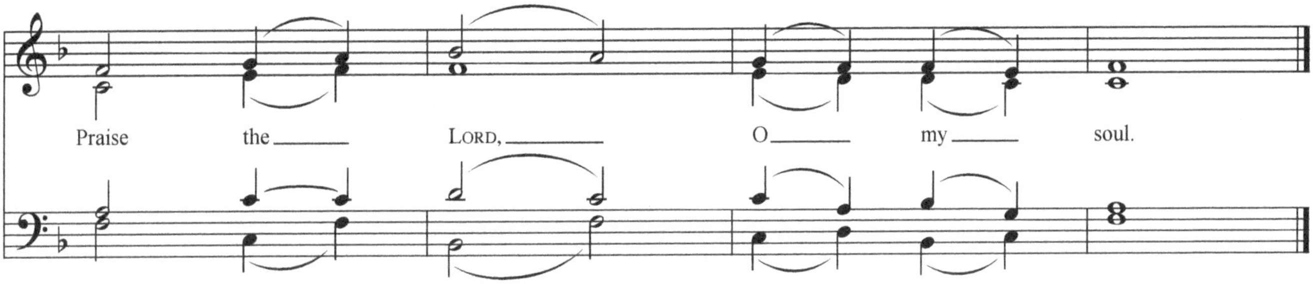

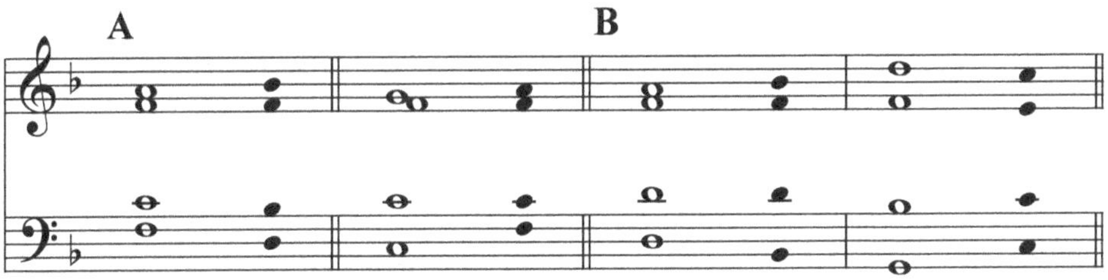

A 1 Hallelujah!
Praise the LORD, O my soul! *
I will praise the LORD as long as I live;
I will sing praises to my God while I have my being.
A 2 Put not your trust in rulers, nor in any child of earth, *
for there is no help in them.
B 3 When they breathe their last, they return to earth, *
and in that day their thoughts perish. [ANT.]

A 4 Happy are they who have the God of Jacob for their help! *
whose hope is in the LORD their God;
A 5 Who made heaven and earth, the seas, and all that is in them; *
who keeps his promise for ever;
B 6 Who gives justice to those who are oppressed, *
and food to those who hunger. [ANT.]

A 7 The LORD sets the prisoners free;
the LORD opens the eyes of the blind; *
the LORD lifts up those who are bowed down;
A 8 The LORD loves the righteous;
the LORD cares for the stranger; *
he sustains the orphan and widow,
but frustrates the way of the wicked.
B 9 The LORD shall reign for ever, *
your God, O Zion, throughout all generations.
Hallelujah! [ANT.]

RCL Proper 28B (C Track) The Song of Hannah

based on "Truro" (H82–436)

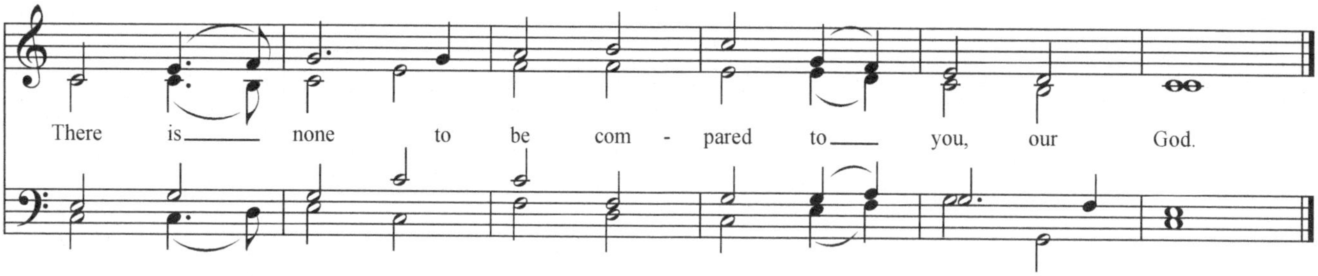

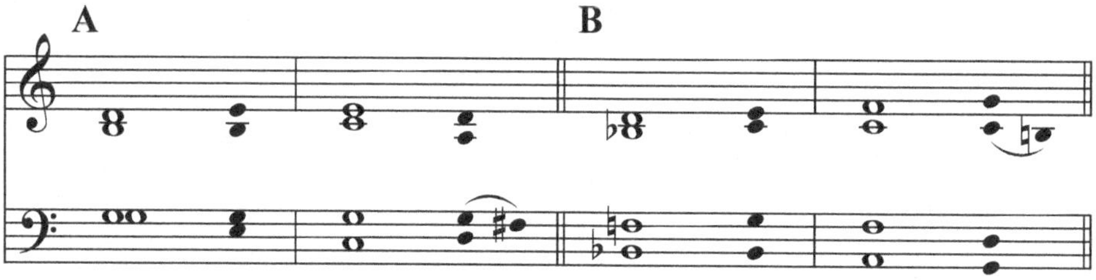

A My heart exults in you, O God; *
my triumph song is lifted in you.
A My mouth derides my enemies, *
for I rejoice in your salvation.
B There is none holy like you, *
nor any rock to be compared to you, our God. [ANT.]

A Do not heap up prideful words or speak in arrogance; *
only God is knowing and weighs all actions.
B The weapons of the mighty are broken, *
but the weak are clothed in strength.
A Those once full now labor for bread, *
those who hungered now are well fed.
B The childless woman finds her life fruitful, *
and the mother of many sits forlorn. [ANT.]

A God destroys and brings to life, casts down and raises up; *
gives wealth or takes it away, humbles and dignifies.
B God raises the poor from the dust; *
and lifts the needy from the ash heap
A To make them sit with the rulers *
and inherit a place of honor.
B For the pillars of the earth are God's *
on which the whole earth is founded. [ANT.]

A God will guide the path of the faithful, *
but the wicked will languish in darkness.
B for it is not by human might *
that any mortal will prevail.
A The foes of our God will be shattered; *
the Most High will thunder through the heavens.
B The Almighty will judge the earth to its ends *
and will give strength to the ruler of God's own choosing. [ANT.]

RCL Proper 28B (G Track) Psalm 16

based on "Rouen" (H82–360)

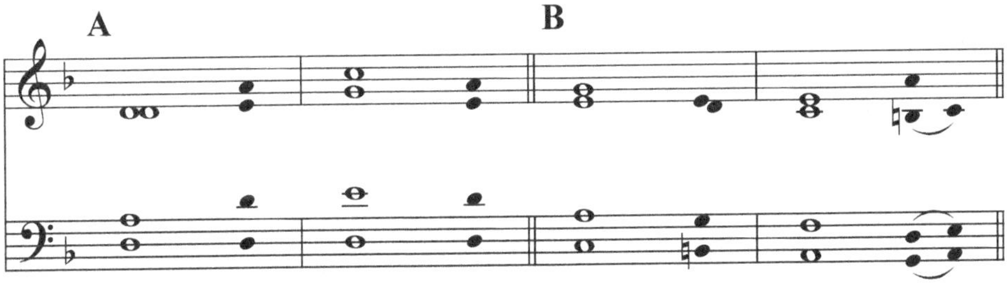

1 Protect me, O God, for I take refuge in you; *
I have said to the LORD, "You are my Lord,
my good above all other."
2 All my delight is upon the godly that are in the land, *
upon those who are noble among the people. [ANT.]

3 But those who run after other gods *
shall have their troubles multiplied.
4 Their libations of blood I will not offer, *
nor take the names of their gods upon my lips. [ANT.]

5 O LORD, you are my portion and my cup; *
it is you who uphold my lot.
6 My boundaries enclose a pleasant land; *
indeed, I have a goodly heritage. [ANT.]

7 I will bless the LORD who gives me counsel; *
my heart teaches me, night after night.
8 I have set the LORD always before me; *
because he is at my right hand I shall not fall. [ANT.]

A 9 My heart, therefore, is glad, and my spirit rejoices; *
my body also shall rest in hope.
A 10 For you will not abandon me to the grave, *
nor let your holy one see the Pit.
B 11 You will show me the path of life; *
in your presence there is fullness of joy,
and in your right hand are pleasures for evermore. [ANT.]

RCL Proper 29B (C Track) Psalm 132: 1–13

based on "Ton-y-Botel" (H82–527)

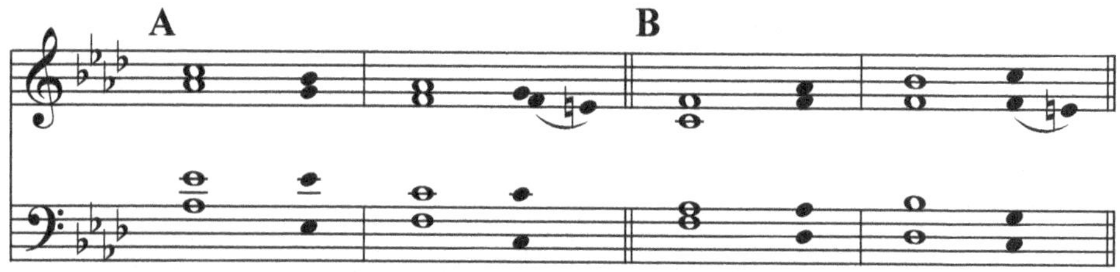

1 Lord, remember David, *
and all the hardships he endured;
2 How he swore an oath to the Lord *
and vowed a vow to the Mighty One of Jacob: [ANT.]

A 3 "I will not come under the roof of my house," *
nor climb up into my bed;
A 4 I will not allow my eyes to sleep, *
nor let my eyelids slumber;
B 5 Until I find a place for the Lord, *
a dwelling for the Mighty One of Jacob." [ANT.]

6 "The ark! We heard it was in Ephratah; *
we found it in the fields of Jearim.
7 Let us go to God's dwelling place; *
let us fall upon our knees before his footstool." [ANT.]

9 Let your priests be clothed with righteousness; *
let your faithful people sing with joy.
10 For your servant David's sake, *
do not turn away the face of your Anointed. [ANT.]

A 11 The Lord has sworn an oath to David; *
in truth, he will not break it:
A 12 "A son, the fruit of your body *
will I set upon your throne.
B 13 If your children keep my covenant
and my testimonies that I shall teach them, *
their children will sit upon your throne for evermore." [ANT.]

RCL Proper 29B (G Track) Psalm 93

based on "Hanover" (H82–388)

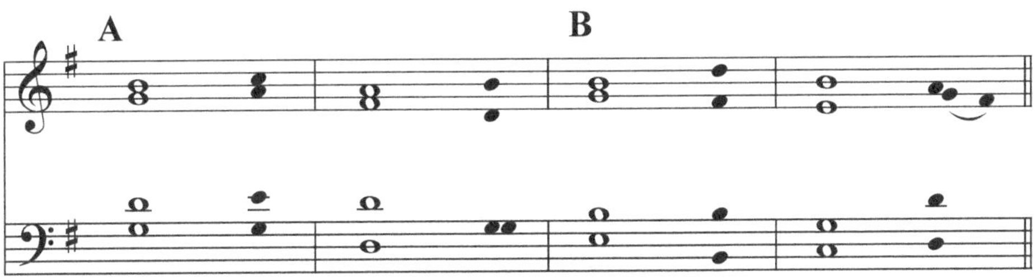

A 1 The LORD is King;
he has put on splendid apparel; *
the LORD has put on his apparel
and girded himself with strength.
A 2 He has made the whole world so sure *
that it cannot be moved;
B 3 Ever since the world began, your throne has been established; *
you are from everlasting. [ANT.]

A 4 The waters have lifted up, O LORD,
the waters have lifted up their voice; *
the waters have lifted up their pounding waves.
A 5 Mightier than the sound of many waters,
mightier than the breakers of the sea, *
mightier is the LORD who dwells on high.
B 6 Your testimonies are very sure, *
and holiness adorns your house, O LORD,
for ever and for evermore. [ANT.]

RCL Year C

Trinity Sunday through Proper 29

RCL Trinity Sunday C Psalm 8

based on "Leoni" (H82–401)

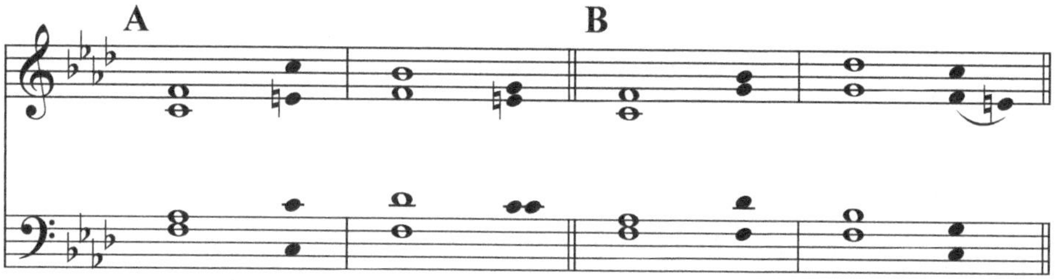

2 Out of the mouths of infants and children *
your majesty is praised above the heavens.
3 You have set up a stronghold against your adversaries, *
to quell the enemy and the avenger. [ANT.]

4 When I consider your heavens, the work of your fingers, *
the moon and the stars you have set in their courses,
5 What is man that you should be mindful of him? *
the son of man that you should seek him out? [ANT.]

A 6 You have made him but little lower than the angels; *
you adorn him with glory and honor;
B 7 You give him mastery over the works of your hands; *
you put all things under his feet:
A 8 All sheep and oxen, *
even the wild beasts of the field,
B 9 The birds of the air, the fish of the sea, *
and whatsoever walks in the paths of the sea. [ANT.]

RCL Trinity Sunday C Canticle 13

based on "Lobe den Herren" (H82–390)

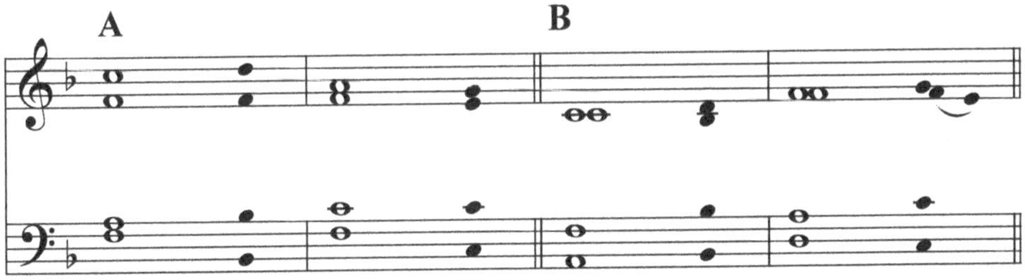

Glory to you, Lord God of our fathers; *
  you are worthy of praise; glory to you.
Glory to you for the radiance of your holy Name; *
  we will praise you and highly exalt you for ever. [ANT.]

Glory to you in the splendor of your temple; *
  on the throne of your majesty, glory to you.
Glory to you, seated between the Cherubim; *
  we will praise you and highly exalt you for ever. [ANT.]

Glory to you, beholding the depths; *
  in the high vault of heaven, glory to you.
Glory to you, Father, Son, and Holy Spirit; *
  we will praise you and highly exalt you for ever. [ANT.]

RCL Proper 1C Psalm 1

based on "Es flog ein kleins Waldvögelein" (H82–616)

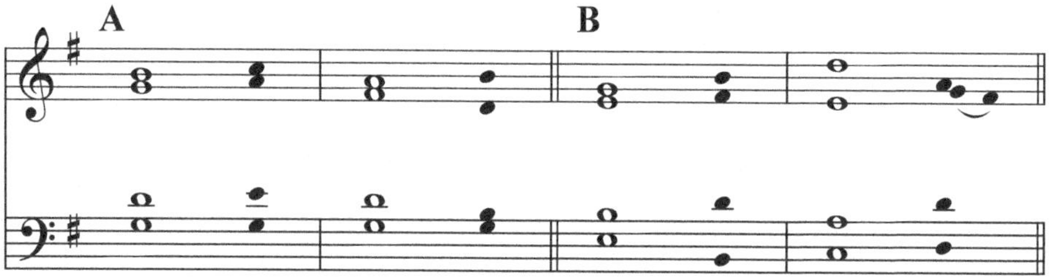

1 Happy are they who have not walked in the counsel of
the wicked, *
nor lingered in the way of sinners,
nor sat in the seats of the scornful!
2 Their delight is in the law of the LORD, *
and they meditate on his law day and night. [ANT.]

3 They are like trees planted by streams of water,
bearing fruit in due season, with leaves that do not wither; *
everything they do shall prosper.
4 It is not so with the wicked; *
they are like chaff which the wind blows away. [ANT.]

5 Therefore the wicked shall not stand upright when
judgment comes, *
nor the sinner in the council of the righteous.
6 For the LORD knows the way of the righteous, *
but the way of the wicked is doomed. [ANT.]

RCL Proper 2C Psalm 37: 1–12, 41–42

based on "Song 1" (H82–499)

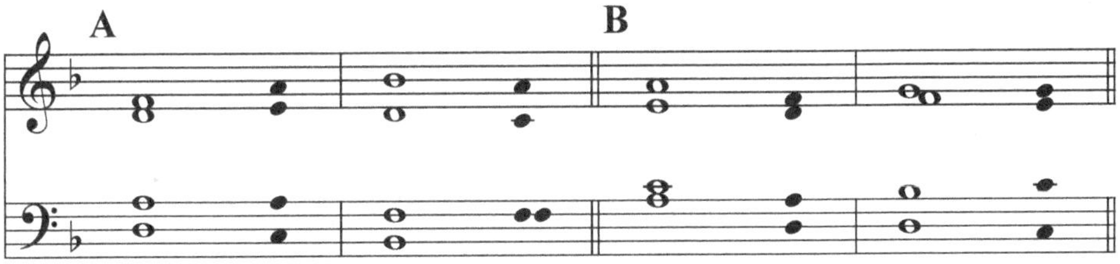

1 Do not fret yourself because of evildoers; *
  do not be jealous of those who do wrong.
2 For they shall soon wither like the grass, *
  and like the green grass fade away. [ANT.]

A 3 Put your trust in the LORD and do good; *
  dwell in the land and feed on its riches.
B 4 Take delight in the LORD, *
  and he shall give you your heart's desire.
A 5 Commit your way to the LORD and put your trust in him, *
  and he will bring it to pass.
B 6 He will make your righteousness as clear as the light *
  and your just dealing as the noonday. [ANT.]

A 7 Be still before the LORD *
  and wait patiently for him.
B 8 Do not fret yourself over the one who prospers, *
  the one who succeeds in evil schemes.
A 9 Refrain from anger, leave rage alone; *
  do not fret yourself; it leads only to evil.
B 10 For evildoers shall be cut off, *
  but those who wait upon the LORD shall possess the land. [ANT.]

11 In a little while the wicked shall be no more; *
  you shall search out their place, but they will not be there.
12 But the lowly shall possess the land; *
  they will delight in abundance of peace. [ANT.]

41 But the deliverance of the righteous comes from the LORD; *
  he is their stronghold in time of trouble.
42 The LORD will help them and rescue them; *
  he will rescue them from the wicked and deliver them,
  because they seek refuge in him. [ANT.]

RCL Proper 3C Psalm 92: 1–4, 11–14

based on "Rouen" (H82–360)

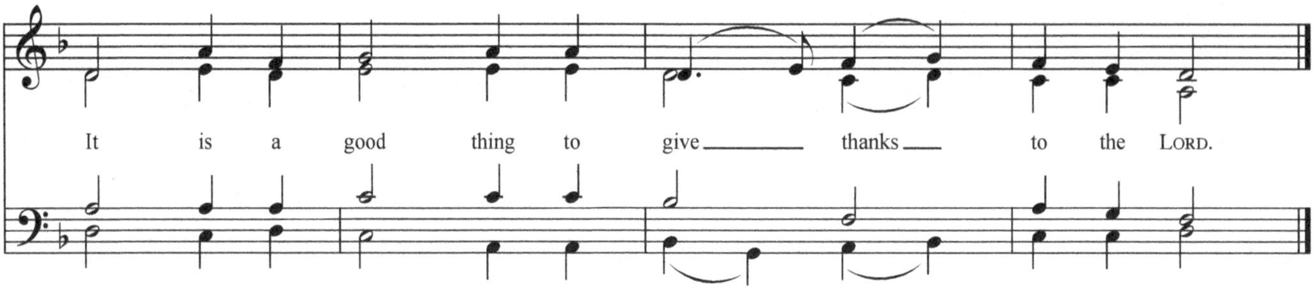

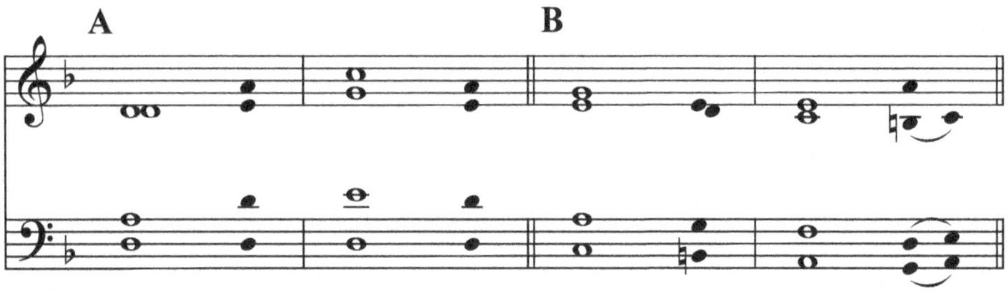

A 1 It is a good thing to give thanks to the LORD, *
and to sing praises to your Name, O Most High;
B 2 To tell of your loving-kindness early in the morning *
and of your faithfulness in the night season;
A 3 On the psaltery, and on the lyre, *
and to the melody of the harp.
B 4 For you have made me glad by your acts, O LORD; *
and I shout for joy because of the works of your hands. [ANT.]

11 The righteous shall flourish like a palm tree, *
and shall spread abroad like a cedar of Lebanon.
12 Those who are planted in the house of the LORD *
shall flourish in the courts of our God; [ANT.]

13 They shall still bear fruit in old age; *
they shall be green and succulent;
14 That they may show how upright the LORD is, *
my Rock, in whom there is no fault. [ANT.]

RCL Proper 4C (C Track) Psalm 96

based on "Liebster Jesu" (H82–440)

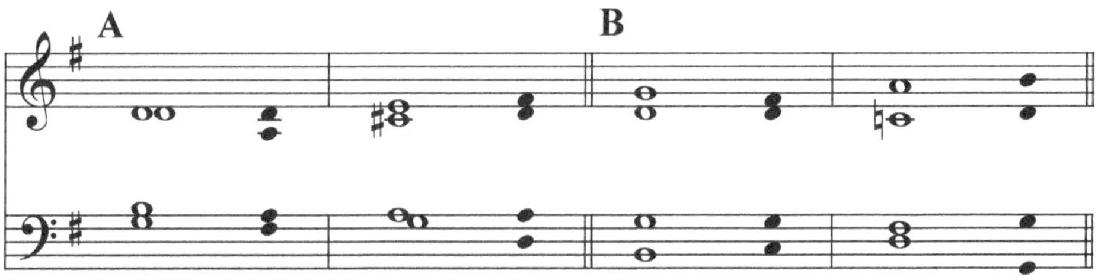

2 Sing to the LORD and bless his Name; *
proclaim the good news of his salvation from day to day.
3 Declare his glory among the nations *
and his wonders among all peoples. [ANT.]

4 For great is the LORD and greatly to be praised; *
he is more to be feared than all gods.
5 As for all the gods of the nations, they are but idols; *
but it is the LORD who made the heavens. [ANT.]

6 Oh, the majesty and magnificence of his presence! *
Oh, the power and the splendor of his sanctuary!
7 Ascribe to the LORD, you families of the peoples; *
ascribe to the LORD honor and power. [ANT.]

8 Ascribe to the LORD the honor due his Name; *
bring offerings and come into his courts.
9 Worship the LORD in the beauty of holiness; *
let the whole earth tremble before him. [ANT.]

10 Tell it out among the nations: "The LORD is King! *
he has made the world so firm that it cannot be moved;
he will judge the peoples with equity."
11 Let the heavens rejoice, and let the earth be glad;
let the sea thunder and all that is in it; *
let the field be joyful and all that is therein. [ANT.]

12 Then shall all the trees of the wood shout for joy
before the LORD when he comes, *
when he comes to judge the earth.
13 He will judge the world with righteousness *
and the peoples with his truth. [ANT.]

RCL Proper 4C (G Track) Psalm 96: 1–9

based on "Liebster Jesu" (H82–440)

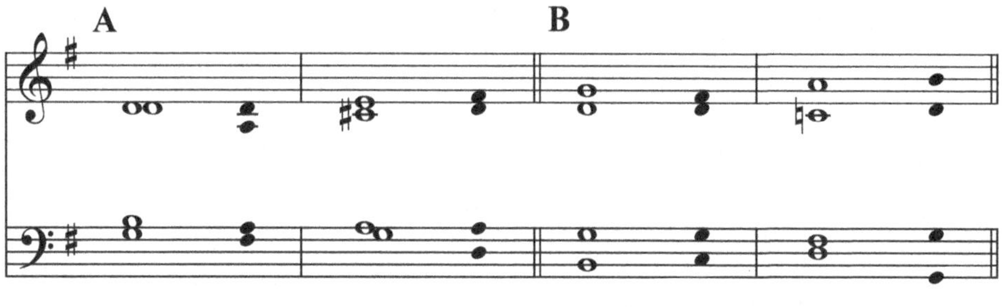

2 Sing to the LORD and bless his Name; *
 proclaim the good news of his salvation from day to day.
3 Declare his glory among the nations *
 and his wonders among all peoples. [ANT.]

4 For great is the LORD and greatly to be praised; *
 he is more to be feared than all gods.
5 As for all the gods of the nations, they are but idols; *
 but it is the LORD who made the heavens. [ANT.]

6 Oh, the majesty and magnificence of his presence! *
 Oh, the power and the splendor of his sanctuary!
7 Ascribe to the LORD, you families of the peoples; *
 ascribe to the LORD honor and power. [ANT.]

8 Ascribe to the LORD the honor due his Name; *
 bring offerings and come into his courts.
9 Worship the LORD in the beauty of holiness; *
 let the whole earth tremble before him. [ANT.]

RCL Proper 5C (C Track) Psalm 146

based on "Old 124th" (H82–404)

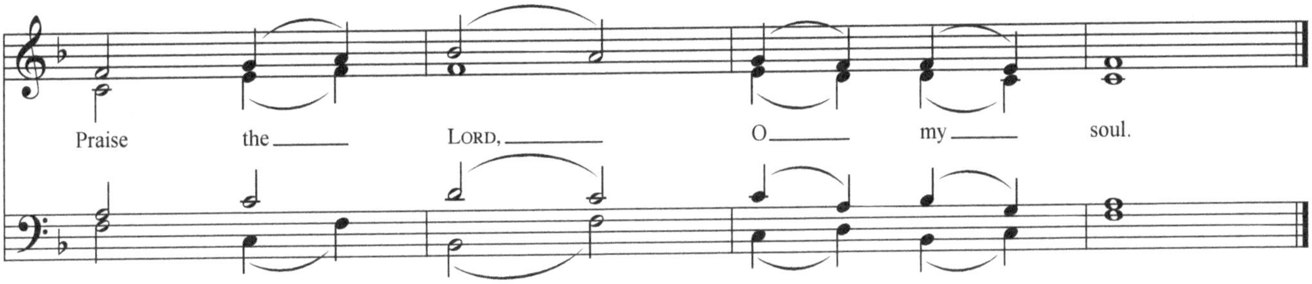

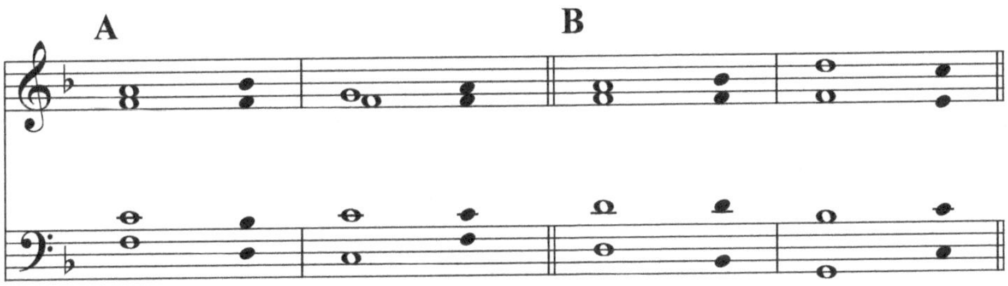

A 1 Hallelujah!
Praise the LORD, O my soul! *
I will praise the LORD as long as I live;
I will sing praises to my God while I have my being.
A 2 Put not your trust in rulers, nor in any child of earth, *
for there is no help in them.
B 3 When they breathe their last, they return to earth, *
and in that day their thoughts perish. [ANT.]

A 4 Happy are they who have the God of Jacob for their help! *
whose hope is in the LORD their God;
A 5 Who made heaven and earth, the seas, and all that is in them; *
who keeps his promise for ever;
B 6 Who gives justice to those who are oppressed, *
and food to those who hunger. [ANT.]

A 7 The LORD sets the prisoners free;
the LORD opens the eyes of the blind; *
the LORD lifts up those who are bowed down;
A 8 The LORD loves the righteous;
the LORD cares for the stranger; *
he sustains the orphan and widow,
but frustrates the way of the wicked.
B 9 The LORD shall reign for ever, *
your God, O Zion, throughout all generations.
Hallelujah! [ANT.]

RCL Proper 5C (G Track) Psalm 30

based on "Truro" (H82–182)

A 1 I will exalt you, O Lord,
because you have lifted me up *
and have not let my enemies triumph over me.
A 2 O Lord my God, I cried out to you, *
and you restored me to health.
B 3 You brought me up, O Lord, from the dead; *
you restored my life as I was going down to the grave. [ANT.]

A 4 Sing to the Lord, you servants of his; *
give thanks for the remembrance of his holiness.
A 5 For his wrath endures but the twinkling of an eye, *
his favor for a lifetime.
B 6 Weeping may spend the night, *
but joy comes in the morning. [ANT.]

7 While I felt secure, I said,
"I shall never be disturbed. *
You, Lord, with your favor, made me as strong as
the mountains."
8 Then you hid your face, *
and I was filled with fear. [ANT.]

A 9 I cried to you, O Lord; *
I pleaded with the Lord, saying,
A 10 "What profit is there in my blood, if I go down to the Pit? *
will the dust praise you or declare your faithfulness?
B 11 Hear, O Lord, and have mercy upon me; *
O Lord, be my helper." [ANT.]

12 You have turned my wailing into dancing; *
you have put off my sack-cloth and clothed me with joy.
13 Therefore my heart sings to you without ceasing; *
O Lord my God, I will give you thanks for ever. [ANT.]

RCL Proper 6C (C Track) Psalm 5: 1–8

based on "Eventide" (H82–662)

A 1 Give ear to my words, O LORD; *
consider my meditation.
A 2 Hearken to my cry for help, my King and my God, *
for I make my prayer to you.
B 3 In the morning, LORD, you hear my voice; *
early in the morning I make my appeal and watch for you. [ANT.]

A 4 For you are not a God who takes pleasure in wickedness, *
and evil cannot dwell with you.
A 5 Braggarts cannot stand in your sight; *
you hate all those who work wickedness.
B 6 You destroy those who speak lies; *
the bloodthirsty and deceitful, O LORD, you abhor. [ANT.]

7 But as for me, through the greatness of your mercy I will go into your house; *
I will bow down toward your holy temple in awe of you.
8 Lead me, O LORD, in your righteousness,
because of those who lie in wait for me; *
make your way straight before me. [ANT.]

RCL Proper 6C (G Track) Psalm 32

based on "Tender Thought" (H82–702)

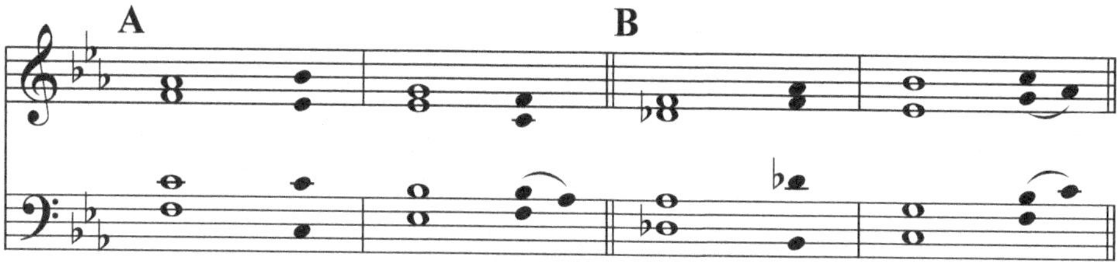

1 Happy are they whose transgressions are forgiven, *
and whose sin is put away!
2 Happy are they to whom the Lord imputes no guilt, *
and in whose spirit there is no guile! [ANT.]

3 While I held my tongue, my bones withered away, *
because of my groaning all day long.
4 For your hand was heavy upon me day and night; *
my moisture was dried up as in the heat of summer.

5 Then I acknowledged my sin to you, *
and did not conceal my guilt.
6 I said, "I will confess my transgressions to the Lord." *
Then you forgave me the guilt of my sin. [ANT.]

7 Therefore all the faithful will make their prayers to you in time of trouble; *
when the great waters overflow, they shall not reach them.
8 You are my hiding-place;
you preserve me from trouble; *
you surround me with shouts of deliverance. [ANT.]

9 "I will instruct you and teach you in the way that you should go; *
I will guide you with my eye.
10 Do not be like horse or mule, which have no understanding; *
who must be fitted with bit and bridle,
or else they will not stay near you." [ANT.]

11 Great are the tribulations of the wicked; *
but mercy embraces those who trust in the Lord.
12 Be glad, you righteous, and rejoice in the Lord; *
shout for joy, all who are true of heart. [ANT.]

This page intentionally left blank

RCL Proper 7C (C Track) **Psalms 42 & 43**

based on "Wondrous Love" (H82–439)

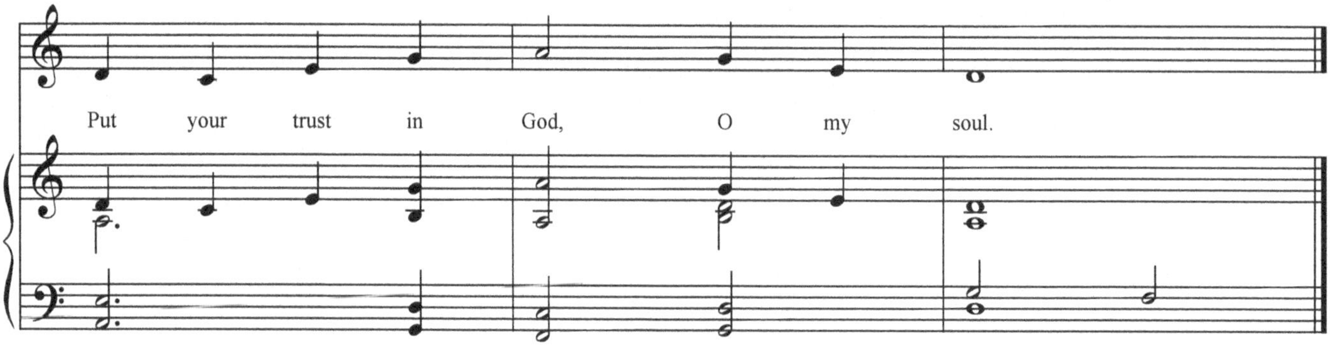

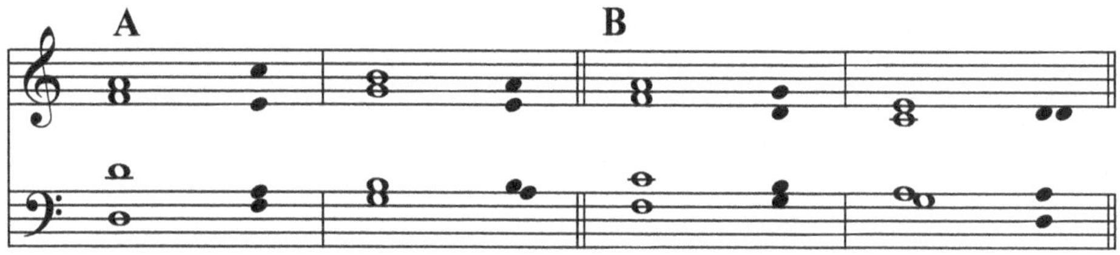

A 1 As the deer longs for the water-brooks, *
so longs my soul for you, O God.
A 2 My soul is athirst for God, athirst for the living God; *
when shall I come to appear before the presence of God?
B 3 My tears have been my food day and night, *
while all day long they say to me,
"Where now is your God?" [ANT.]

A 4 I pour out my soul when I think on these things: *
how I went with the multitude and led them into the house of God,
B 5 With the voice of praise and thanksgiving, *
among those who keep holy-day. [ANT.]

A 6 Why are you so full of heaviness, O my soul? *
and why are you so disquieted within me?
B 7 Put your trust in God; *
for I will yet give thanks to him,
who is the help of my countenance, and my God. [ANT.]

A 8 My soul is heavy within me; *
therefore I will remember you from the land of Jordan,
and from the peak of Mizar among the heights of Hermon.
A 9 One deep calls to another in the noise of your cataracts; *
all your rapids and floods have gone over me.
B 10 The LORD grants his loving-kindness in the daytime; *
in the night season his song is with me,
a prayer to the God of my life. [ANT.]

A 11 I will say to the God of my strength,
"Why have you forgotten me? *
and why do I go so heavily while the enemy
oppresses me?"
A 12 While my bones are being broken, *
my enemies mock me to my face;
B 13 All day long they mock me *
and say to me, "Where now is your God?" [ANT.]

14 Why are you so full of heaviness, O my soul? *
and why are you so disquieted within me?
15 Put your trust in God; *
for I will yet give thanks to him,
who is the help of my countenance, and my God. [ANT.]

1 Give judgment for me, O God,
and defend my cause against an ungodly people; *
deliver me from the deceitful and the wicked.
2 For you are the God of my strength;
why have you put me from you? *
and why do I go so heavily while the enemy
oppresses me? [ANT.]

3 Send out your light and your truth, that they may lead me, *
and bring me to your holy hill
and to your dwelling;
4 That I may go to the altar of God,
to the God of my joy and gladness; *
and on the harp I will give thanks to you,
O God my God. [ANT.]

5 Why are you so full of heaviness, O my soul? *
and why are you so disquieted within me?
6 Put your trust in God; *
for I will yet give thanks to him,
who is the help of my countenance, and my God. [ANT.]

RCL Proper 7C (G Track) Psalm 22: 18–27

based on "Holy Manna" (H82–580)

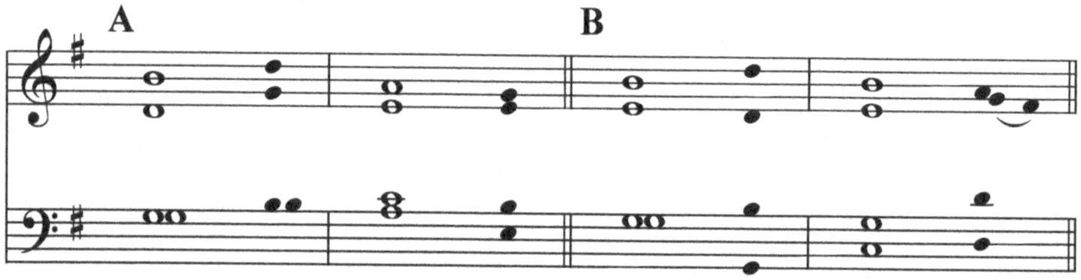

A 18 Be not far away, O Lord; *
you are my strength; hasten to help me.
A 19 Save me from the sword, *
my life from the power of the dog.
B 20 Save me from the lion's mouth, *
my wretched body from the horns of wild bulls. [ANT.]

A 21 I will declare your Name to my brethren; *
in the midst of the congregation I will praise you.
A 22 Praise the Lord, you that fear him; *
stand in awe of him, O offspring of Israel;
all you of Jacob's line, give glory.
B 23 For he does not despise nor abhor the poor in their poverty;
neither does he hide his face from them; *
but when they cry to him he hears them. [ANT.]

24 My praise is of him in the great assembly; *
I will perform my vows in the presence of those who worship him.
25 The poor shall eat and be satisfied,
and those who seek the Lord shall praise him: *
"May your heart live for ever!" [ANT.]

26 All the ends of the earth shall remember and turn to the Lord, *
and all the families of the nations shall bow before him.
27 For kingship belongs to the Lord; *
he rules over the nations. [ANT.]

RCL Proper 8C (C Track) Psalm 77: 1–2, 11–20

based on "Wareham" (H82–137)

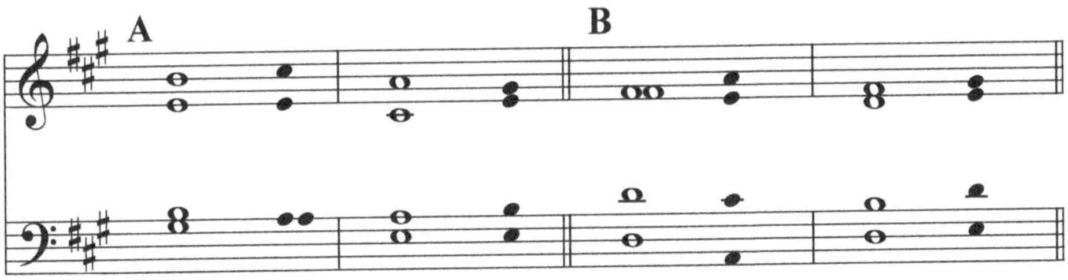

1 I will cry aloud to God; *
 I will cry aloud, and he will hear me.
2 In the day of my trouble I sought the Lord; *
 my hands were stretched out by night and did not tire;
 I refused to be comforted. [ANT.]

11 I will remember the works of the LORD, *
 and call to mind your wonders of old time.
12 I will meditate on all your acts *
 and ponder your mighty deeds. [ANT.]

A 13 Your way, O God, is holy; *
 who is so great a god as our God?
A 14 You are the God who works wonders *
 and have declared your power among the peoples.
B 15 By your strength you have redeemed your people, *
 the children of Jacob and Joseph. [ANT.]

A 16 The waters saw you, O God;
 the waters saw you and trembled; *
 the very depths were shaken.
A 17 The clouds poured out water;
 the skies thundered; *
 your arrows flashed to and fro;
B 18 The sound of your thunder was in the whirlwind;
 your lightnings lit up the world; *
 the earth trembled and shook. [ANT.]

19 Your way was in the sea,
 and your paths in the great waters, *
 yet your footsteps were not seen.
20 You led your people like a flock *
 by the hand of Moses and Aaron. [ANT.]

RCL Proper 8C (G Track) Psalm 16

based on "Rouen" (H82–360)

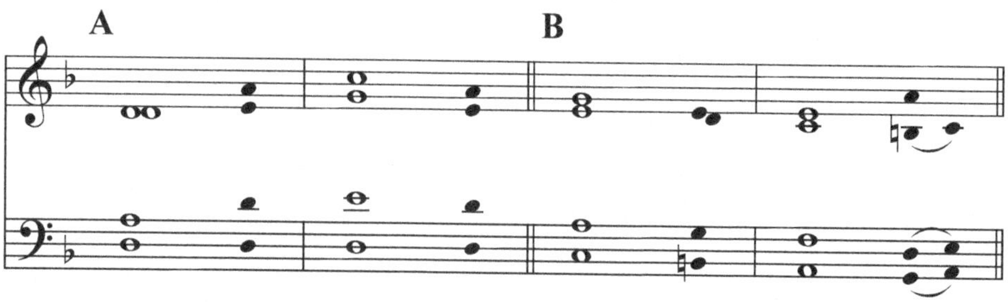

A 1 Protect me, O God, for I take refuge in you; *
I have said to the LORD, "You are my Lord,
my good above all other."
B 2 All my delight is upon the godly that are in the land, *
upon those who are noble among the people.
A 3 But those who run after other gods *
shall have their troubles multiplied.
B 4 Their libations of blood I will not offer, *
nor take the names of their gods upon my lips. [ANT.]

5 O LORD, you are my portion and my cup; *
it is you who uphold my lot.
6 My boundaries enclose a pleasant land; *
indeed, I have a goodly heritage. [ANT.]

A 7 I will bless the LORD who gives me counsel; *
my heart teaches me, night after night.
A 8 I have set the LORD always before me; *
because he is at my right hand I shall not fall.
B 9 My heart, therefore, is glad, and my spirit rejoices; *
my body also shall rest in hope. [ANT.]

10 For you will not abandon me to the grave, *
nor let your holy one see the Pit.
11 You will show me the path of life; *
in your presence there is fullness of joy,
and in your right hand are pleasures for evermore. [ANT.]

RCL Proper 9C (C Track) Psalm 30

based on "Truro" (H82–182)

A 1 I will exalt you, O LORD,
because you have lifted me up *
and have not let my enemies triumph over me.
A 2 O LORD my God, I cried out to you, *
and you restored me to health.
B 3 You brought me up, O LORD, from the dead; *
you restored my life as I was going down to the grave. [ANT.]

A 4 Sing to the LORD, you servants of his; *
give thanks for the remembrance of his holiness.
A 5 For his wrath endures but the twinkling of an eye, *
his favor for a lifetime.
B 6 Weeping may spend the night, *
but joy comes in the morning. [ANT.]

7 While I felt secure, I said,
"I shall never be disturbed. *
You, LORD, with your favor, made me as strong as
the mountains."
8 Then you hid your face, *
and I was filled with fear. [ANT.]

A 9 I cried to you, O LORD; *
I pleaded with the LORD, saying,
A 10 "What profit is there in my blood, if I go down to the Pit? *
will the dust praise you or declare your faithfulness?
B 11 Hear, O LORD, and have mercy upon me; *
O LORD, be my helper." [ANT.]

12 You have turned my wailing into dancing; *
you have put off my sack-cloth and clothed me with joy.
13 Therefore my heart sings to you without ceasing; *
O LORD my God, I will give you thanks for ever. [ANT.]

RCL Proper 9C (G Track) **Psalm 66: 1–8**

based on "Paderborn" (H82–535)

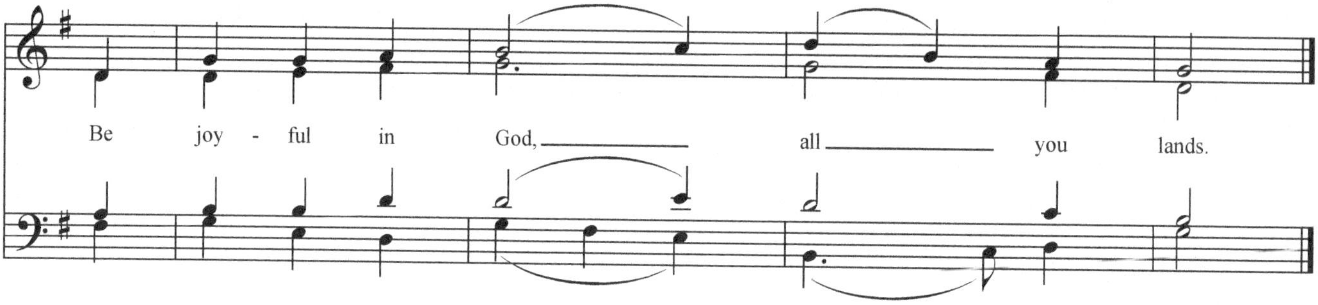

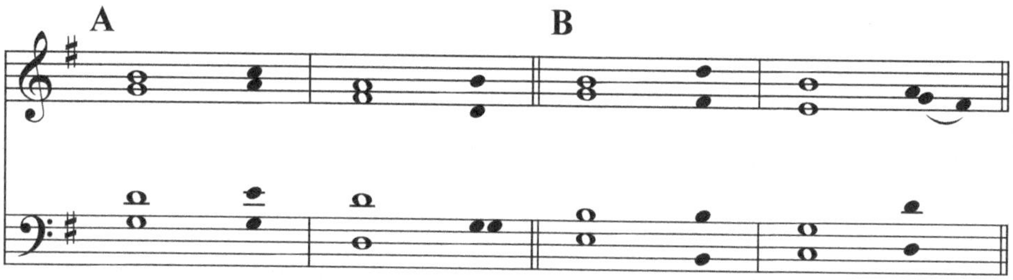

1 Be joyful in God, all you lands; *
sing the glory of his Name;
sing the glory of his praise.
2 Say to God, "How awesome are your deeds! *
because of your great strength your enemies
cringe before you. [ANT.]

3 All the earth bows down before you, *
sings to you, sings out your Name."
4 Come now and see the works of God, *
how wonderful he is in his doing toward all people. [ANT.]

5 He turned the sea into dry land,
so that they went through the water on foot, *
and there we rejoiced in him.
6 In his might he rules for ever;
his eyes keep watch over the nations; *
let no rebel rise up against him. [ANT.]

7 Bless our God, you peoples; *
make the voice of his praise to be heard;
8 Who holds our souls in life, *
and will not allow our feet to slip. [ANT.]

RCL Proper 10C (C Track) Psalm 82

based on "In Babilone" (H82–215)

1 God takes his stand in the council of heaven; *
he gives judgment in the midst of the gods:
2 "How long will you judge unjustly, *
and show favor to the wicked? [ANT.]

3 Save the weak and the orphan; *
defend the humble and needy;
4 Rescue the weak and the poor; *
deliver them from the power of the wicked. [ANT.]

5 They do not know,
neither do they understand;
they go about in darkness; *
all the foundations of the earth are shaken. [ANT.]

A 6 Now I say to you, 'You are gods, *
and all of you children of the Most High;
A 7 Nevertheless, you shall die like mortals, *
and fall like any prince.'"
B 8 Arise, O God, and rule the earth, *
for you shall take all nations for your own. [ANT.]

RCL Proper 10C (G Track) Psalm 25: 1–9

based on "Picardy" (H82–324)

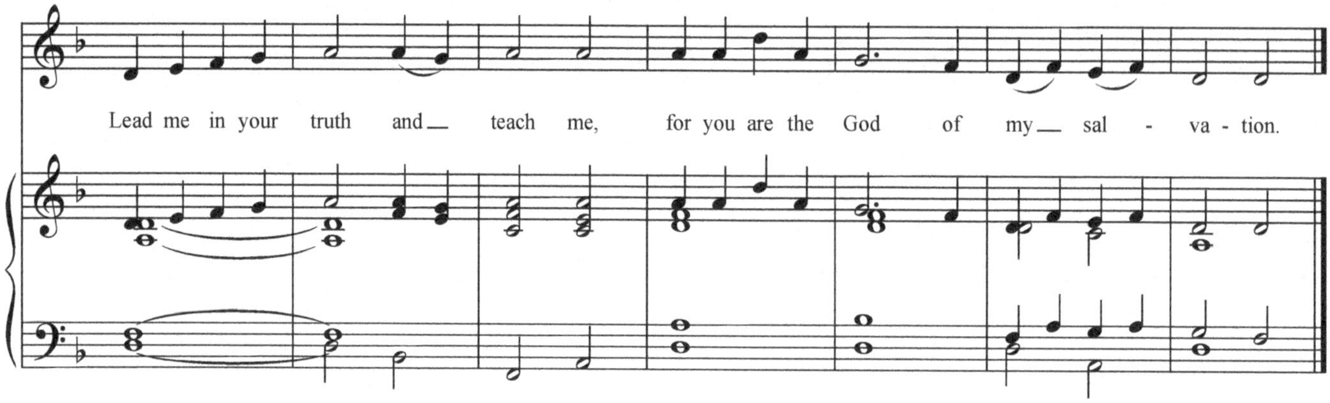

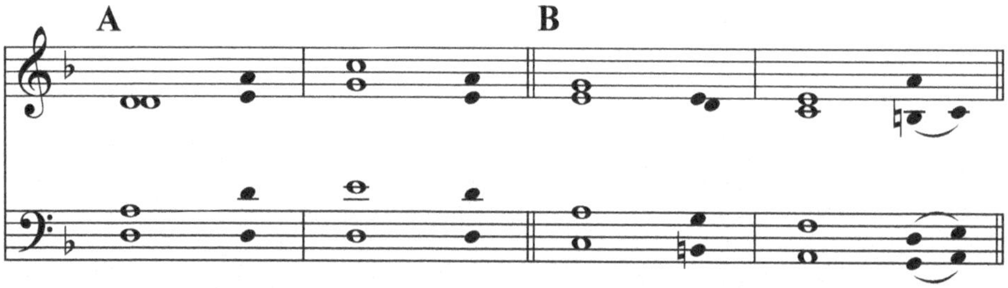

A 1 To you, O Lord, I lift up my soul;
my God, I put my trust in you; *
A let me not be humiliated,
nor let my enemies triumph over me.
B 2 Let none who look to you be put to shame; *
let the treacherous be disappointed in their schemes. [ANT.]

A 3 Show me your ways, O Lord, *
and teach me your paths.
A 4 Lead me in your truth and teach me, *
for you are the God of my salvation;
in you have I trusted all the day long.
B 5 Remember, O Lord, your compassion and love, *
for they are from everlasting. [ANT.]

6 Remember not the sins of my youth and my transgressions; *
remember me according to your love
and for the sake of your goodness, O Lord.
7 Gracious and upright is the Lord; *
therefore he teaches sinners in his way. [ANT.]

8 He guides the humble in doing right *
and teaches his way to the lowly.
9 All the paths of the Lord are love and faithfulness *
to those who keep his covenant and his testimonies. [ANT.]

RCL Proper 11C (C Track) Psalm 52

based on "Charlestown" (H82–571)

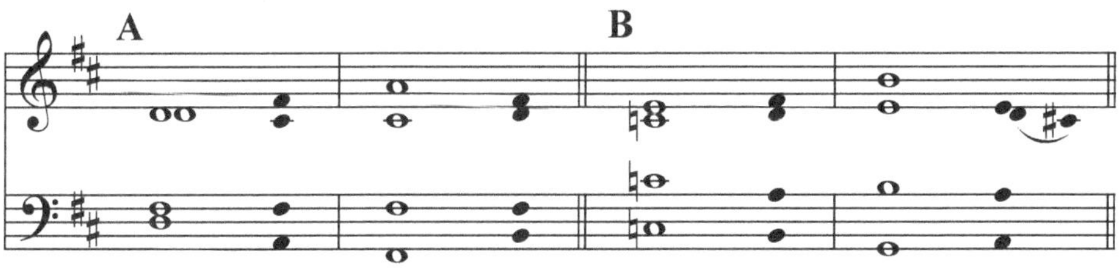

A 1 You tyrant, why do you boast of wickedness *
against the godly all day long?
B 2 You plot ruin;
your tongue is like a sharpened razor, *
O worker of deception.
A 3 You love evil more than good *
and lying more than speaking the truth.
B 4 You love all words that hurt, *
O you deceitful tongue. [ANT.]

A 5 Oh, that God would demolish you utterly, *
topple you, and snatch you from your dwelling,
and root you out of the land of the living!
A 6 The righteous shall see and tremble, *
and they shall laugh at him, saying,
B 7 "This is the one who did not take God for a refuge, *
but trusted in great wealth
and relied upon wickedness." [ANT.]

8 But I am like a green olive tree in the house of God; *
I trust in the mercy of God for ever and ever.
9 I will give you thanks for what you have done *
and declare the goodness of your Name in the presence
of the godly. [ANT.]

RCL Proper 11C (G Track) Psalm 15

based on "Festal Song" (H82–551)

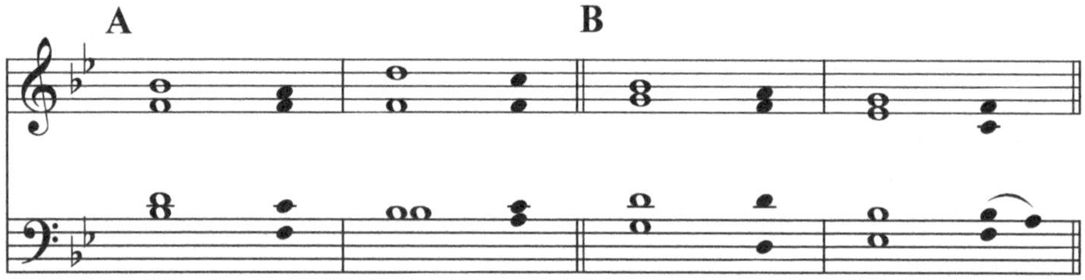

1 LORD, who may dwell in your tabernacle? *
who may abide upon your holy hill?
2 Whoever leads a blameless life and does what is right, *
who speaks the truth from his heart. [ANT.]

A 3 There is no guile upon his tongue;
he does no evil to his friend; *
B he does not heap contempt
upon his neighbor. [ANT.]

4 In his sight the wicked is rejected, *
but he honors those who fear the LORD.
5 He has sworn to do no wrong *
and does not take back his word. [ANT.]

6 He does not give his money in hope of gain, *
nor does he take a bribe against the innocent.
7 Whoever does these things *
shall never be overthrown. [ANT.]

RCL Proper 12C (C Track) Psalm 85

based on "Aus tiefer Not" (H82–151)

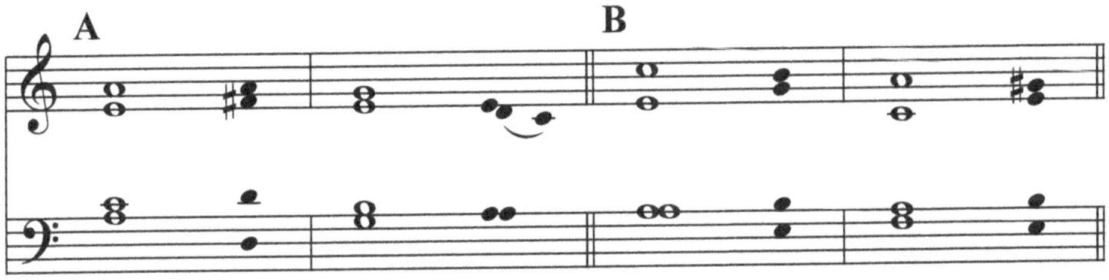

A 1 You have been gracious to your land, O LORD, *
you have restored the good fortune of Jacob.
A 2 You have forgiven the iniquity of your people *
and blotted out all their sins.
B 3 You have withdrawn all your fury *
and turned yourself from your wrathful indignation. [ANT.]

A 4 Restore us then, O God our Savior; *
let your anger depart from us.
A 5 Will you be displeased with us for ever? *
will you prolong your anger from age to age?
B 6 Will you not give us life again, *
that your people may rejoice in you? [ANT.]

8 I will listen to what the LORD God is saying, *
for he is speaking peace to his faithful people
and to those who turn their hearts to him.
9 Truly, his salvation is very near to those who fear him, *
that his glory may dwell in our land. [ANT.]

10 Mercy and truth have met together; *
righteousness and peace have kissed each other.
11 Truth shall spring up from the earth, *
and righteousness shall look down from heaven. [ANT.]

12 The LORD will indeed grant prosperity, *
and our land will yield its increase.
13 Righteousness shall go before him, *
and peace shall be a pathway for his feet. [ANT.]

RCL Proper 12C (G Track) Psalm 138

based on "St. Clement" (H82–24)

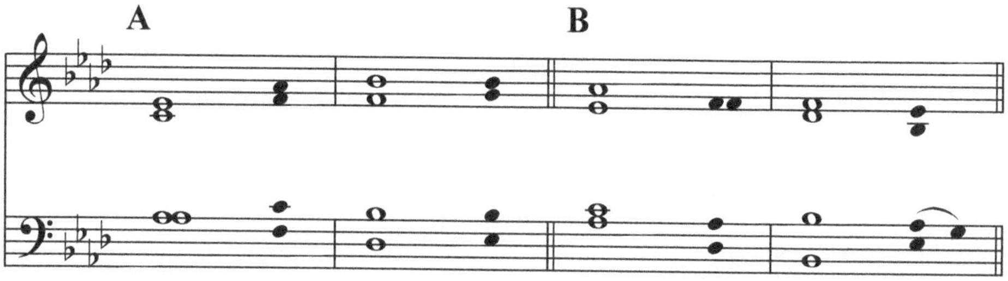

1 I will give thanks to you, O LORD, with my whole heart; *
before the gods I will sing your praise.
2 I will bow down toward your holy temple
and praise your Name, *
because of your love and faithfulness; [ANT.]

3 For you have glorified your Name *
and your word above all things.
4 When I called, you answered me; *
you increased my strength within me. [ANT.]

5 All the kings of the earth will praise you, O LORD, *
when they have heard the words of your mouth.
6 They will sing of the ways of the LORD, *
that great is the glory of the LORD. [ANT.]

A 7 Though the LORD be high, he cares for the lowly; *
he perceives the haughty from afar.
A 8 Though I walk in the midst of trouble, you keep me safe; *
you stretch forth your hand against the fury of my enemies;
your right hand shall save me.
B 9 The LORD will make good his purpose for me; *
O LORD, your love endures for ever;
do not abandon the works of your hands. [ANT.]

RCL Proper 13C (C Track) Psalm 107: 1–9, 43

based on "Darwall's 148th" (H82–625)

A 1 Give thanks to the LORD, for he is good, *
and his mercy endures for ever.
A 2 Let all those whom the LORD has redeemed proclaim *
that he redeemed them from the hand of the foe.
B 3 He gathered them out of the lands; *
from the east and from the west,
from the north and from the south. [ANT.]

A 4 Some wandered in desert wastes; *
they found no way to a city where they might dwell.
B 5 They were hungry and thirsty; *
their spirits languished within them.
A 6 Then they cried to the LORD in their trouble, *
and he delivered them from their distress.
B 7 He put their feet on a straight path *
to go to a city where they might dwell. [ANT.]

A 8 Let them give thanks to the Lord for his mercy *
and the wonders he does for his children.
A 9 For he satisfies the thirsty *
and fills the hungry with good things.
B 43 Whoever is wise will ponder these things, *
and consider well the mercies of the LORD. [ANT.]

RCL Proper 13C (G Track) Psalm 49: 1–11

based on "Holy Manna" (H82–580)

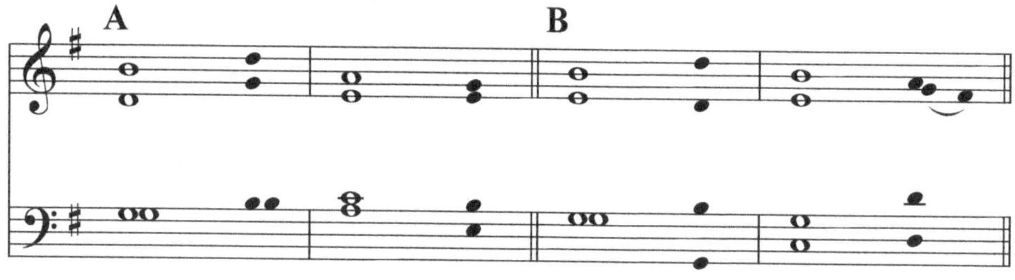

A 1 Hear this, all you peoples;
hearken, all you who dwell in the world, *
you of high degree and low, rich and poor together.
A 2 My mouth shall speak of wisdom, *
and my heart shall meditate on understanding.
B 3 I will incline my ear to a proverb *
and set forth my riddle upon the harp. [ANT.]

4 Why should I be afraid in evil days, *
when the wickedness of those at my heels surrounds me,
5 The wickedness of those who put their trust in their goods, *
and boast of their great riches? [ANT.]

7 For the ransom of our life is so great, *
that we should never have enough to pay it,
8 In order to live for ever and ever, *
and never see the grave. [ANT.]

A 9 For we see that the wise die also;
like the dull and stupid they perish *
and leave their wealth to those who come after them.
A 10 Their graves shall be their homes for ever,
their dwelling places from generation to generation, *
though they call the lands after their own names.
B 11 Even though honored, they cannot live for ever; *
they are like the beasts that perish. [ANT.]

RCL Transfiguration ABC August 6 Psalm 99

based on "Old 124th" (H82–404)

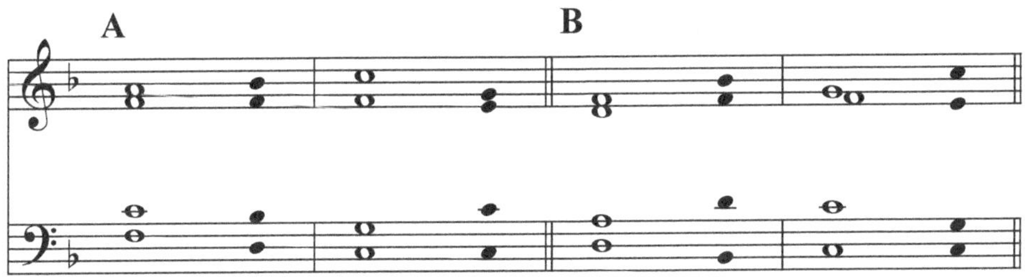

A 1 The LORD is King;
let the people tremble; *
he is enthroned upon the cherubim;
let the earth shake.
A 2 The LORD is great in Zion; *
he is high above all peoples.
B 3 Let them confess his Name, which is great and awesome; *
he is the Holy One. [ANT.]

4 "O mighty King, lover of justice,
you have established equity; *
you have executed justice and righteousness in Jacob."
5 Proclaim the greatness of the LORD our God
and fall down before his footstool; *
he is the Holy One. [ANT.]

6 Moses and Aaron among his priests,
and Samuel among those who call upon his Name, *
they called upon the LORD, and he answered them.
7 He spoke to them out of the pillar of cloud; *
they kept his testimonies and the decree that he gave them. [ANT.]

8 "O LORD our God, you answered them indeed; *
you were a God who forgave them,
yet punished them for their evil deeds."
9 Proclaim the greatness of the LORD our God
and worship him upon his holy hill; *
for the LORD our God is the Holy One. [ANT.]

RCL Proper 14C (C Track) Psalm 50: 1–8, 23–24

based on "Nyland" (H82–232)

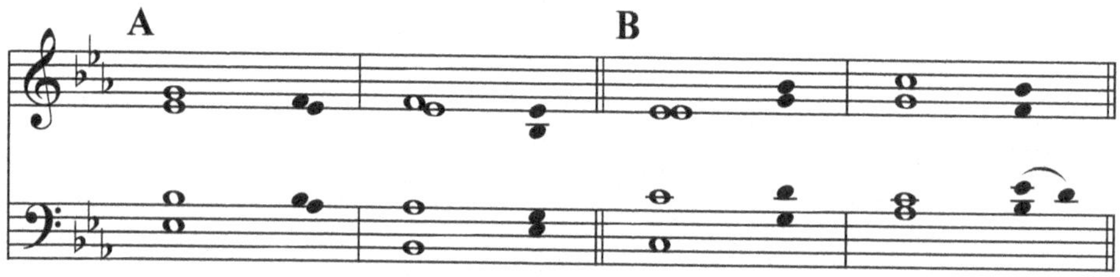

A 1 The LORD, the God of gods, has spoken; *
he has called the earth from the rising of the sun to its setting.

A 2 Out of Zion, perfect in its beauty, *
God reveals himself in glory.

B 3 Our God will come and will not keep silence; *
before him there is a consuming flame,
and round about him a raging storm. [ANT.]

A 4 He calls the heavens and the earth from above *
to witness the judgment of his people.

A 5 "Gather before me my loyal followers, *
those who have made a covenant with me
and sealed it with sacrifice."

B 6 Let the heavens declare the rightness of his cause; *
for God himself is judge. [ANT.]

7 Hear, O my people, and I will speak:
"O Israel, I will bear witness against you; *
for I am God, your God.

8 I do not accuse you because of your sacrifices; *
your offerings are always before me. [ANT.]

23 Consider this well, you who forget God, *
lest I rend you and there be none to deliver you.

24 Whoever offers me the sacrifice of thanksgiving honors me; *
but to those who keep in my way will I show the salvation of God." [ANT.]

RCL Proper 14C (G Track) Psalm 33: 12–22

based on "Nyland" (H82–232)

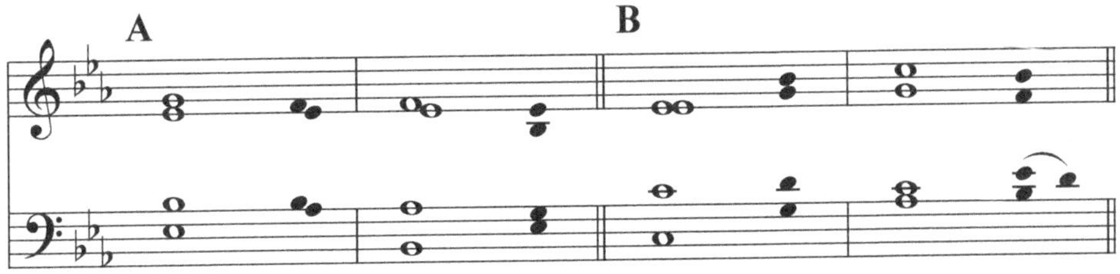

12 Happy is the nation whose God is the LORD! *
happy the people he has chosen to be his own!
13 The LORD looks down from heaven, *
and beholds all the people in the world. [ANT.]

14 From where he sits enthroned he turns his gaze *
on all who dwell on the earth.
15 He fashions all the hearts of them *
and understands all their works. [ANT.]

16 There is no king that can be saved by a mighty army;
a strong man is not delivered by his great strength.
17 The horse is a vain hope for deliverance; *
or all its strength it cannot save. [ANT.]

18 Behold, the eye of the LORD is upon those who fear him, *
on those who wait upon his love,
19 To pluck their lives from death, *
and to feed them in time of famine. [ANT.]

21 Indeed, our heart rejoices in him, *
for in his holy Name we put our trust.
22 Let your loving-kindness, O LORD, be upon us, *
as we have put our trust in you. [ANT.]

RCL Proper 15C (C Track) Psalm 80: 1–2, 8–18

based on "Picardy" (H82–324)

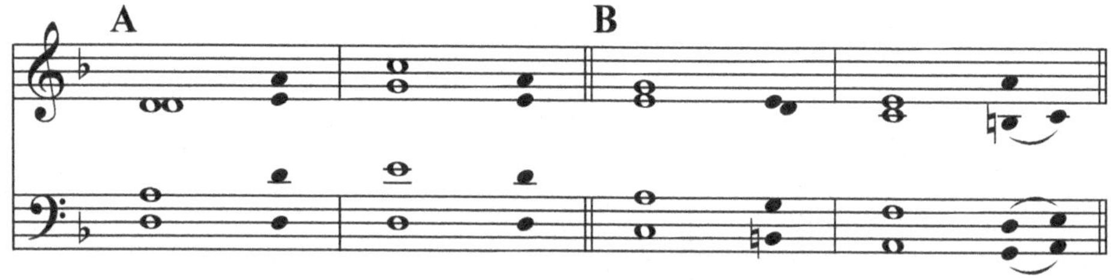

1 Hear, O Shepherd of Israel, leading Joseph like a flock; *
shine forth, you that are enthroned upon the cherubim.
2 In the presence of Ephraim, Benjamin, and Manasseh, *
stir up your strength and come to help us. [ANT.]

A 8 You have brought a vine out of Egypt; *
you cast out the nations and planted it.
B 9 You prepared the ground for it; *
it took root and filled the land.
A 10 The mountains were covered by its shadow *
and the towering cedar trees by its boughs.
B 11 You stretched out its tendrils to the Sea *
and its branches to the River. [ANT.]

12 Why have you broken down its wall, *
so that all who pass by pluck off its grapes?
13 The wild boar of the forest has ravaged it, *
and the beasts of the field have grazed upon it. [ANT.]

14 Turn now, O God of hosts, look down from heaven;
behold and tend this vine; *
preserve what your right hand has planted.
15 They burn it with fire like rubbish; *
at the rebuke of your countenance let them perish. [ANT.]

A 16 Let your hand be upon the man of your right hand, *
the son of man you have made so strong for yourself.
A 17 And so will we never turn away from you; *
give us life, that we may call upon your Name.
B 18 Restore us, O LORD God of hosts; *
show the light of your countenance, and we shall be saved. [ANT.]

RCL Proper 15C (G Track) Psalm 82

based on "Birmingham" (H82–437)

1 God takes his stand in the council of heaven; *
he gives judgment in the midst of the gods:
2 "How long will you judge unjustly, *
and show favor to the wicked? [ANT.]

3 Save the weak and the orphan; *
defend the humble and needy;
4 Rescue the weak and the poor; *
deliver them from the power of the wicked. [ANT.]

5 They do not know,
neither do they understand;
they go about in darkness; *
all the foundations of the earth are shaken. [ANT.]

A 6 Now I say to you, 'You are gods, *
and all of you children of the Most High;
A 7 Nevertheless, you shall die like mortals, *
and fall like any prince.'"
B 8 Arise, O God, and rule the earth, *
for you shall take all nations for your own. [ANT.]

RCL Proper16C (C Track) Psalm 71: 1–6

based on "Paderborn" (H82–535)

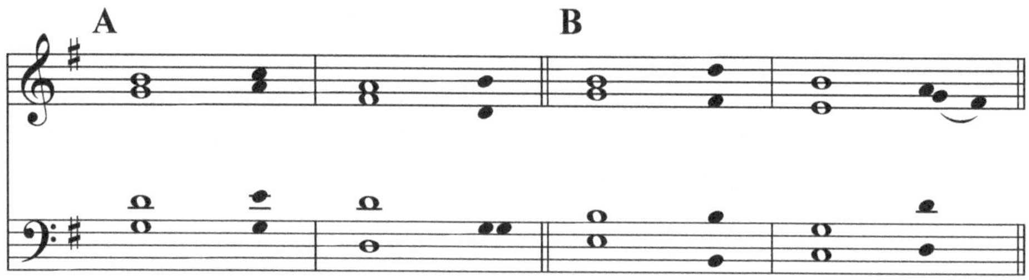

1 In you, O Lord, have I taken refuge; *
let me never be ashamed.
2 In your righteousness, deliver me and set me free; *
incline your ear to me and save me. [ANT.]

3 Be my strong rock, a castle to keep me safe; *
you are my crag and my stronghold.
4 Deliver me, my God, from the hand of the wicked, *
from the clutches of the evildoer and the oppressor. [ANT.]

5 For you are my hope, O Lord God, *
my confidence since I was young.
6 I have been sustained by you ever since I was born;
from my mother's womb you have been my strength; *
my praise shall be always of you. [ANT.]

RCL Proper 16C (G Track) Psalm 103: 1–8

based on "Wondrous Love" (H82–439)

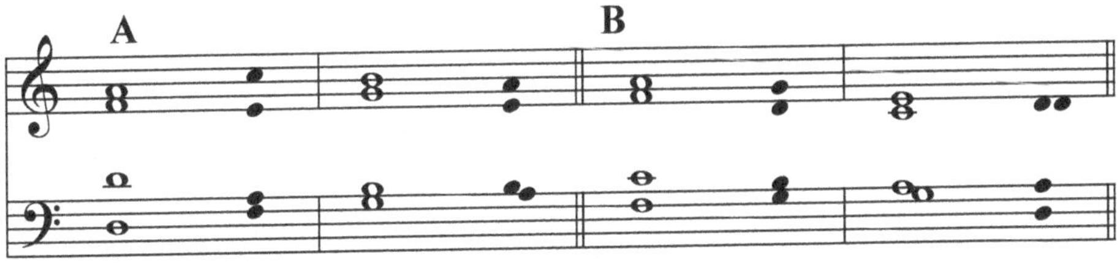

1 Bless the LORD, O my soul, *
  and all that is within me, bless his holy Name.
2 Bless the LORD, O my soul, *
  and forget not all his benefits. [ANT.]

3 He forgives all your sins *
  and heals all your infirmities;
4 He redeems your life from the grave *
  and crowns you with mercy and loving-kindness; [ANT.]

5 He satisfies you with good things, *
  and your youth is renewed like an eagle's.
6 The LORD executes righteousness *
  and judgment for all who are oppressed. [ANT.]

7 He made his ways known to Moses *
  and his works to the children of Israel.
8 The LORD is full of compassion and mercy, *
  slow to anger and of great kindness. [ANT.]

RCL Proper 17C (C Track) Psalm 81: 1, 10–16

based on "Gott sei Dank" (H82–47)

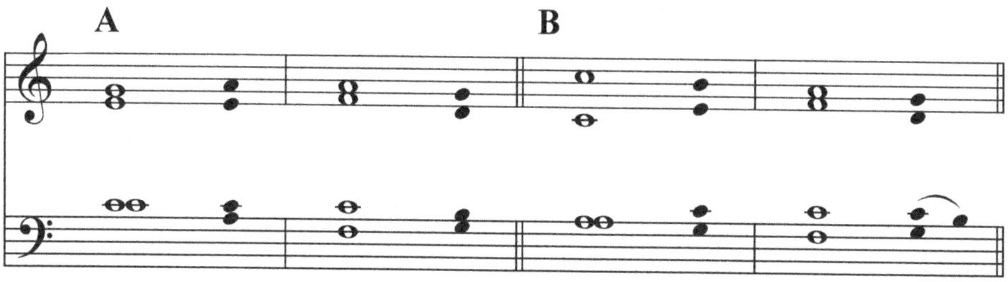

1 Sing with joy to God our strength *
 and raise a loud shout to the God of Jacob.
10 I am the LORD your God,
 who brought you out of the land of Egypt and said, *
 "Open your mouth wide, and I will fill it." [ANT.]

11 And yet my people did not hear my voice, *
 and Israel would not obey me.
12 So I gave them over to the stubbornness of their hearts, *
 to follow their own devices. [ANT.]

13 Oh, that my people would listen to me! *
 that Israel would walk in my ways!
14 I should soon subdue their enemies *
 and turn my hand against their foes. [ANT.]

15 Those who hate the LORD would cringe before him, *
 and their punishment would last for ever.
16 But Israel would I feed with the finest wheat *
 and satisfy him with honey from the rock. [ANT.]

RCL Proper 17C (G Track) Psalm 112

based on "Gelobt sei Gott" (H82–205)

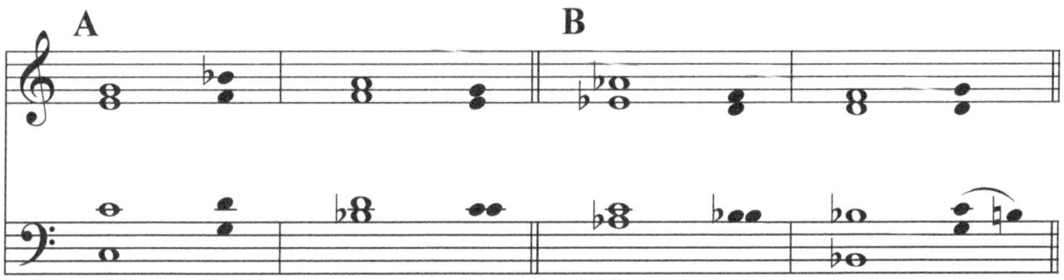

A 1 Hallelujah!
Happy are they who fear the LORD *
and have great delight in his commandments!
A 2 Their descendants will be mighty in the land; *
the generation of the upright will be blessed.
B 3 Wealth and riches will be in their house, *
and their righteousness will last for ever. [ANT.]

A 4 Light shines in the darkness for the upright; *
the righteous are merciful and full of compassion.
A 5 It is good for them to be generous in lending *
and to manage their affairs with justice.
B 6 For they will never be shaken; *
the righteous will be kept in everlasting remembrance. [ANT.]

7 They will not be afraid of any evil rumors; *
their heart is right;
they put their trust in the LORD.
8 Their heart is established and will not shrink, *
until they see their desire upon their enemies. [ANT.]

9 They have given freely to the poor, *
and their righteousness stands fast for ever;
they will hold up their head with honor.
10 The wicked will see it and be angry;
they will gnash their teeth and pine away; *
the desires of the wicked will perish. [ANT.]

RCL Proper 18C (C Track) Psalm 139: 1–5, 12–17

based on "Tender Thought" (H82–702)

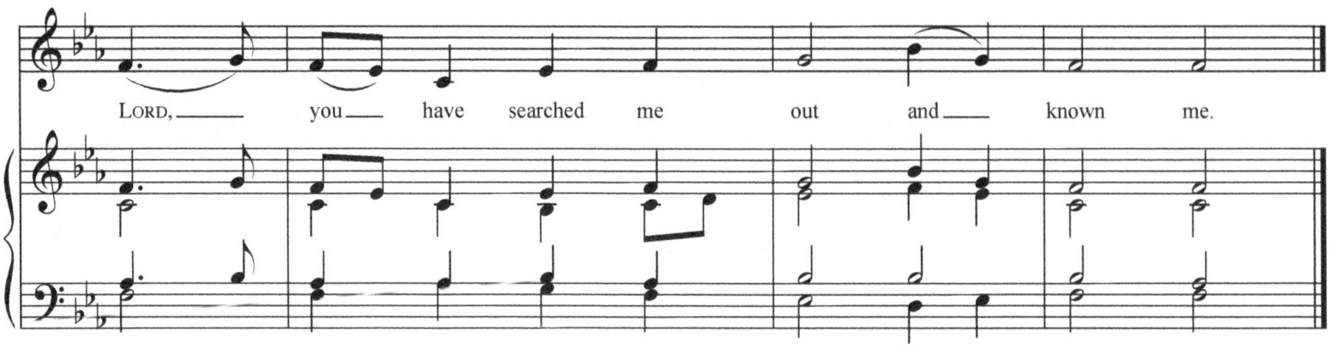

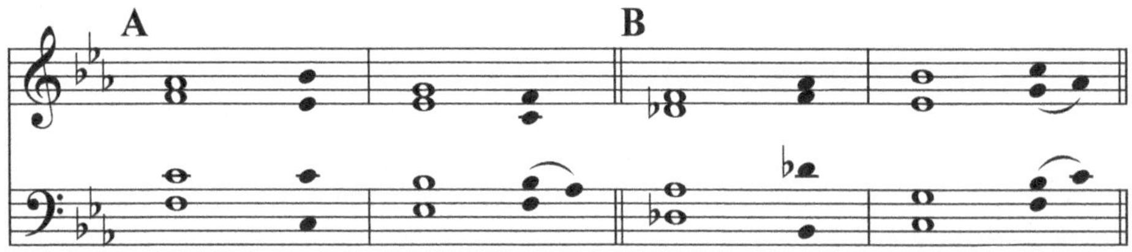

1 LORD, you have searched me out and known me; *
you know my sitting down and my rising up;
you discern my thoughts from afar.
2 You trace my journeys and my resting-places *
and are acquainted with all my ways. [ANT.]

A 3 Indeed, there is not a word on my lips, *
but you, O LORD, know it altogether.
A 4 You press upon me behind and before *
and lay your hand upon me.
B 5 Such knowledge is too wonderful for me; *
it is so high that I cannot attain to it. [ANT.]

12 For you yourself created my inmost parts; *
you knit me together in my mother's womb.
13 I will thank you because I am marvelously made; *
your works are wonderful, and I know it well. [ANT.]

14 My body was not hidden from you, *
while I was being made in secret
and woven in the depths of the earth.
15 Your eyes beheld my limbs, yet unfinished in the womb;
all of them were written in your book; *
they were fashioned day by day,
when as yet there was none of them. [ANT.]

16 How deep I find your thoughts, O God! *
how great is the sum of them!
17 If I were to count them,
they would be more in number than the sand; *
to count them all,
my life span would need to be like yours. [ANT.]

RCL Proper 18C (G Track) Psalm 1

based on "Es flog ein kleins Waldvögelein" (H82–616)

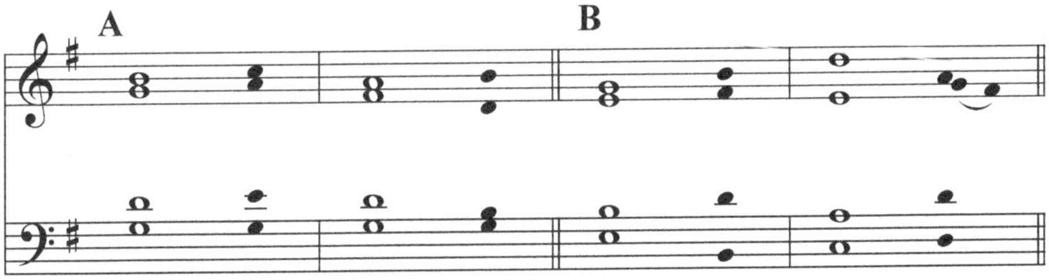

1 Happy are they who have not walked in the counsel of
the wicked, *
nor lingered in the way of sinners,
nor sat in the seats of the scornful!
2 Their delight is in the law of the LORD, *
and they meditate on his law day and night. [ANT.]

3 They are like trees planted by streams of water,
bearing fruit in due season, with leaves that do not wither; *
everything they do shall prosper.
4 It is not so with the wicked; *
they are like chaff which the wind blows away. [ANT.]

5 Therefore the wicked shall not stand upright when
judgment comes, *
nor the sinner in the council of the righteous.
6 For the LORD knows the way of the righteous, *
but the way of the wicked is doomed. [ANT.]

RCL Proper 19C (C Track) Psalm 14

based on "Martyrdom" (H82–658)

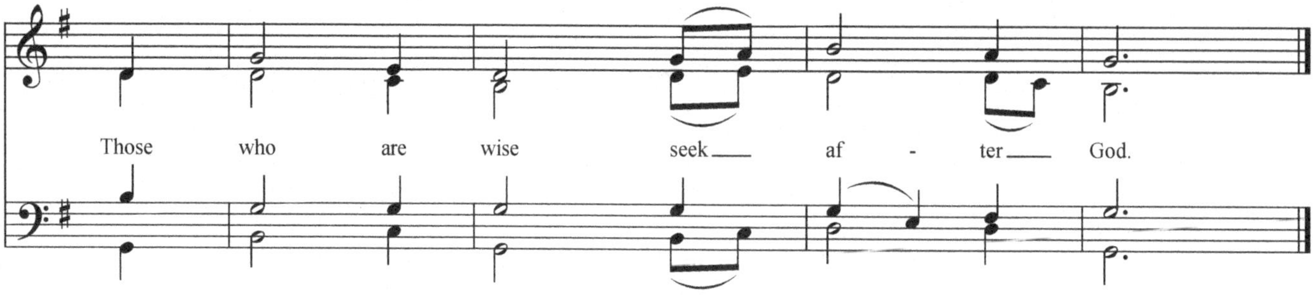

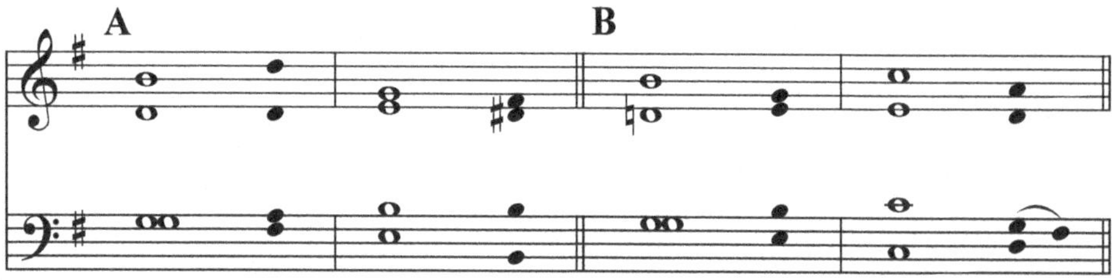

A 1 The fool has said in his heart, "There is no God." *
All are corrupt and commit abominable acts;
there is none who does any good.
B 2 The LORD looks down from heaven upon us all, *
to see if there is any who is wise,
if there is one who seeks after God.
B 3 Every one has proved faithless;
all alike have turned bad; *
there is none who does good; no, not one. [ANT.]

4 Have they no knowledge, all those evildoers *
who eat up my people like bread
and do not call upon the LORD?
5 See how they tremble with fear, *
because God is in the company of the righteous. [ANT.]

6 Their aim is to confound the plans of the afflicted, *
but the LORD is their refuge.
7 Oh, that Israel's deliverance would come out of Zion! *
when the LORD restores the fortunes of his people,
Jacob will rejoice and Israel be glad. [ANT.]

RCL Proper 19C (G Track) **Psalm 51: 1–11**

based on "Eventide" (H82–662)

1 Have mercy on me, O God, according to your loving-kindness; *
in your great compassion blot out my offenses.
2 Wash me through and through from my wickedness *
and cleanse me from my sin. [ANT.]

3 For I know my transgressions, *
and my sin is ever before me.
4 Against you only have I sinned *
and done what is evil in your sight. [ANT.]

5 And so you are justified when you speak *
and upright in your judgment.
6 Indeed, I have been wicked from my birth, *
a sinner from my mother's womb. [ANT.]

7 For behold, you look for truth deep within me, *
and will make me understand wisdom secretly.
8 Purge me from my sin, and I shall be pure; *
wash me, and I shall be clean indeed. [ANT.]

A 9 Make me hear of joy and gladness, *
that the body you have broken may rejoice.
A 10 Hide your face from my sins *
and blot out all my iniquities.
B 11 Create in me a clean heart, O God, *
and renew a right spirit within me. [ANT.]

RCL Proper 20C (C Track) Psalm 79: 1–9

based on "St. Anne" (H82–680)

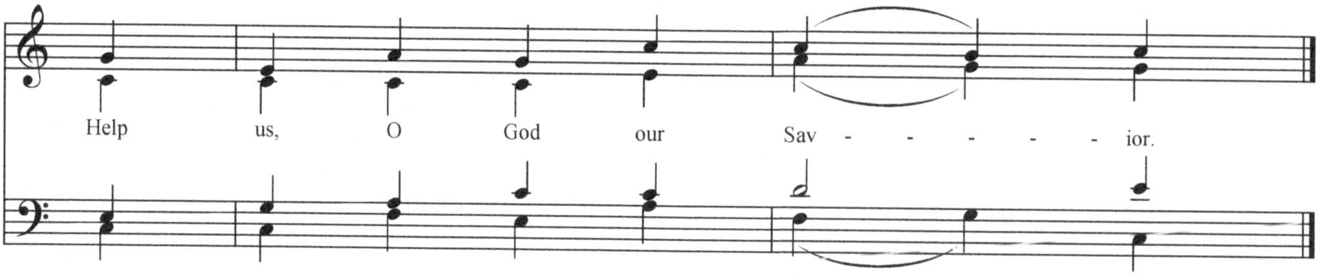

A 1 O God, the heathen have come into your inheritance;
they have profaned your holy temple; *
they have made Jerusalem a heap of rubble.
A 2 They have given the bodies of your servants as food for the birds of the air, *
and the flesh of your faithful ones to the beasts of the field.
B 3 They have shed their blood like water on every side of Jerusalem, *
and there was no one to bury them. [ANT.]

4 We have become a reproach to our neighbors, *
an object of scorn and derision to those around us.
5 How long will you be angry, O LORD? *
will your fury blaze like fire for ever? [ANT.]

6 Pour out your wrath upon the heathen who have not known you *
and upon the kingdoms that have not called upon your Name.
7 For they have devoured Jacob *
and made his dwelling a ruin. [ANT.]

8 Remember not our past sins;
let your compassion be swift to meet us; *
for we have been brought very low.
9 Help us, O God our Savior, for the glory of your Name; *
deliver us and forgive us our sins, for your Name's sake. [ANT.]

RCL Proper 20C (G Track) Psalm 113

based on "Duke Street" (H82–544)

1 Hallelujah!
Give praise, you servants of the LORD; *
praise the Name of the LORD.
2 Let the Name of the LORD be blessed, *
from this time forth for evermore. [ANT.]

3 From the rising of the sun to its going down *
let the Name of the LORD be praised.
4 The LORD is high above all nations, *
and his glory above the heavens. [ANT.]

5 Who is like the LORD our God, who sits enthroned on high *
but stoops to behold the heavens and the earth?
6 He takes up the weak out of the dust *
and lifts up the poor from the ashes. [ANT.]

7 He sets them with the princes, *
with the princes of his people.
8 He makes the woman of a childless house *
to be a joyful mother of children. [ANT.]

RCL Proper 21C (C Track) Psalm 91: 1–6, 14–16

based on "Grosser Gott" (H82–366)

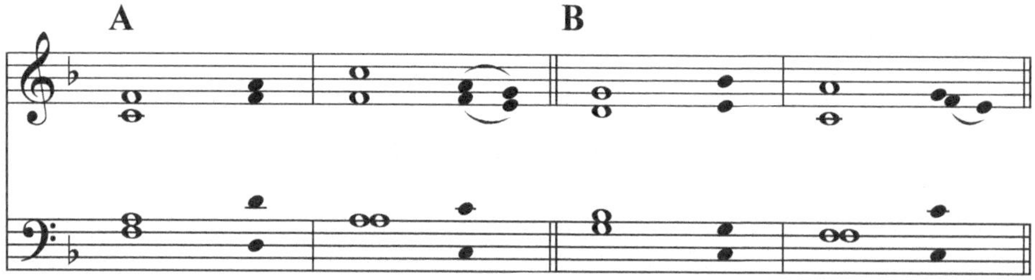

1 He who dwells in the shelter of the Most High, *
abides under the shadow of the Almighty.
2 He shall say to the LORD,
"You are my refuge and my stronghold, *
my God in whom I put my trust." [ANT.]

3 He shall deliver you from the snare of the hunter *
and from the deadly pestilence.
4 He shall cover you with his pinions,
and you shall find refuge under his wings; *
his faithfulness shall be a shield and buckler. [ANT.]

5 You shall not be afraid of any terror by night, *
nor of the arrow that flies by day;
6 Of the plague that stalks in the darkness, *
nor of the sickness that lays waste at mid-day. [ANT.]

A 14 Because he is bound to me in love,
therefore will I deliver him; *
I will protect him, because he knows my Name.
A 15 He shall call upon me, and I will answer him; *
I am with him in trouble;
I will rescue him and bring him to honor.
B 16 With long life will I satisfy him, *
and show him my salvation. [ANT.]

RCL Proper 21C (G Track) Psalm 146

based on "Old 124th" (H82–404)

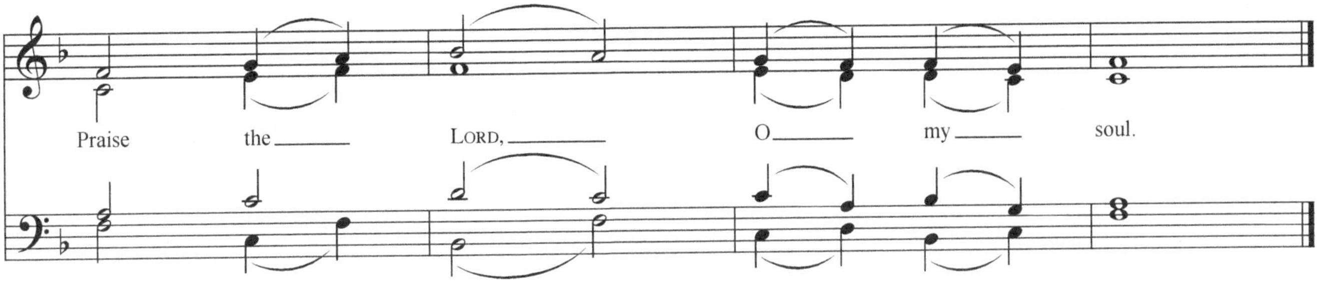

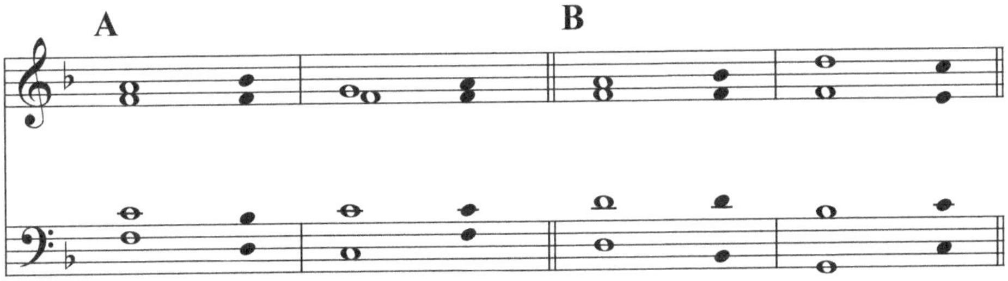

A 1 Hallelujah!
Praise the LORD, O my soul! *
I will praise the LORD as long as I live;
I will sing praises to my God while I have my being.
A 2 Put not your trust in rulers, nor in any child of earth, *
for there is no help in them.
B 3 When they breathe their last, they return to earth, *
and in that day their thoughts perish. [ANT.]

A 4 Happy are they who have the God of Jacob for their help! *
whose hope is in the LORD their God;
A 5 Who made heaven and earth, the seas, and all that is in them; *
who keeps his promise for ever;
B 6 Who gives justice to those who are oppressed, *
and food to those who hunger. [ANT.]

A 7 The LORD sets the prisoners free;
the LORD opens the eyes of the blind; *
the LORD lifts up those who are bowed down;
A 8 The LORD loves the righteous;
the LORD cares for the stranger; *
he sustains the orphan and widow,
but frustrates the way of the wicked.
B 9 The LORD shall reign for ever, *
your God, O Zion, throughout all generations.
Hallelujah! [ANT.]

RCL Proper 22C (C Track) A Song of Waiting

based on "Nyland" (H82–655)

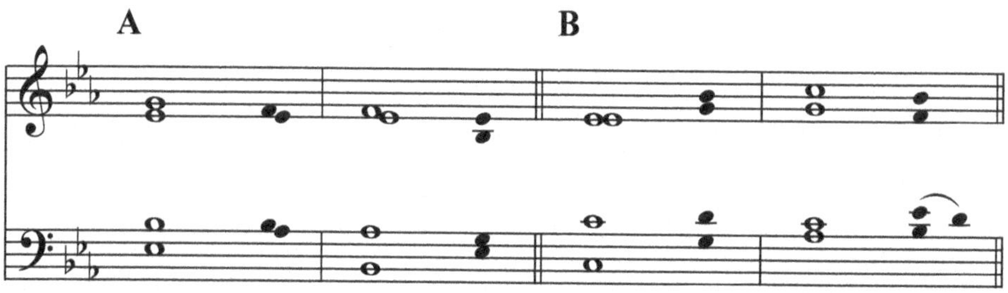

The thought of my trouble and my homelessness *
  is as bitter as wormwood and gall.
My mind dwells on it continually; *
  my soul is weighed down within me. [ANT.]

When I remember this, I have hope:
  by God's kindness, we are not destroyed;
for God's mercies are never-ending *
  and are new every morning. [ANT.]

A How great is your faithfulness, O God! *
  "You are my portion," says my soul,
  "therefore I hope in you."
A You are good to those who wait with patience, *
  to every soul that seeks you.
B It is good to wait, even in silence,
  for the salvation of the Lord. [ANT.]

RCL Proper 22C (C Track, alt.) Psalm 137

based on "Resignation" (H82–664)

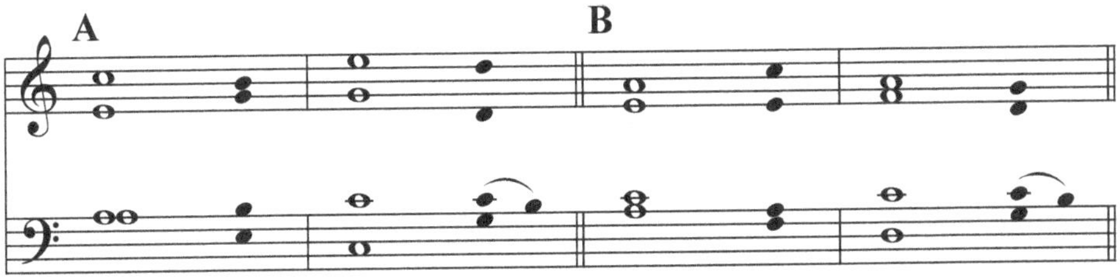

1 By the waters of Babylon we sat down and wept, *
when we remembered you, O Zion.
2 As for our harps, we hung them up *
on the trees in the midst of that land. [ANT.]

3 For those who led us away captive asked us for a song,
and our oppressors called for mirth: *
"Sing us one of the songs of Zion."
4 How shall we sing the LORD's song *
upon an alien soil? [ANT.]

5 If I forget you, O Jerusalem, *
let my right hand forget its skill.
6 Let my tongue cleave to the roof of my mouth
if I do not remember you, *
if I do not set Jerusalem above my highest joy. [ANT.]

A 7 Remember the day of Jerusalem, O LORD,
against the people of Edom, *
who said, "Down with it! down with it!
even to the ground!"
A 8 O Daughter of Babylon, doomed to destruction, *
happy the one who pays you back
for what you have done to us!
B 9 Happy shall he be who takes your little ones, *
and dashes them against the rock! [ANT.]

RCL Proper 22C (G Track) Psalm 37: 1–10

based on "Song 1" (H82–499)

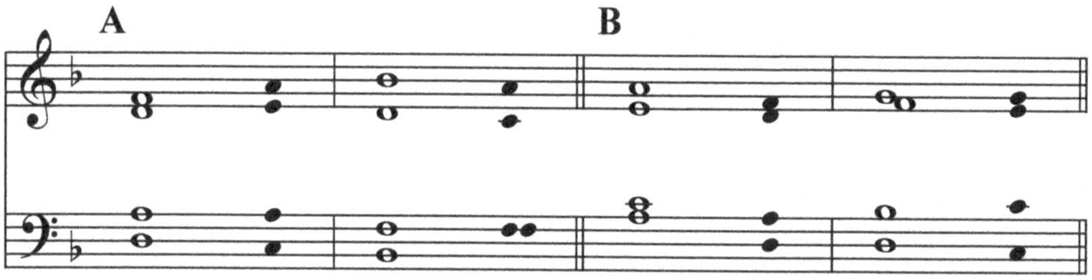

1 Do not fret yourself because of evildoers; *
do not be jealous of those who do wrong.
2 For they shall soon wither like the grass, *
and like the green grass fade away. [ANT.]

3 Put your trust in the LORD and do good; *
dwell in the land and feed on its riches.
4 Take delight in the LORD, *
and he shall give you your heart's desire. [ANT.]

5 Commit your way to the LORD and put your trust in him, *
and he will bring it to pass.
6 He will make your righteousness as clear as the light *
and your just dealing as the noonday. [ANT.]

7 Be still before the LORD *
and wait patiently for him.
8 Do not fret yourself over the one who prospers, *
the one who succeeds in evil schemes. [ANT.]

9 Refrain from anger, leave rage alone; *
do not fret yourself; it leads only to evil.
10 For evildoers shall be cut off, *
but those who wait upon the LORD shall possess the land. [ANT.]

RCL Proper 23C (C Track) Psalm 66: 1–11

based on "Paderborn" (H82–535)

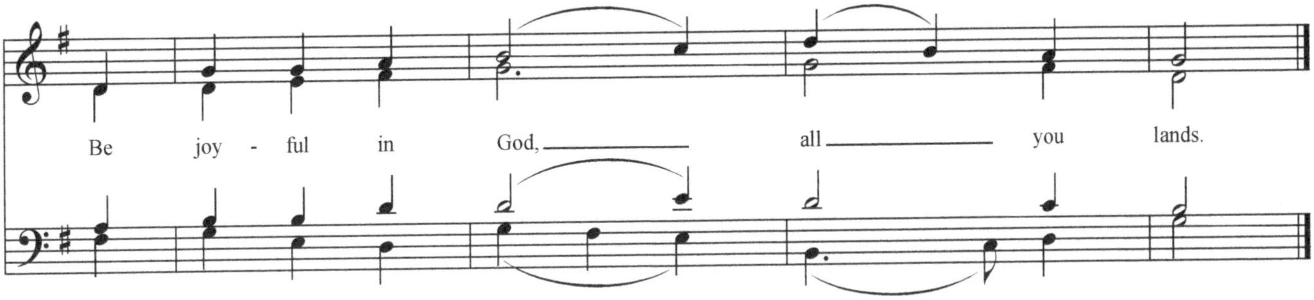

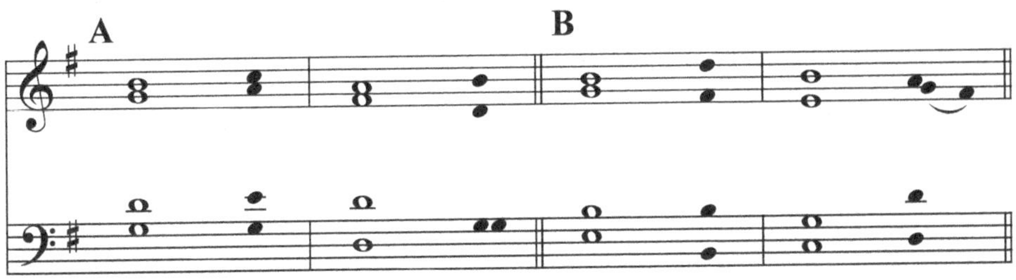

1 Be joyful in God, all you lands; *
sing the glory of his Name;
sing the glory of his praise.
2 Say to God, "How awesome are your deeds! *
because of your great strength your enemies
cringe before you. [ANT.]

3 All the earth bows down before you, *
sings to you, sings out your Name."
4 Come now and see the works of God, *
how wonderful he is in his doing toward all people. [ANT.]

5 He turned the sea into dry land,
so that they went through the water on foot, *
and there we rejoiced in him.
6 In his might he rules for ever;
his eyes keep watch over the nations; *
let no rebel rise up against him. [ANT.]

7 Bless our God, you peoples; *
make the voice of his praise to be heard;
8 Who holds our souls in life, *
and will not allow our feet to slip. [ANT.]

A 9 For you, O God, have proved us; *
you have tried us just as silver is tried.
A 10 You brought us into the snare; *
you laid heavy burdens upon our backs.
B 11 You let enemies ride over our heads;
we went through fire and water; *
but you brought us out into a place of refreshment. [ANT.]

RCL Proper 23C (G Track) **Psalm 111**

based on "Picardy" (H82–324)

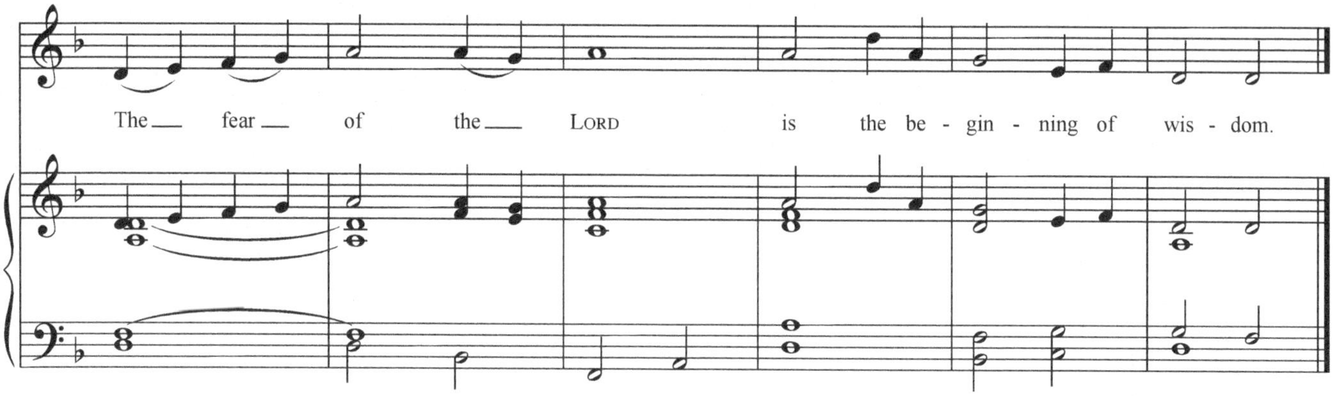

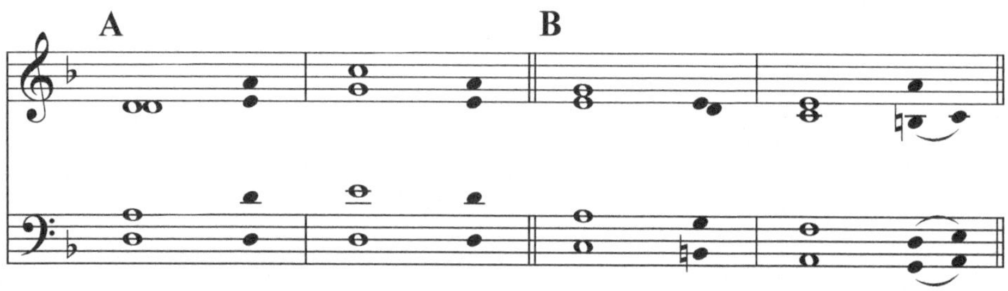

1 Hallelujah!
I will give thanks to the LORD with my whole heart, *
in the assembly of the upright, in the congregation.
2 Great are the deeds of the LORD! *
they are studied by all who delight in them. [ANT.]

3 His work is full of majesty and splendor, *
and his righteousness endures for ever.
4 He makes his marvelous works to be remembered; *
the LORD is gracious and full of compassion. [ANT.]

5 He gives food to those who fear him; *
he is ever mindful of his covenant.
6 He has shown his people the power of his works *
in giving them the lands of the nations. [ANT.]

7 The works of his hands are faithfulness and justice; *
all his commandments are sure.
8 They stand fast for ever and ever, *
because they are done in truth and equity. [ANT.]

9 He sent redemption to his people;
he commanded his covenant for ever; *
holy and awesome is his Name.
10 The fear of the LORD is the beginning of wisdom; *
those who act accordingly have a good understanding;
his praise endures for ever. [ANT.]

RCL Proper 24C (C Track) Psalm 119: 97–104

based on "Eventide" (H82–662)

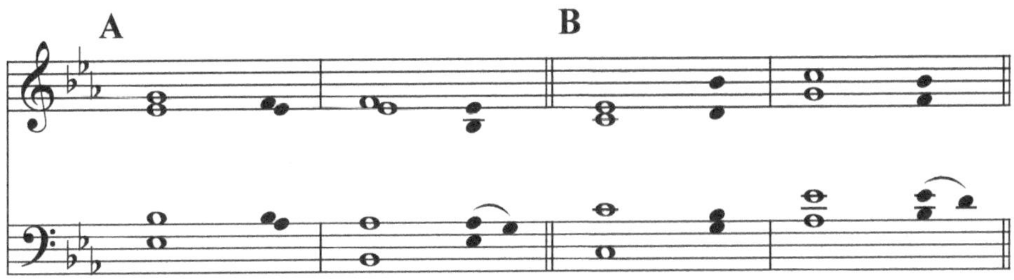

97 Oh, how I love your law! *
all the day long it is in my mind.
98 Your commandment has made me wiser than my enemies, *
and it is always with me. [ANT.]

99 I have more understanding than all my teachers, *
for your decrees are my study.
100 I am wiser than the elders, *
because I observe your commandments. [ANT.]

101 I restrain my feet from every evil way, *
that I may keep your word.
102 I do not shrink from your judgments, *
because you yourself have taught me. [ANT.]

103 How sweet are your words to my taste! *
they are sweeter than honey to my mouth.
104 Through your commandments I gain understanding; *
therefore I hate every lying way. [ANT.]

RCL Proper 24C (G Track) Psalm 121

based on "Munich" (H82–632)

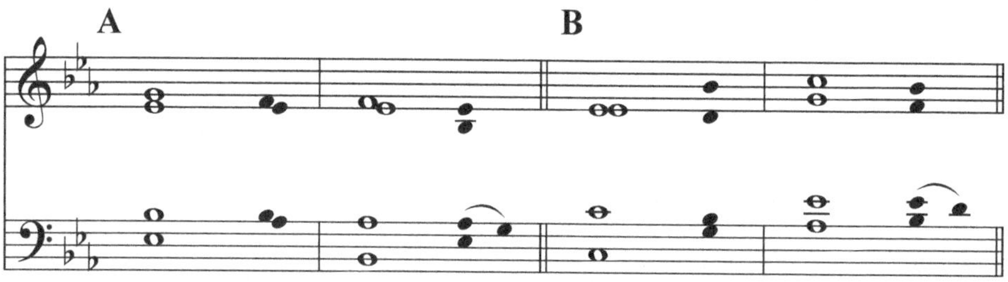

1 I lift up my eyes to the hills; *
from where is my help to come?
2 My help comes from the LORD, *
the maker of heaven and earth. [ANT.]

3 He will not let your foot be moved *
and he who watches over you will not fall asleep.
4 Behold, he who keeps watch over Israel *
shall neither slumber nor sleep; [ANT.]

5 The LORD himself watches over you; *
the LORD is your shade at your right hand,
6 So that the sun shall not strike you by day, *
nor the moon by night. [ANT.]

7 The LORD shall preserve you from all evil; *
it is he who shall keep you safe.
8 The LORD shall watch over your going out and
your coming in, *
from this time forth for evermore. [ANT.]

RCL Proper 25C (C Track) Psalm 65

based on "St. Denio" (H82–423)

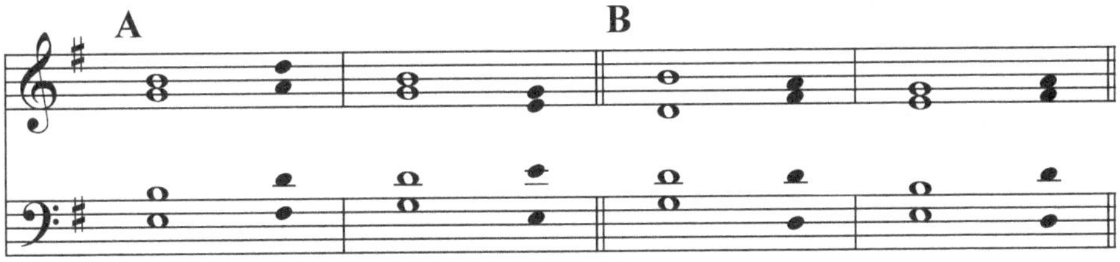

A 1 You are to be praised, O God, in Zion; *
to you shall vows be performed in Jerusalem.

A 2 To you that hear prayer shall all flesh come, *
because of their transgressions.

B 3 Our sins are stronger than we are, *
but you will blot them out. [ANT.]

A 4 Happy are they whom you choose
and draw to your courts to dwell there! *

A they will be satisfied by the beauty of your house,
by the holiness of your temple.

B 5 Awesome things will you show us in your righteousness,
O God of our salvation, *
O Hope of all the ends of the earth
and of the seas that are far away. [ANT.]

A 6 You make fast the mountains by your power; *
they are girded about with might.

A 7 You still the roaring of the seas, *
the roaring of their waves,
and the clamor of the peoples.

B 8 Those who dwell at the ends of the earth will tremble at your marvelous signs; *
you make the dawn and the dusk to sing for joy. [ANT.]

A 9 You visit the earth and water it abundantly;
you make it very plenteous; *
the river of God is full of water.

B 10 You prepare the grain, *
for so you provide for the earth.

A 11 You drench the furrows and smooth out the ridges; *
with heavy rain you soften the ground and bless its increase.

B 12 You crown the year with your goodness, *
and your paths overflow with plenty. [ANT.]

13 May the fields of the wilderness be rich for grazing, *
and the hills be clothed with joy.

14 May the meadows cover themselves with flocks,
and the valleys cloak themselves with grain; *
let them shout for joy and sing. [ANT.]

RCL Proper 25C (G Track) Psalm 84: 1–6

based on "Brother James' Air" (H82–517)

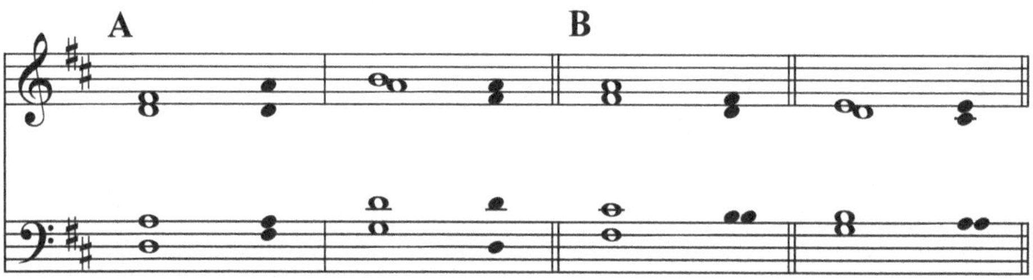

A 1 How dear to me is your dwelling,
O LORD of hosts! *
B My soul has a desire and longing for the courts of
the LORD;
my heart and my flesh rejoice in the living God. [ANT.]

A 2 The sparrow has found her a house
and the swallow a nest where she may lay her young; *
B by the side of your altars, O LORD of hosts,
my King and my God. [ANT.]

3 Happy are they who dwell in your house! *
they will always be praising you.
4 Happy are the people whose strength is in you! *
whose hearts are set on the pilgrims' way. [ANT.]

5 Those who go through the desolate valley will find
it a place of springs, *
for the early rains have covered it with pools of water.
6 They will climb from height to height, *
and the God of gods will reveal himself in Zion. [ANT.]

RCL All Saints' Day C Psalm 149

based on "Mit Freuden zart" (H82–408)

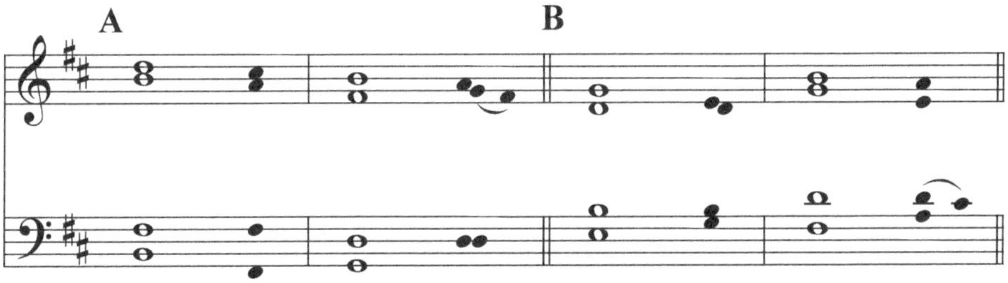

A 1 Hallelujah!
Sing to the LORD a new song; *
sing his praise in the congregation of the faithful.
A 2 Let Israel rejoice in his Maker; *
let the children of Zion be joyful in their King.
B 3 Let them praise his Name in the dance; *
let them sing praise to him with timbrel and harp. [ANT.]

4 For the LORD takes pleasure in his people *
and adorns the poor with victory.
5 Let the faithful rejoice in triumph; *
let them be joyful on their beds. [ANT.]

6 Let the praises of God be in their throat *
and a two-edged sword in their hand;
7 To wreak vengeance on the nations *
and punishment on the peoples; [ANT.]

8 To bind their kings in chains *
and their nobles with links of iron;
9 To inflict on them the judgment decreed; *
this is glory for all his faithful people.
Hallelujah! [ANT.]

RCL Proper 26C (C Track) Psalm 119: 137–144

based on "Rouen" (H82–360)

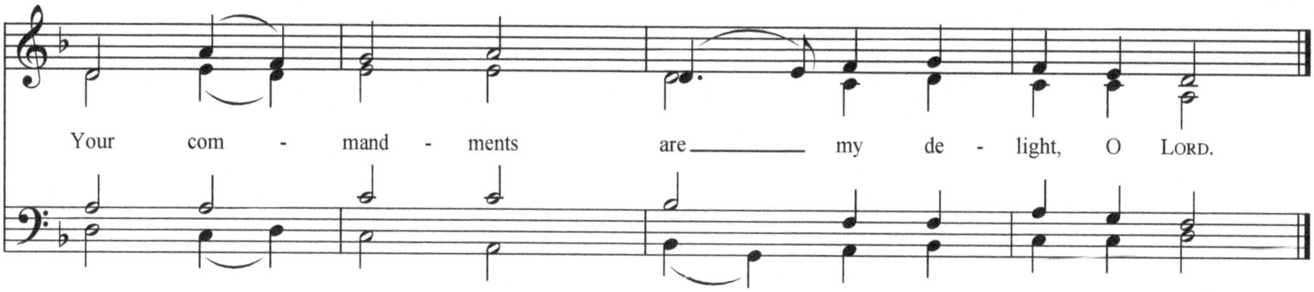

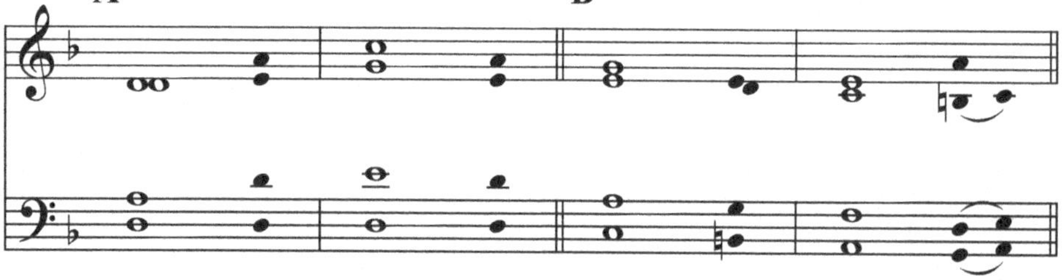

137 You are righteous, O LORD, *
and upright are your judgments.
138 You have issued your decrees *
with justice and in perfect faithfulness. [ANT.]

139 My indignation has consumed me, *
because my enemies forget your words.
140 Your word has been tested to the uttermost, *
and your servant holds it dear. [ANT.]

141 I am small and of little account, *
yet I do not forget your commandments.
142 Your justice is an everlasting justice *
and your law is the truth. [ANT.]

143 Trouble and distress have come upon me, *
yet your commandments are my delight.
144 The righteousness of your decrees is everlasting; *
grant me understanding, that I may live. [ANT.]

RCL Proper 26C (G Track) Psalm 32: 1–8

based on "O quanta qualia" (H82–623)

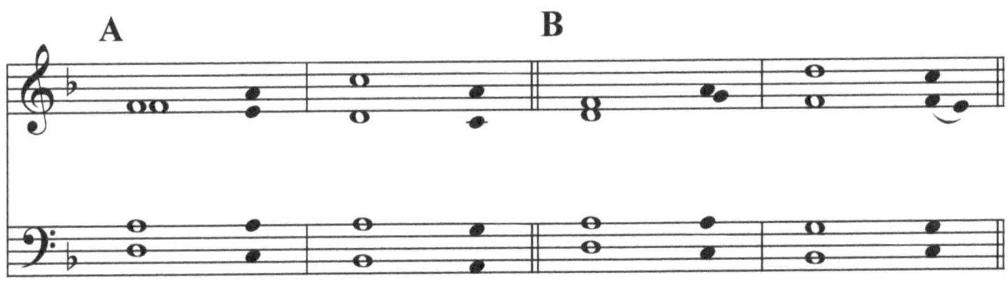

1 Happy are they whose transgressions are forgiven, *
and whose sin is put away!
2 Happy are they to whom the LORD imputes no guilt, *
and in whose spirit there is no guile! [ANT.]

3 While I held my tongue, my bones withered away, *
because of my groaning all day long.
4 For your hand was heavy upon me day and night; *
my moisture was dried up as in the heat of summer. [ANT.]

5 Then I acknowledged my sin to you, *
and did not conceal my guilt.
6 I said, "I will confess my transgressions to the LORD." *
Then you forgave me the guilt of my sin. [ANT.]

7 Therefore all the faithful will make their prayers to you in time of trouble; *
when the great waters overflow, they shall not reach them.
8 You are my hiding-place;
you preserve me from trouble; *
you surround me with shouts of deliverance. [ANT.]

RCL Proper 27C (C Track) Psalm 145: 1–5, 18–22

based on "Foundation" (H82–636)

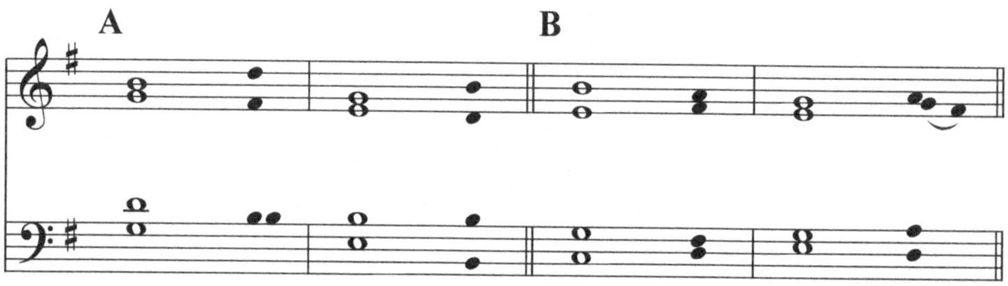

1 I will exalt you, O God my King, *
and bless your Name for ever and ever.
2 Every day will I bless you *
and praise your Name for ever and ever. [ANT.]

A 3 Great is the LORD and greatly to be praised; *
there is no end to his greatness.
A 4 One generation shall praise your works to another *
and shall declare your power.
B 5 I will ponder the glorious splendor of your majesty *
and all your marvelous works. [ANT.]

A 18 The LORD is righteous in all his ways *
and loving in all his works.
A 19 The LORD is near to those who call upon him, *
to all who call upon him faithfully.
B 20 He fulfills the desire of those who fear him; *
he hears their cry and helps them. [ANT.]

21 The LORD preserves all those who love him, *
but he destroys all the wicked.
22 My mouth shall speak the praise of the LORD; *
let all flesh bless his holy Name for ever and ever. [ANT.]

RCL Proper 27C (C Track, alt.) Psalm 98

based on "Song 1" (H82–499)

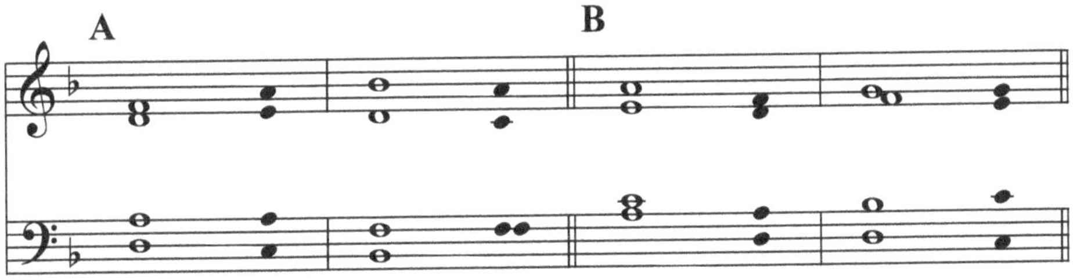

1 Sing to the LORD a new song, *
for he has done marvelous things.
2 With his right hand and his holy arm *
has he won for himself the victory. [ANT.]

3 The LORD has made known his victory; *
his righteousness has he openly shown in
the sight of the nations.
4 He remembers his mercy and faithfulness to
the house of Israel, *
and all the ends of the earth have seen the
victory of our God. [ANT.]

5 Shout with joy to the LORD, all you lands; *
lift up your voice, rejoice, and sing.
6 Sing to the LORD with the harp, *
with the harp and the voice of song. [ANT.]

7 With trumpets and the sound of the horn *
shout with joy before the King, the LORD.
8 Let the sea make a noise and all that is in it, *
the lands and those who dwell therein. [ANT.]

9 Let the rivers clap their hands, *
and let the hills ring out with joy before the LORD,
when he comes to judge the earth.
10 In righteousness shall he judge the world *
and the peoples with equity. [ANT.]

RCL Proper 27C (G Track) Psalm 17: 1–9

based on "Tender Thought" (H82–702)

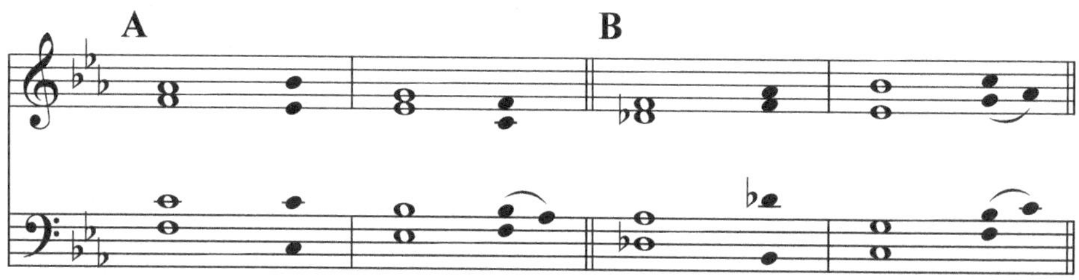

1 Hear my plea of innocence, O LORD;
give heed to my cry; *
listen to my prayer, which does not come from lying lips.
2 Let my vindication come forth from your presence; *
let your eyes be fixed on justice. [ANT.]

3 Weigh my heart, summon me by night, *
melt me down; you will find no impurity in me.
4 I give no offense with my mouth as others do; *
I have heeded the words of your lips. [ANT.]

5 My footsteps hold fast to the ways of your law; *
in your paths my feet shall not stumble.
6 I call upon you, O God, for you will answer me; *
incline your ear to me and hear my words. [ANT.]

A 7 Show me your marvelous loving-kindness, *
O Savior of those who take refuge at your right hand
from those who rise up against them.
A 8 Keep me as the apple of your eye; *
hide me under the shadow of your wings,
B 9 From the wicked who assault me, *
from my deadly enemies who surround me. [ANT.]

RCL Proper 28C (C Track) Canticle 9

based on "Birmingham" (H82–437)

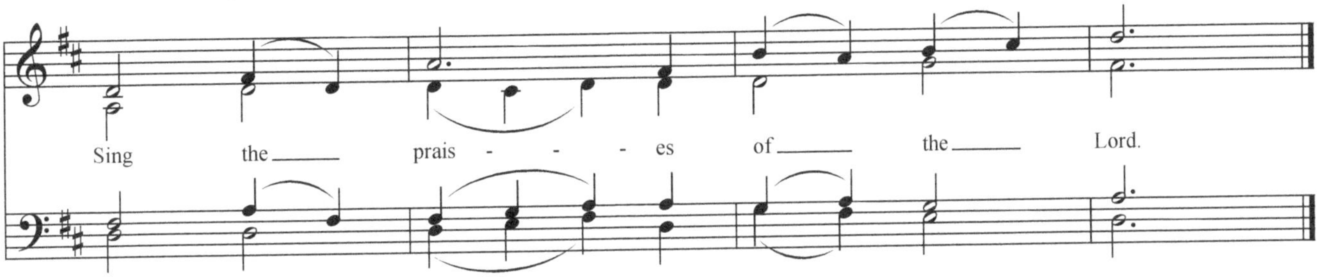

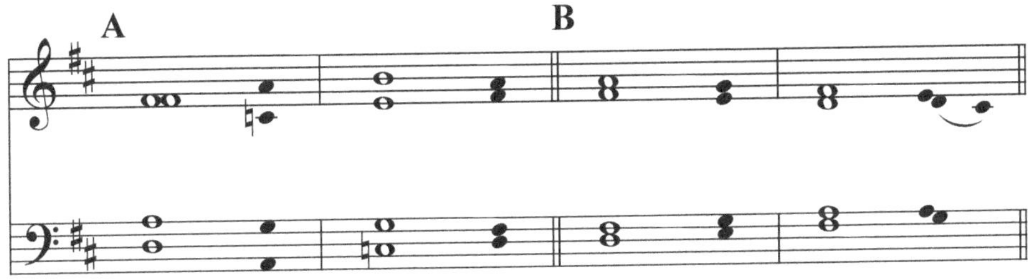

Surely, it is God who saves me; *
   I will trust in him and not be afraid.
For the Lord is my stronghold and my sure defense, *
   and he will be my Savior. [ANT.]

A Therefore you shall draw water with rejoicing *
   from the springs of salvation.
A And on that day you shall say, *
   Give thanks to the Lord and call upon his Name;
B Make his deeds known among the peoples; *
   see that they remember that his Name is exalted. [ANT.]

Sing the praises of the Lord, for he has done great things, *
   and this is known in all the world.
Cry aloud, inhabitants of Zion, ring out your joy, *
   for the great one in the midst of you is the Holy One of Israel. [ANT.]

RCL Proper 28C (G Track) Psalm 98

based on "Song 1" (H82–499)

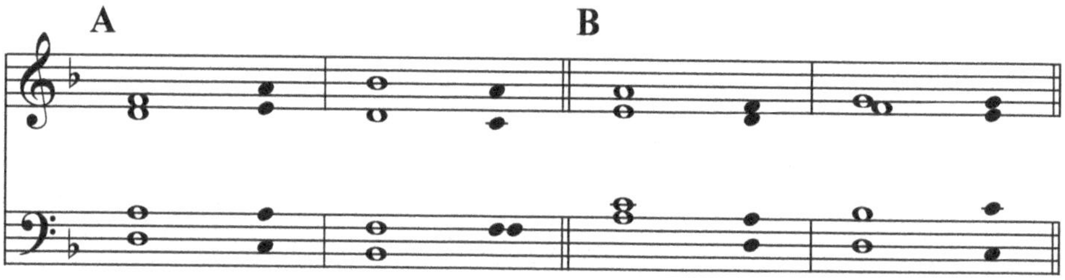

1 Sing to the LORD a new song, *
for he has done marvelous things.
2 With his right hand and his holy arm *
has he won for himself the victory. [ANT.]

3 The LORD has made known his victory; *
his righteousness has he openly shown in
the sight of the nations.
4 He remembers his mercy and faithfulness to
the house of Israel, *
and all the ends of the earth have seen the
victory of our God. [ANT.]

5 Shout with joy to the LORD, all you lands; *
lift up your voice, rejoice, and sing.
6 Sing to the LORD with the harp, *
with the harp and the voice of song. [ANT.]

7 With trumpets and the sound of the horn *
shout with joy before the King, the LORD.
8 Let the sea make a noise and all that is in it, *
the lands and those who dwell therein. [ANT.]

9 Let the rivers clap their hands, *
and let the hills ring out with joy before the LORD,
when he comes to judge the earth.
10 In righteousness shall he judge the world *
and the peoples with equity. [ANT.]

RCL Proper 29C (C Track) Canticle 16

based on "Bereden väg för Herran" (H82–65)

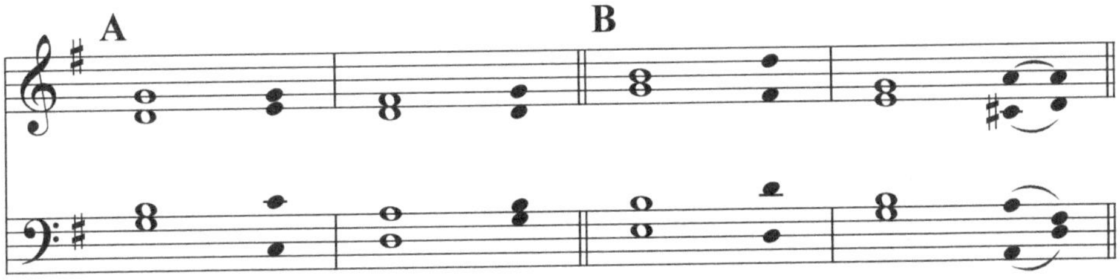

Blessed be the Lord, the God of Israel, *
he has come to his people and set them free.
He has raised up for us a mighty savior, *
born of the house of his servant David. [ANT.]

A Through his holy prophets he promised of old
that he would save us from our enemies, *
from the hands of all who hate us,
B He promised to show mercy to our fathers, *
and to remember his holy covenant.
A This was the oath he swore to our father Abraham, *
to set us free from the hands of our enemies,
B Free to worship him without fear, *
holy and righteous in his sight
all the days of our life. [ANT.]

You, my child, shall be called the prophet of the Most High, *
for you will go before the Lord to prepare his way,
To give his people knowledge of salvation *
by the forgiveness of their sins. [ANT.]

In the tender compassion of our God *
the dawn from on high shall break upon us,
To shine on those who dwell in darkness and the shadow of death, *
and to guide our feet into the way of peace. [ANT.]

RCL Proper 29C (G Track) Psalm 46

based on "Ein feste burg" (H82–688)

A 1 God is our refuge and strength, *
a very present help in trouble.
A 2 Therefore we will not fear, though the earth be moved, *
and though the mountains be toppled into the
depths of the sea;
B 3 Though its waters rage and foam, *
and though the mountains tremble at its tumult. [ANT.]

A 5 There is a river whose streams make glad the city of God, *
the holy habitation of the Most High.
A 6 God is in the midst of her;
she shall not be overthrown; *
God shall help her at the break of day.
B 7 The nations make much ado, and the kingdoms are shaken; *
God has spoken, and the earth shall melt away. [ANT.]

A 9 Come now and look upon the works of the LORD, *
what awesome things he has done on earth.
A 10 It is he who makes war to cease in all the world; *
he breaks the bow, and shatters the spear,
and burns the shields with fire.
B 11 "Be still, then, and know that I am God; *
I will be exalted among the nations;
I will be exalted in the earth." [ANT.]

APPENDIX

RCL Trinity Sunday A Psalm 8

RCL Trinity Sunday A Canticle 13

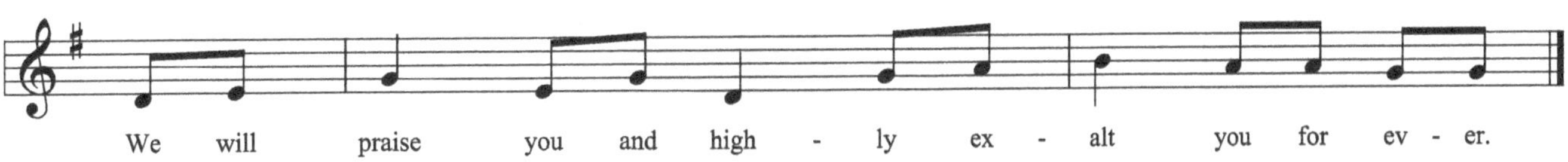

RCL Proper 1A Psalm 119: 1–8

RCL Proper 2A Psalm 119: 33–40

RCL Proper 3A Psalm 131

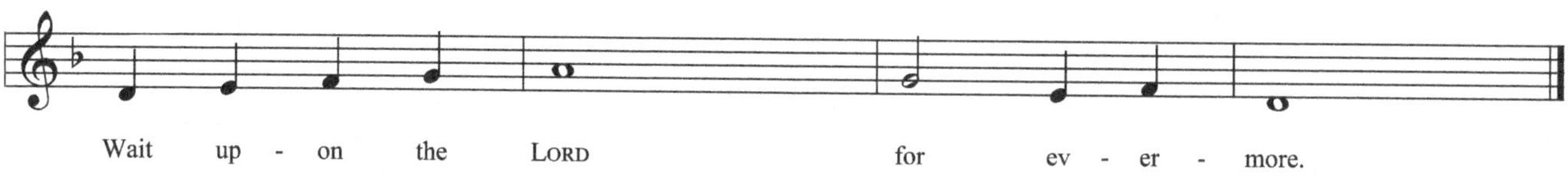

RCL Proper 4A (C Track) Psalm 46

RCL Proper 4A (G Track) Psalm 31: 1–5, 19–24

RCL Proper 5A (C Track) Psalm 33: 1–12

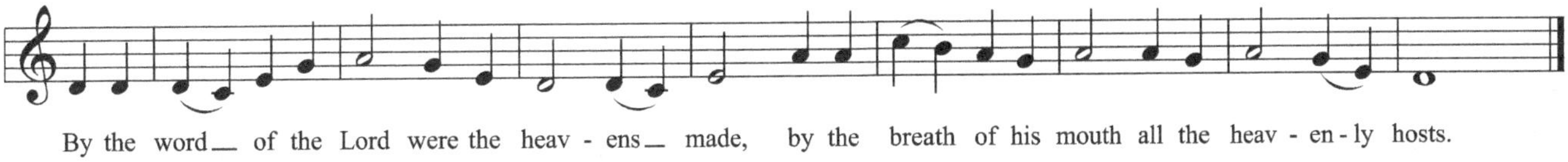

RCL Proper 5A (G Track) Psalm 50: 7–15

RCL Proper 6A (C Track) Psalm 116: 1, 10–17

RCL Proper 6A (G Track) Psalm 100

RCL Proper 7A (C Track) Psalm 86: 1–10, 16–17

RCL Proper 7A (G Track) Psalm 69: 8–11, (12–17), 18–20

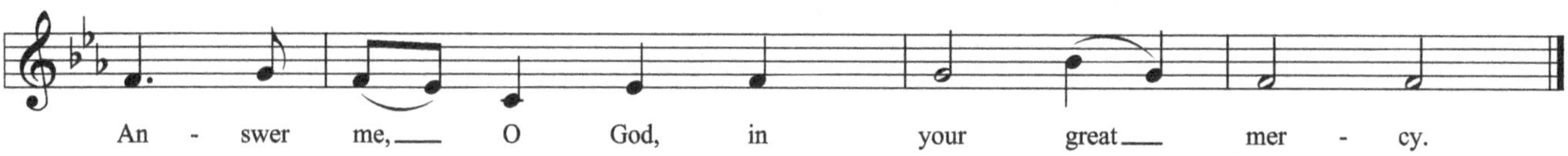

RCL Proper 8A (C Track) Psalm 13

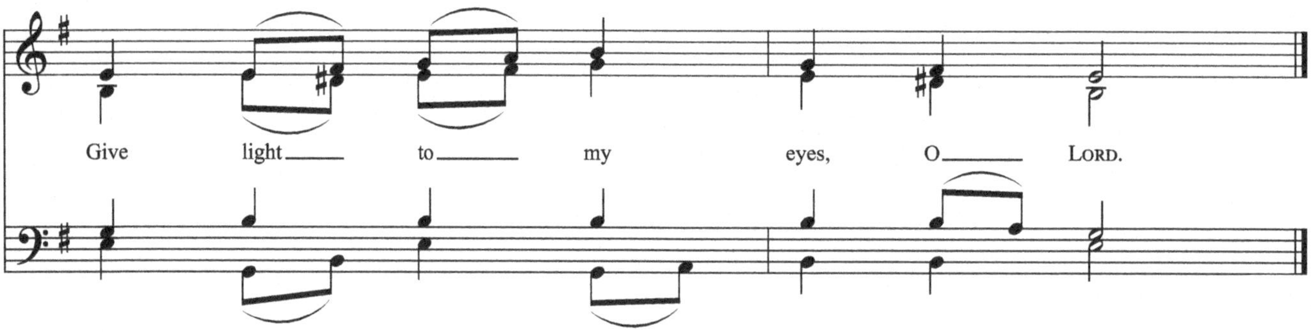

RCL Proper 8A (G Track) **Psalm 89: 1–4, 15–18**

RCL Proper 9A (C Track) **Psalm 45: 11–18**

RCL Proper 9A (C Track, alt.) **The Song of My Beloved (Song of Solomon 2: 8–13)**

RCL Proper 9A (G Track) **Psalm 145: 8–15**

RCL Proper 10A (C Track) **Psalm 119: 105–112**

RCL Proper 10A (G Track) **Psalm 65: (1–8), 9–14**

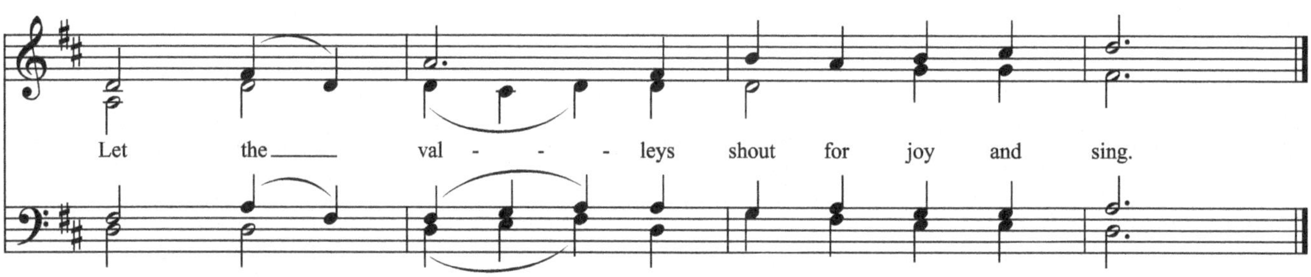

RCL Proper 11A (C Track) **Psalm 139: 1–11, 22–23**

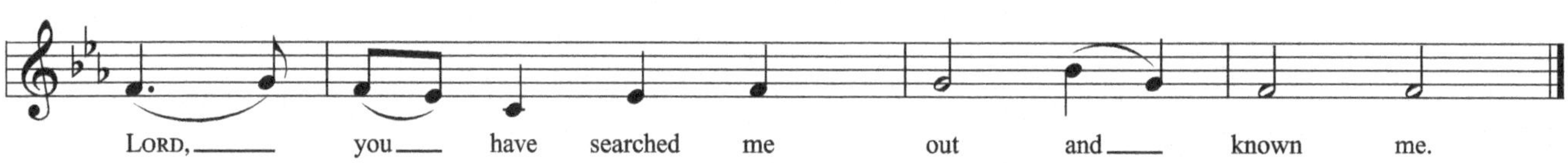

RCL Proper 11A (C Track, alt.) A Song of God's Strength in Mercy (Wisdom 12: 13, 16–19)

RCL Proper 11A (G Track) Psalm 86: 11–17

RCL Proper 12A (C Track) Psalm 105: 1–11, 45b

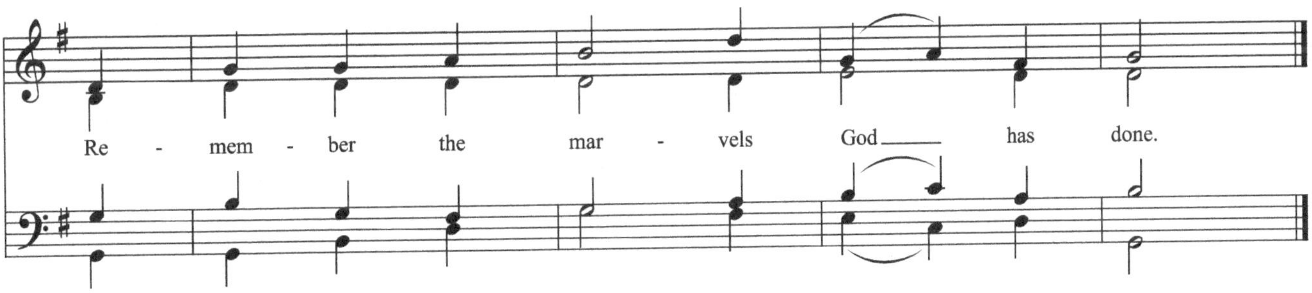

RCL Proper 12A (C Track, alt.) Psalm 128

RCL Proper 12A (G Track) Psalm 119: 129–136

RCL Proper 13A (C Track) Psalm 17: 1–7, 16

RCL Proper 13A (G Track) Psalm 145: 8–9, 15–22

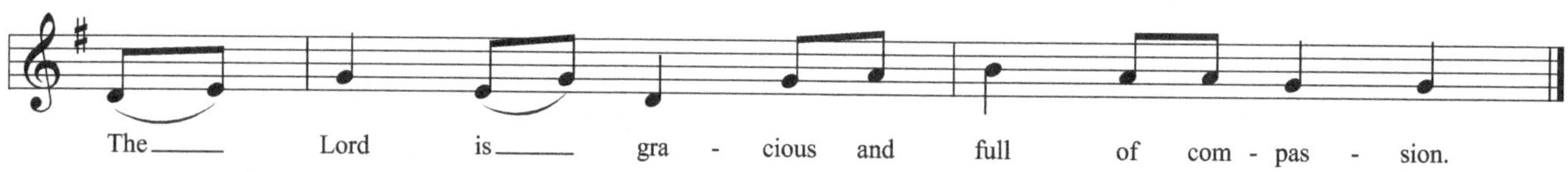

RCL Transfiguration ABC August 6 Psalm 99

RCL Proper 14A (C Track) Psalm 105: 1–6, 16–22, 45b

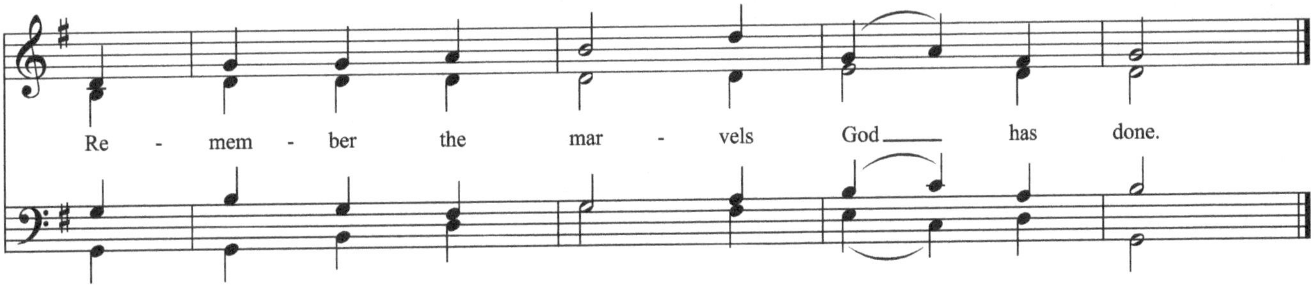

RCL Proper 14A (G Track) Psalm 85: 7–13

RCL Proper 15A (C Track) Psalm 133

RCL Proper 15A (G Track) Psalm 67

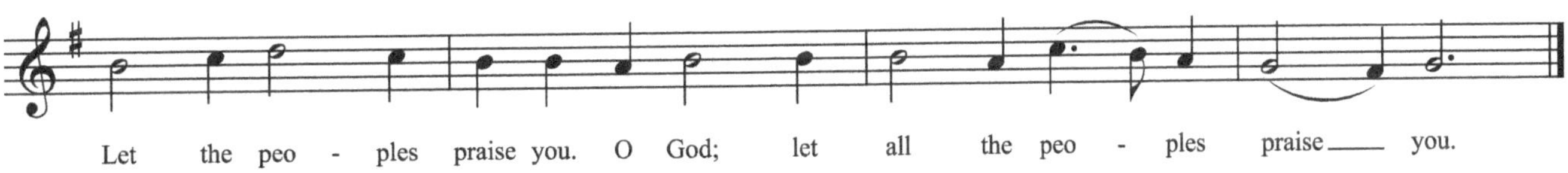

RCL Proper 16A (C Track) Psalm 124

RCL Proper 16A (G Track) Psalm 138

RCL Proper 17A (C Track) Psalm 105: 1–6, 23–26, 45b

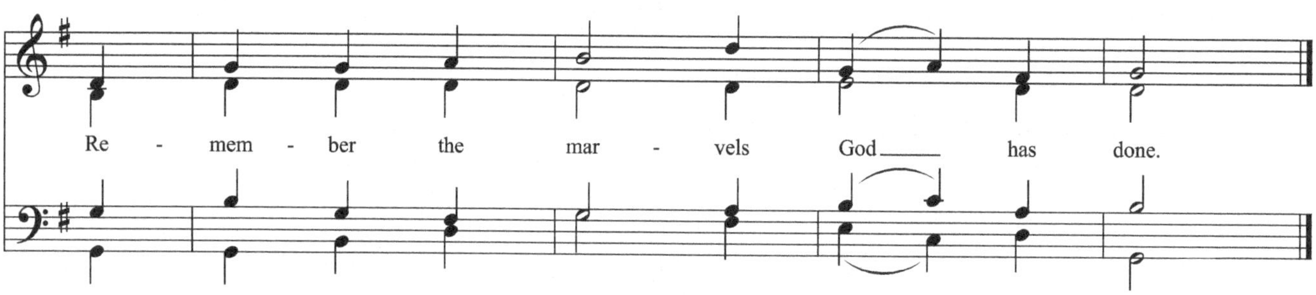

RCL Proper 17A (G Track) Psalm 26: 1–8

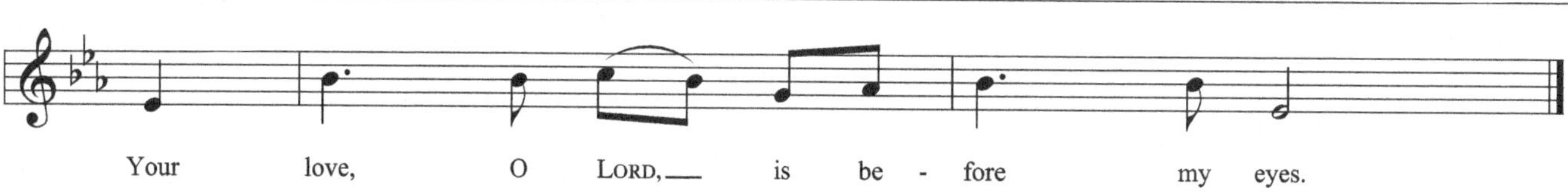

RCL Proper 18A (C Track) Psalm 149

RCL Proper 18A (G Track) Psalm 119: 33–40

RCL Proper 19A (C Track) Psalm 114

RCL Proper 19A (C Track, alt.) **The Songs of Moses and Miriam (Exodus 15: 1b–11, 20–21)**

RCL Proper 19A (G Track) **Psalm 103: (1–7), 8–13**

RCL Proper 20A (C Track) **Psalm 105: 1–6, 37–45**

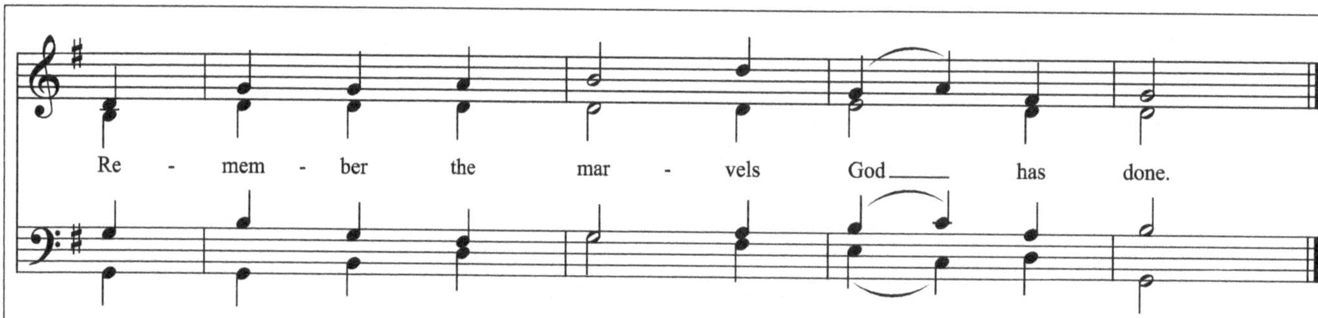

RCL Proper 20A (G Track) Psalm 145: 1–8

RCL Proper 21A (C Track) Psalm 78: 1–4, 12–16

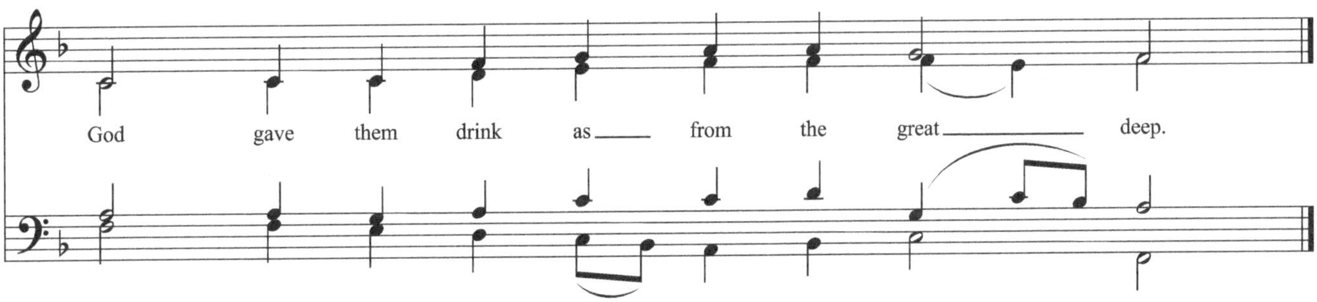

RCL Proper 21A (G Track) Psalm 25: 1–8

RCL Proper 22A (C Track) Psalm 19

RCL Proper 22A (G Track) Psalm 80: 7–14

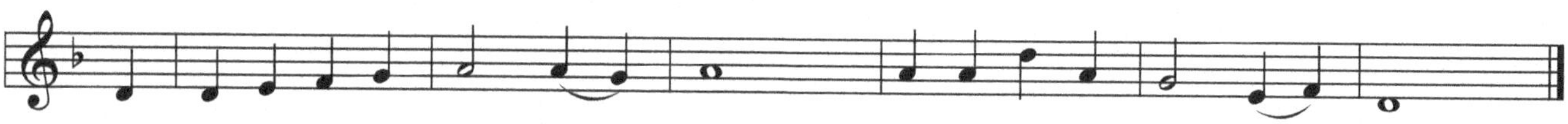

RCL Proper 23A (C Track) Psalm 106: 1–6, 19–23

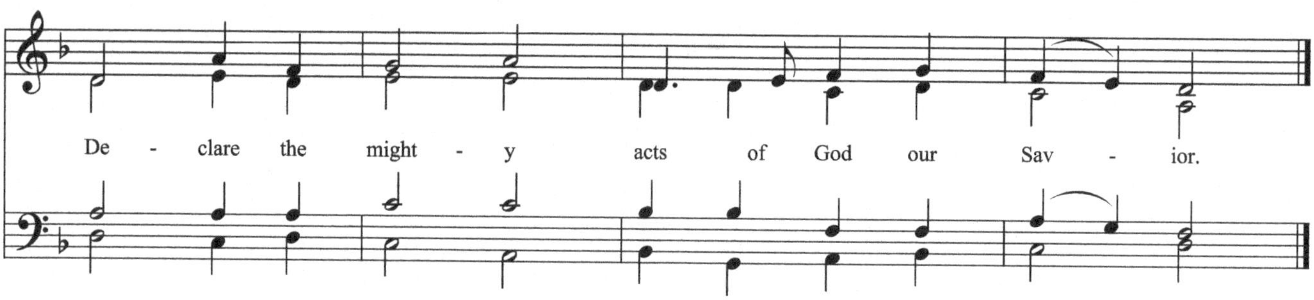

RCL Proper 23A (G Track) Psalm 23

RCL Proper 24A (C Track) Psalm 99

RCL Proper 24A (G Track) Psalm 96: 1–9, (10–13)

RCL Proper 25A (C Track) Psalm 90: 1–6, 13–17

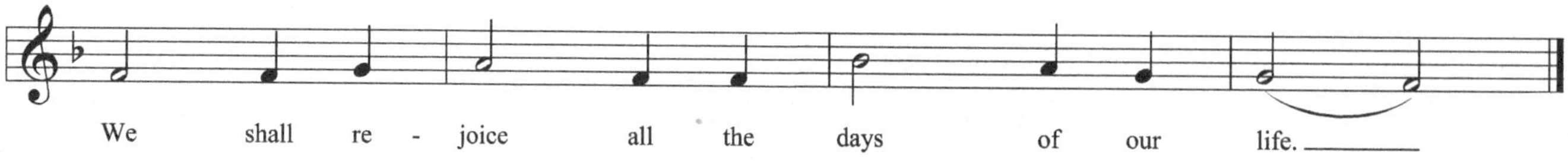

RCL Proper 25A (G Track) Psalm 1

RCL All Saints' Day A Psalm 34: 1–10, 22

RCL Proper 26A (C Track) **Psalm 107: 1–7, 33–37**

From *A HymnTune Psalter, Revised Common Lectionary Edition* © 2007 by Carl P. Daw, Jr. and Kevin R. Hackett. Church Publishing Incorporated.

RCL Proper 26A (G Track) **Psalm 43**

From *A HymnTune Psalter, Revised Common Lectionary Edition* © 2007 by Carl P. Daw, Jr. and Kevin R. Hackett. Church Publishing Incorporated.

RCL Proper 27A (C Track) **Psalm 78: 1–7**

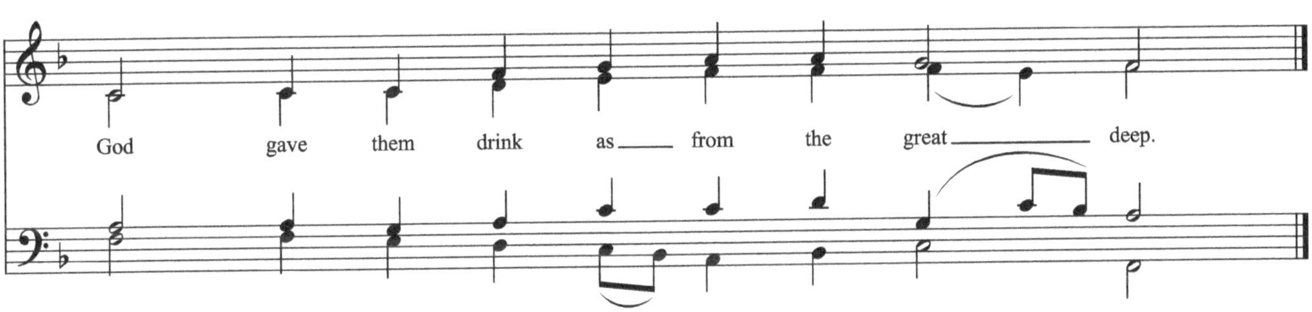

From *A HymnTune Psalter, Revised Common Lectionary Edition* © 2007 by Carl P. Daw, Jr. and Kevin R. Hackett. Church Publishing Incorporated.

RCL Proper 27A (C Track, alt.) A Song of the Love of Wisdom (Wisdom of Solomon 6: 17–20)

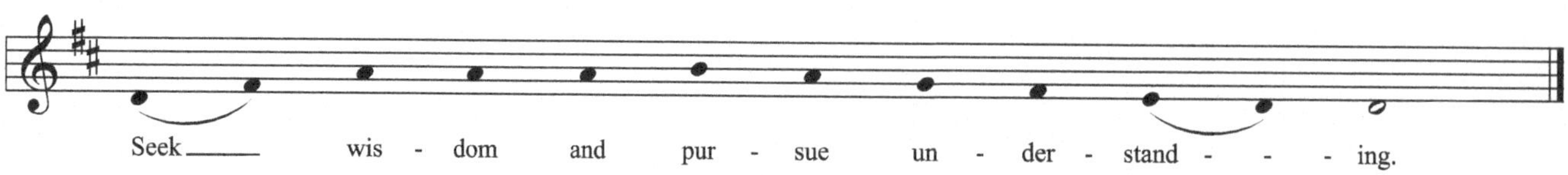

RCL Proper 27A (G Track) Psalm 70

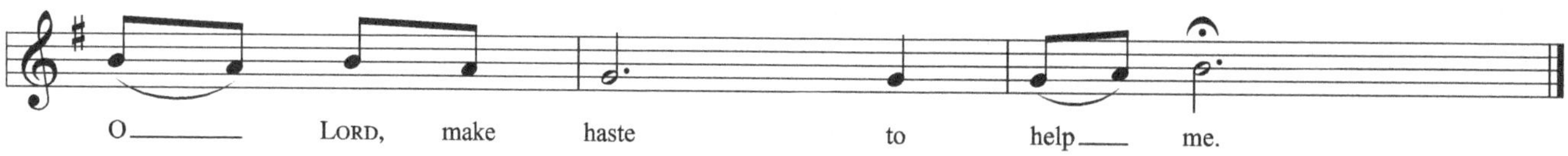

RCL Proper 28A (C Track) Psalm 123

RCL Proper 28A (G Track) Psalm 90: 1–12

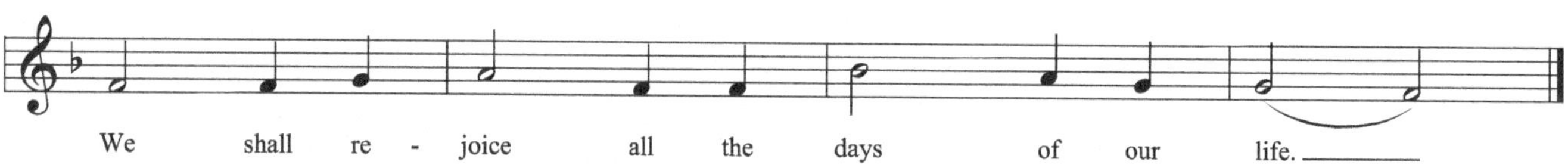

RCL Proper 29A (C Track) Psalm 100

RCL Proper 29A (G Track) Psalm 95: 1–7a

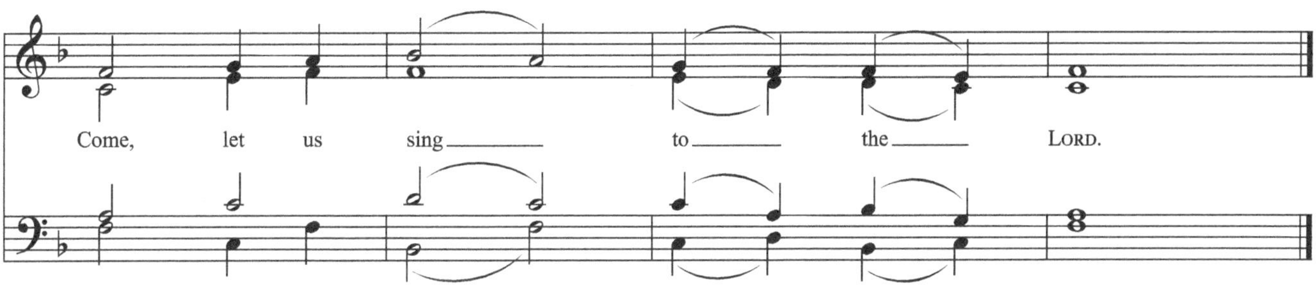

RCL Trinity Sunday B Psalm 29

RCL Trinity Sunday B Canticle 13

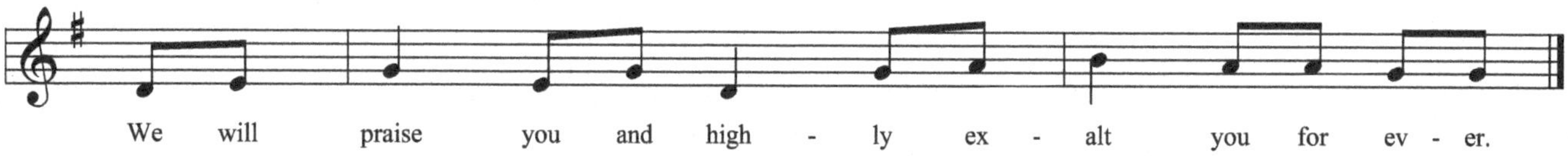

RCL Proper 1B Psalm 30

RCL Proper 2B Psalm 41

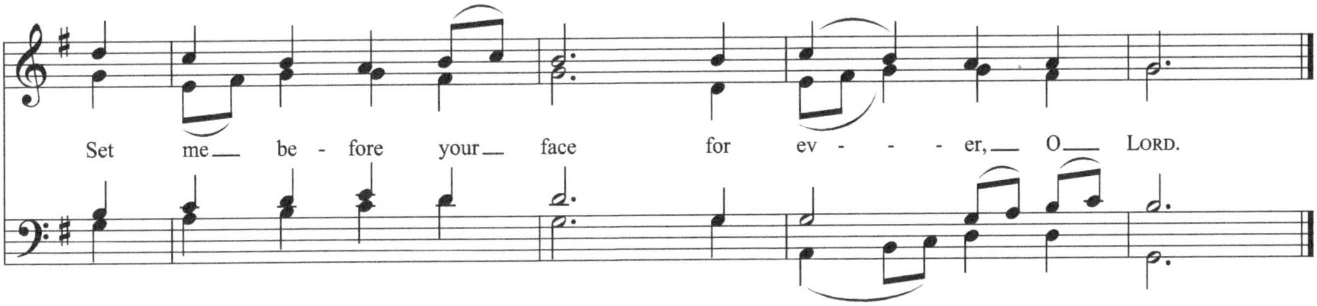

RCL Proper 3B Psalm 103: 1–13, 22

RCL Proper 4B (C Track) Psalm 139: 1–5, 12–17

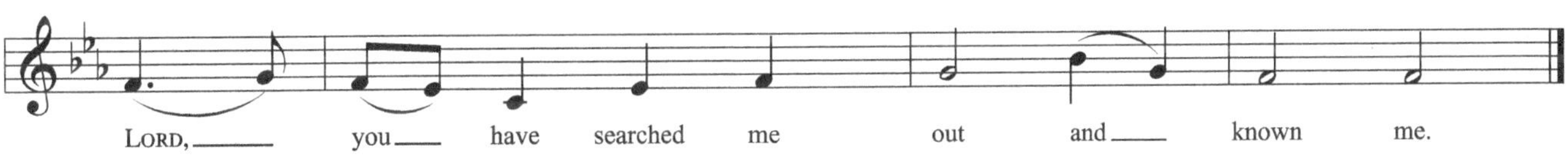

RCL Proper 4B (G Track) Psalm 81: 1–10

RCL Proper 5B (C Track) Psalm 138

RCL Proper 5B (G Track) Psalm 130

RCL Proper 6B (C Track) Psalm 20

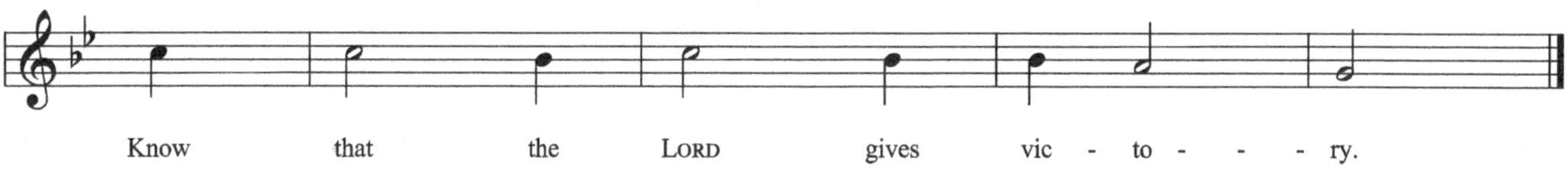

RCL Proper 6B (G Track) Psalm 92: 1–4, 11–14

RCL Proper 7B (C Track) Psalm 9: 9–20

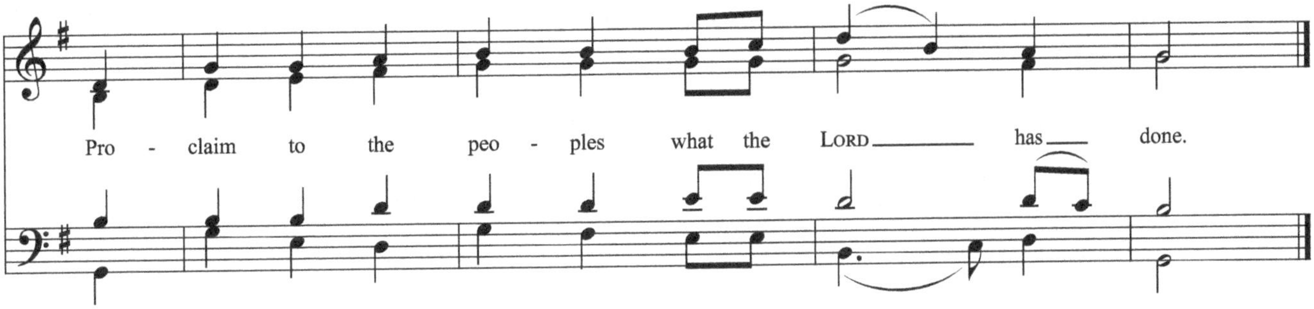

RCL Proper 7B (C Track, alt.) Psalm 133

RCL Proper 7B (G Track) Psalm 107: 1–3, 23–32

RCL Proper 8B (C Track) Psalm 130

RCL Proper 8B (C Track, alt.) A Song of God's Mercy

RCL Proper 8B (G Track) Psalm 30

RCL Proper 9B (C Track) **Psalm 48**

RCL Proper 9B (G Track) **Psalm 123**

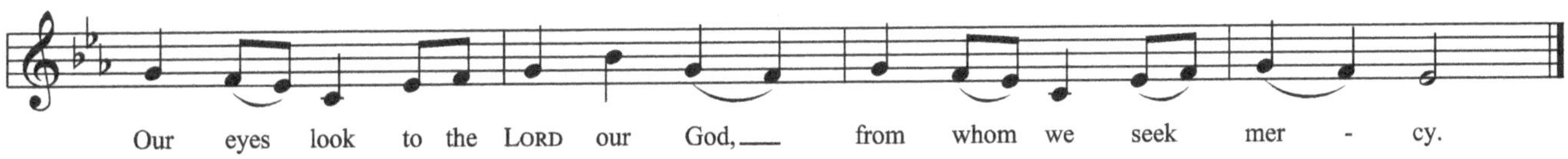

RCL Proper 10B (C Track) **Psalm 24**

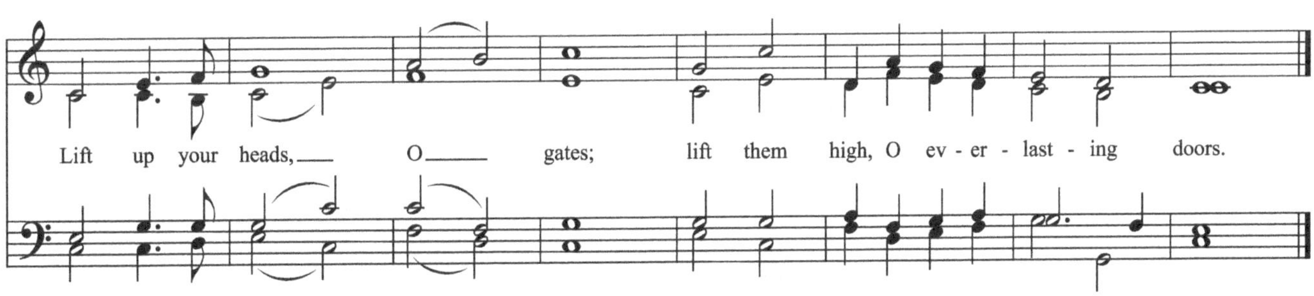

RCL Proper 10B (G Track) **Psalm 85: 7–13**

RCL Proper 11B (C Track) Psalm 89: 20–37

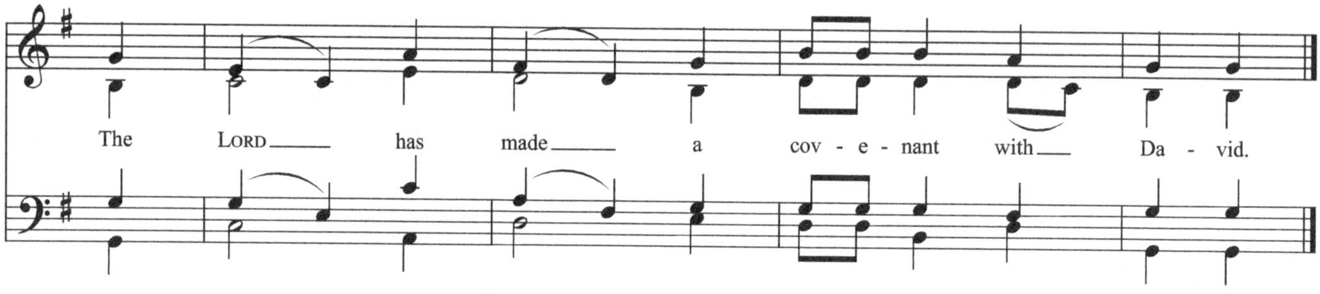

RCL Proper 11B (G Track) Psalm 23

RCL Proper 12B (C Track) Psalm 14

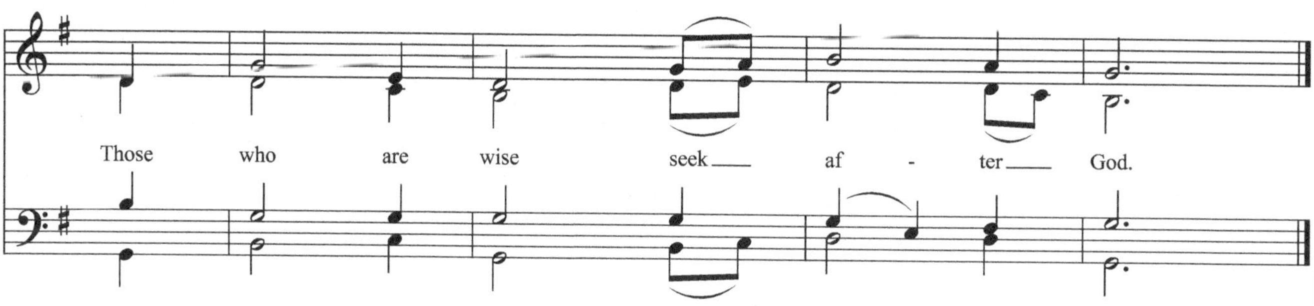

RCL Proper 12B (G Track) Psalm 145: 10–19

RCL Proper 13B (C Track) Psalm 51: 1–13

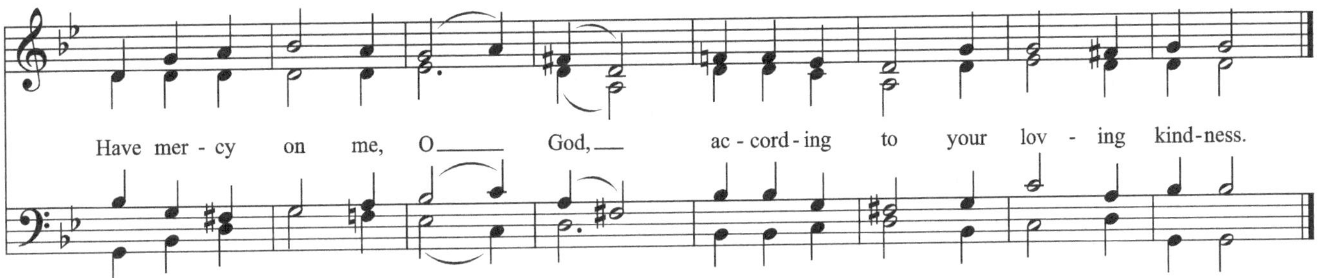

RCL Proper 13B (G Track) Psalm 78: 23–29

RCL Transfiguration ABC August 6 Psalm 99

From *A HymnTune Psalter, Revised Common Lectionary Edition* © 2007 by Carl P. Daw, Jr. and Kevin R. Hackett. Church Publishing Incorporated.

RCL Proper 14B (C Track) Psalm 130

From *A HymnTune Psalter, Revised Common Lectionary Edition* © 2007 by Carl P. Daw, Jr. and Kevin R. Hackett. Church Publishing Incorporated.

RCL Proper 14B (G Track) Psalm 34: 1–8

From *A HymnTune Psalter, Revised Common Lectionary Edition* © 2007 by Carl P. Daw, Jr. and Kevin R. Hackett. Church Publishing Incorporated.

RCL Proper 15B (C Track) Psalm 111

From *A HymnTune Psalter, Revised Common Lectionary Edition* © 2007 by Carl P. Daw, Jr. and Kevin R. Hackett. Church Publishing Incorporated.

RCL Proper 15B (G Track) Psalm 34: 9–14

From *A HymnTune Psalter, Revised Common Lectionary Edition*

RCL Proper 16B (C Track) Psalm 84

From *A HymnTune Psalter, Revised Common Lectionary Edition*

RCL Proper 16B (G Track) Psalm 34: 15–22

From *A HymnTune Psalter, Revised Common Lectionary Edition*

RCL Proper 17B (C Track) Psalm 45: 1–2, 7–10

RCL Proper 17B (G Track) Psalm 15

RCL Proper 18B (C Track) Psalm 125

RCL Proper 18B (G Track) Psalm 146

RCL Proper 19B (C Track) Psalm 19

RCL Proper 19B (C Track, alt.) A Song in Praise of Wisdom

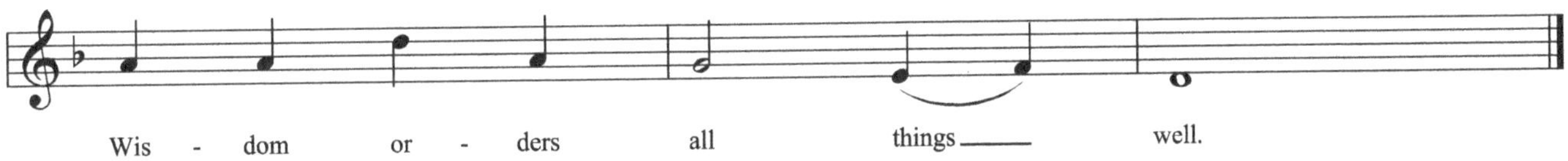

RCL Proper 19B (G Track) Psalm 116: 1–8

RCL Proper 20B (C Track) Psalm 1

RCL Proper 20B (G Track) Psalm 54

Alternate harmonization for choir

RCL Proper 21B (C Track) Psalm 124

RCL Proper 21B (G Track) Psalm 19: 7–14

RCL Proper 22B (C Track) Psalm 26

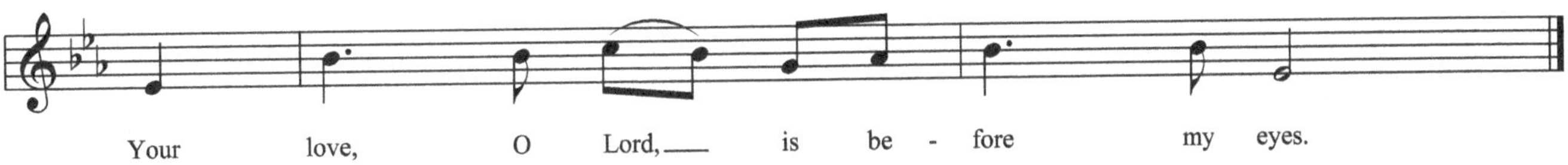

RCL Proper 22B (G Track) Psalm 8

RCL Proper 23B (C Track) Psalm 22: 1–15

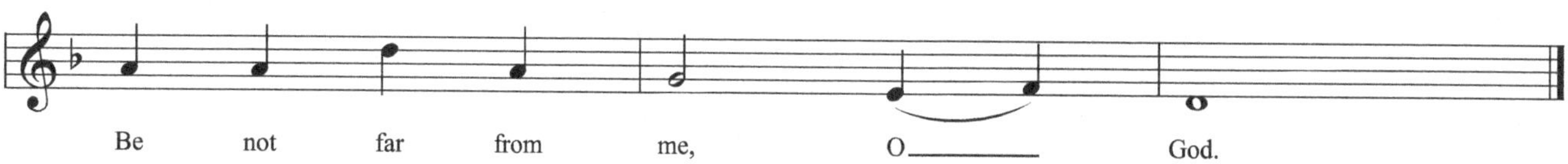

RCL Proper 23B (G Track) Psalm 90: 12–17

RCL Proper 24B (C Track) Psalm 104: 1–9, 25, 37b

RCL Proper 24B (G Track) Psalm 91: 9–16

RCL Proper 25B (C Track) Psalm 34: 1–8, 19–22

RCL Proper 25B (G Track) Psalm 126

RCL All Saints' Day B Psalm 24

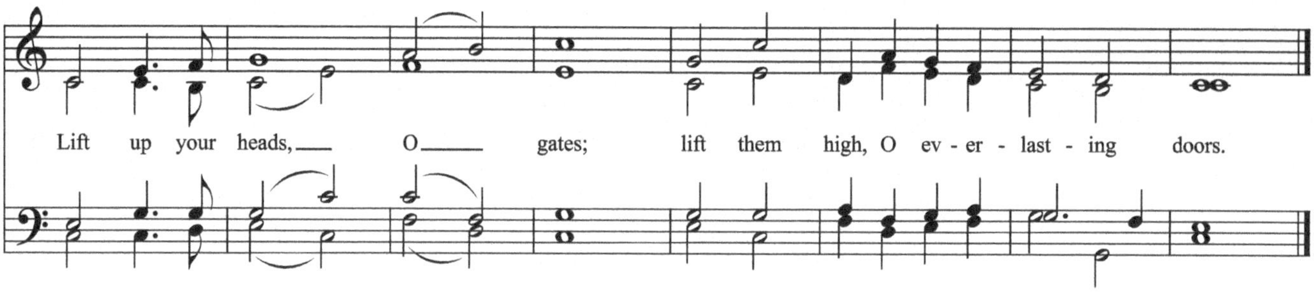

RCL Proper 26B (C Track) Psalm 146

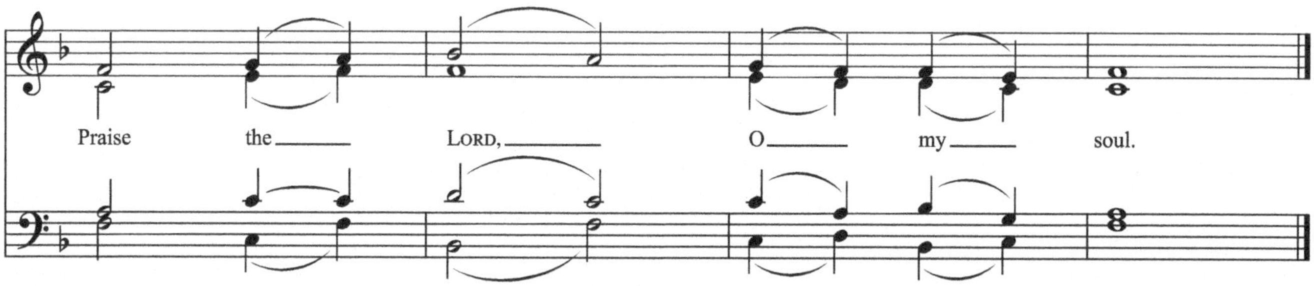

RCL Proper 26B (G Track) Psalm 119: 1–8

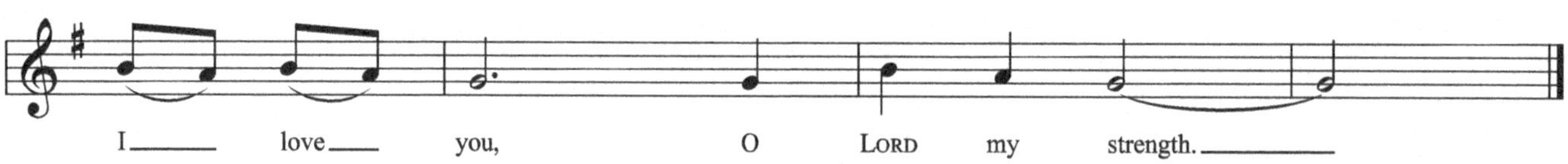

RCL Proper 27B (C Track) Psalm 127

RCL Proper 27B (G Track) Psalm 146

RCL Proper 28B (C Track) The Song of Hannah

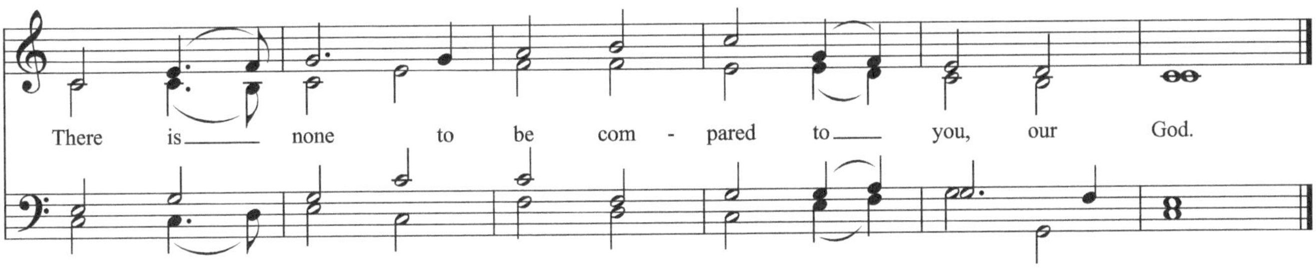

RCL Proper 28B (G Track) Psalm 16

RCL Proper 29B (C Track) Psalm 132: 1–13

RCL Proper 29B (G Track) Psalm 93

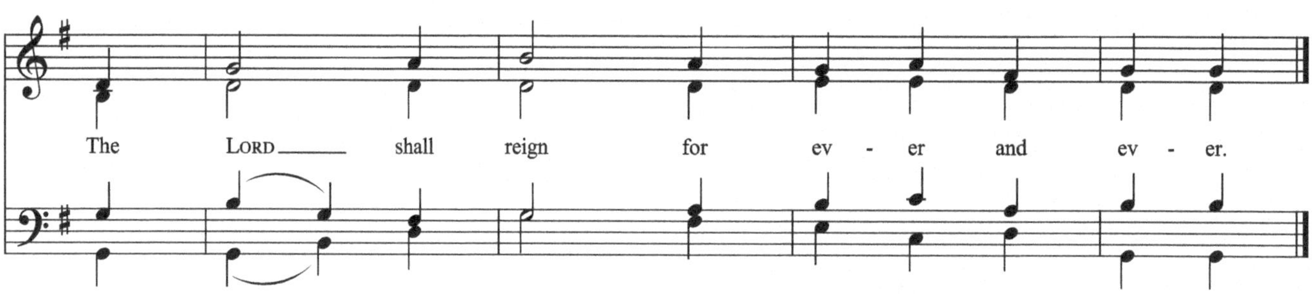

RCL Trinity Sunday C Psalm 8

RCL Trinity Sunday C Canticle 13

RCL Proper 1C Psalm 1

RCL Proper 2C Psalm 37: 1–12, 41–42

RCL Proper 3C Psalm 92: 1–4, 11–14

RCL Proper 4C (C Track) Psalm 96

RCL Proper 4C (G Track) Psalm 96: 1–9

RCL Proper 5C (C Track) Psalm 146

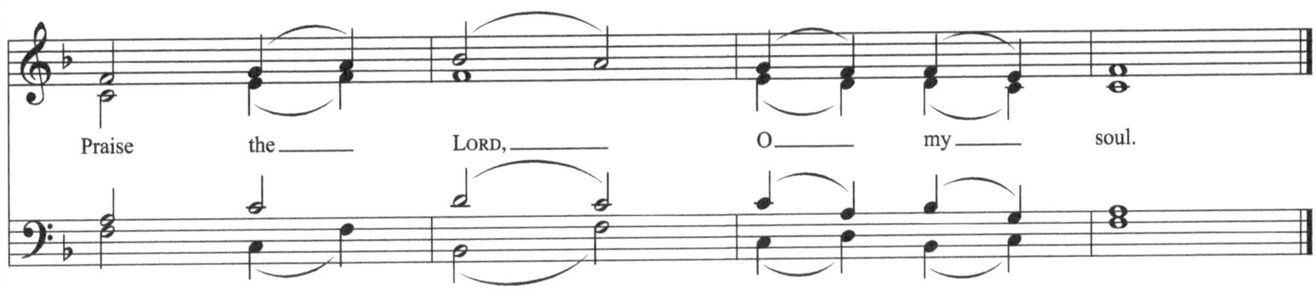

RCL Proper 5C (G Track) Psalm 30

RCL Proper 6C (C Track) Psalm 5: 1–8

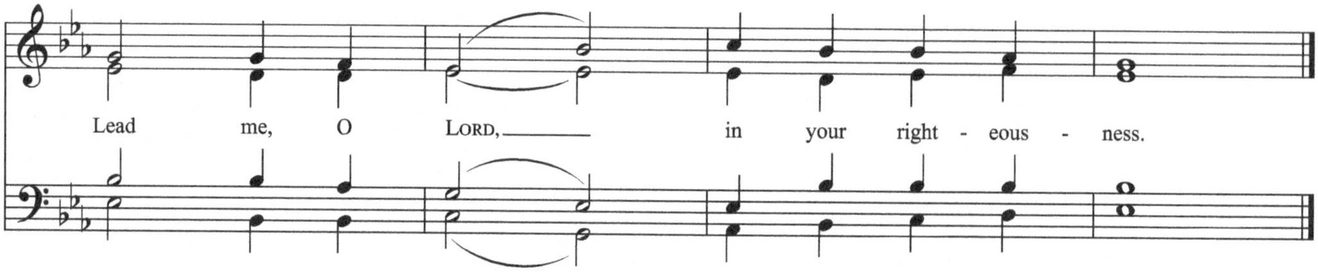

RCL Proper 6C (G Track) Psalm 32

RCL Proper 7C (C Track) Psalms 42 & 43

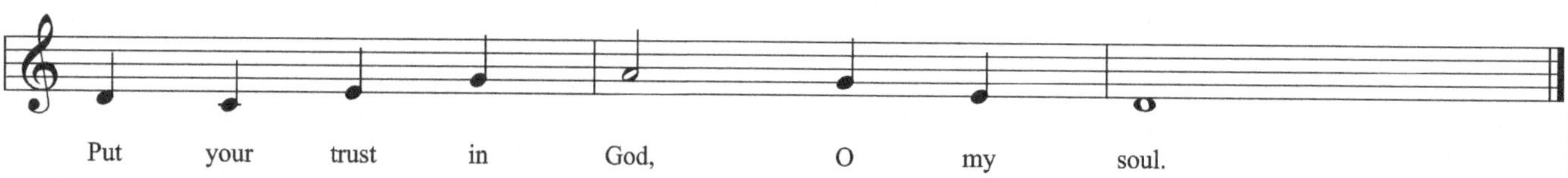

RCL Proper 7C (G Track) Psalm 22: 18–27

RCL Proper 8C (C Track) Psalm 77: 1–2, 11–20

RCL Proper 8C (G Track) Psalm 16

RCL Proper 9C (C Track) Psalm 30

RCL Proper 9C (G Track) Psalm 66: 1–8

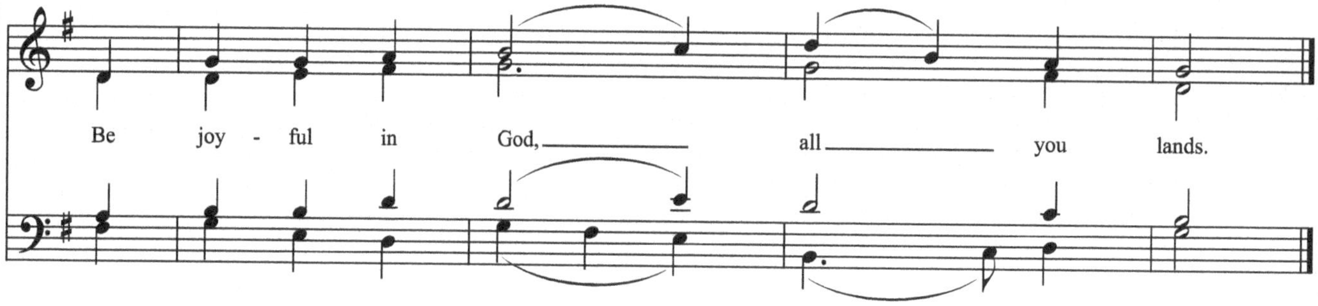

RCL Proper 10C (C Track) Psalm 82

RCL Proper 10C (G Track) Psalm 25: 1–9

RCL Proper 11C (C Track) Psalm 52

RCL Proper 11C (G Track) Psalm 15

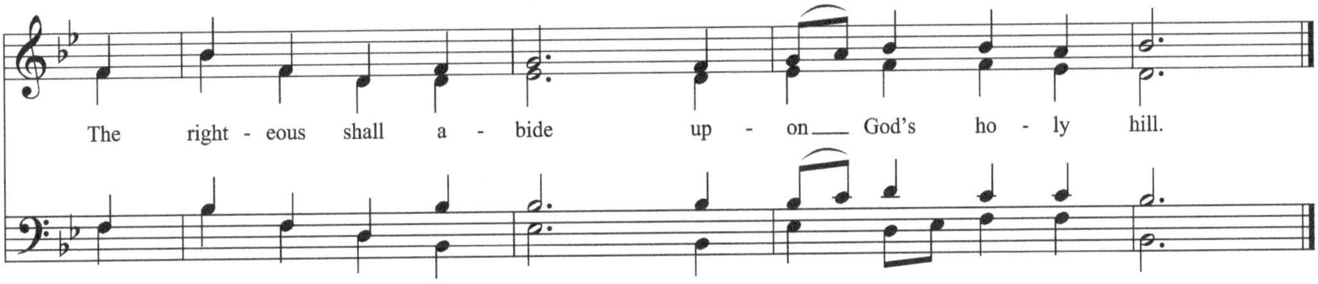

RCL Proper 12C (C Track) Psalm 85

RCL Proper 12C (G Track) Psalm 138

RCL Proper 13C (C Track) Psalm 107: 1–9, 43

RCL Proper 13C (G Track) Psalm 49: 1–11

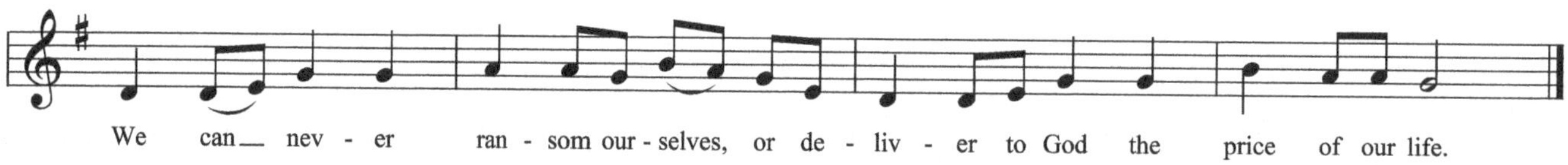

RCL Transfiguration ABC August 6 Psalm 99

RCL Proper 14C (C Track) Psalm 50: 1–8, 23–24

RCL Proper 14C (G Track) Psalm 33: 12–22

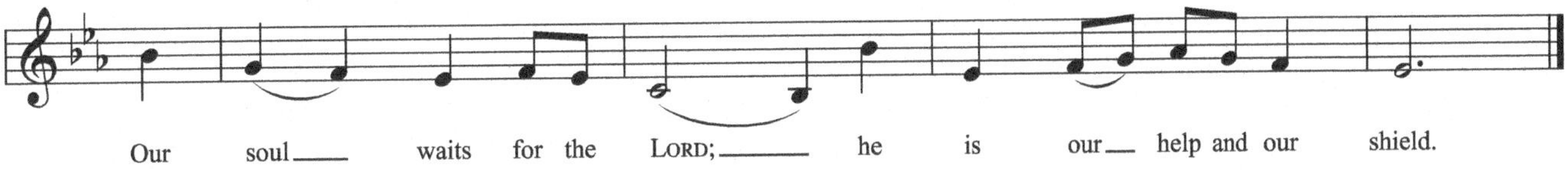

RCL Proper 15C (C Track) Psalm 80: 1–2, 8–18

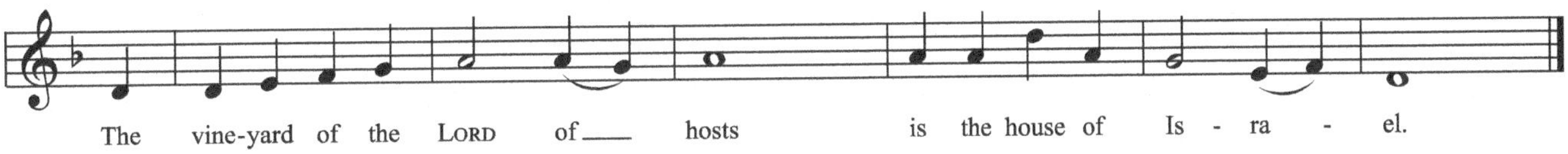

RCL Proper 15C (G Track) Psalm 82

RCL Proper16C (C Track) Psalm 71: 1–6

RCL Proper 16C (G Track) Psalm 103: 1–8

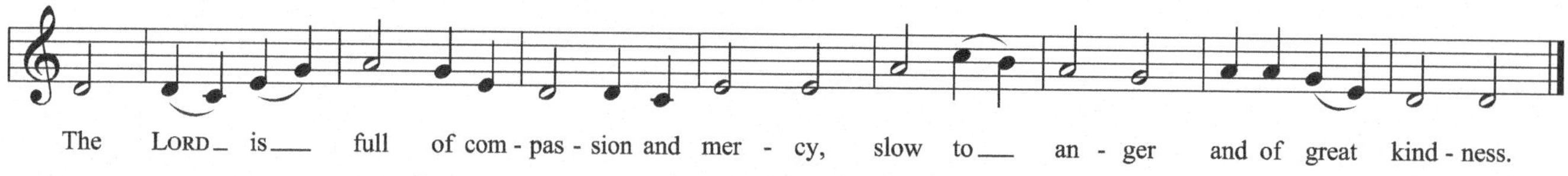

From *A HymnTune Psalter, Revised Common Lectionary Edition* © 2007 by Carl P. Daw, Jr. and Kevin R. Hackett. Church Publishing Incorporated.

RCL Proper 17C (C Track) Psalm 81: 1, 10–16

From *A HymnTune Psalter, Revised Common Lectionary Edition* © 2007 by Carl P. Daw, Jr. and Kevin R. Hackett. Church Publishing Incorporated.

RCL Proper 17C (G Track) Psalm 112

From *A HymnTune Psalter, Revised Common Lectionary Edition* © 2007 by Carl P. Daw, Jr. and Kevin R. Hackett. Church Publishing Incorporated.

RCL Proper 18C (C Track) Psalm 139: 1–5, 12–17

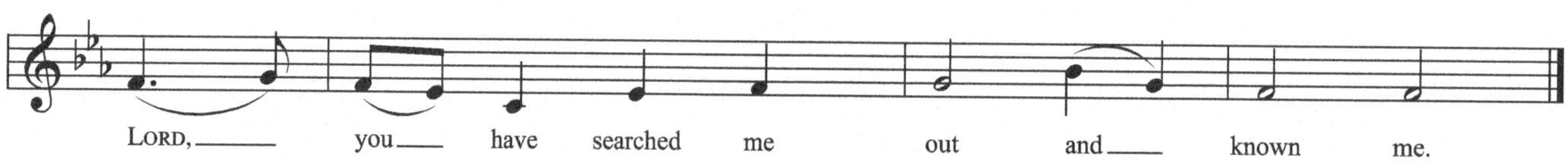

From *A HymnTune Psalter, Revised Common Lectionary Edition* © 2007 by Carl P. Daw, Jr. and Kevin R. Hackett. Church Publishing Incorporated.

RCL Proper 18C (G Track) Psalm 1

RCL Proper 19C (C Track) Psalm 14

RCL Proper 19C (G Track) Psalm 51: 1–11

RCL Proper 20C (C Track) Psalm 79: 1–9

RCL Proper 20C (G Track) Psalm 113

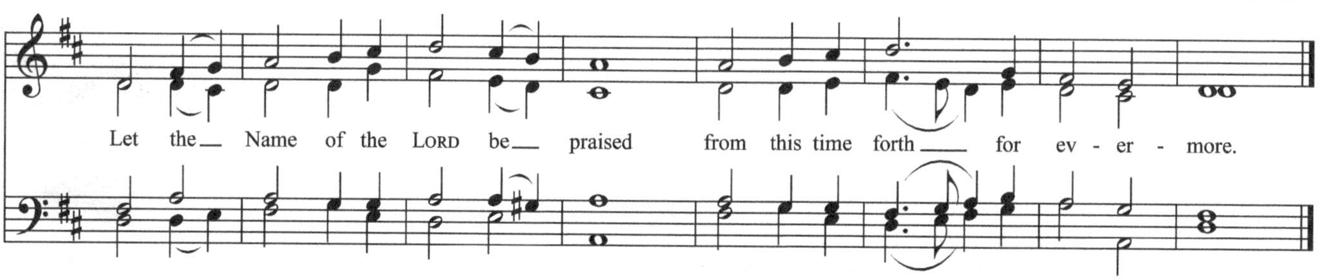

RCL Proper 21C (C Track) Psalm 91: 1–6, 14–16

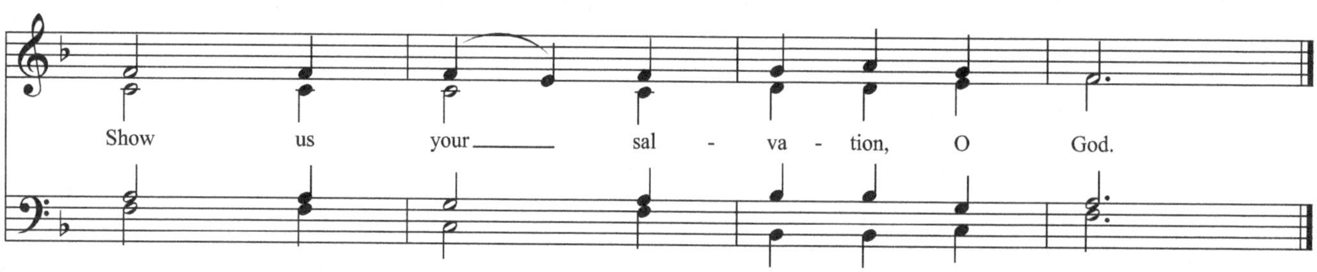

RCL Proper 21C (G Track) **Psalm 146**

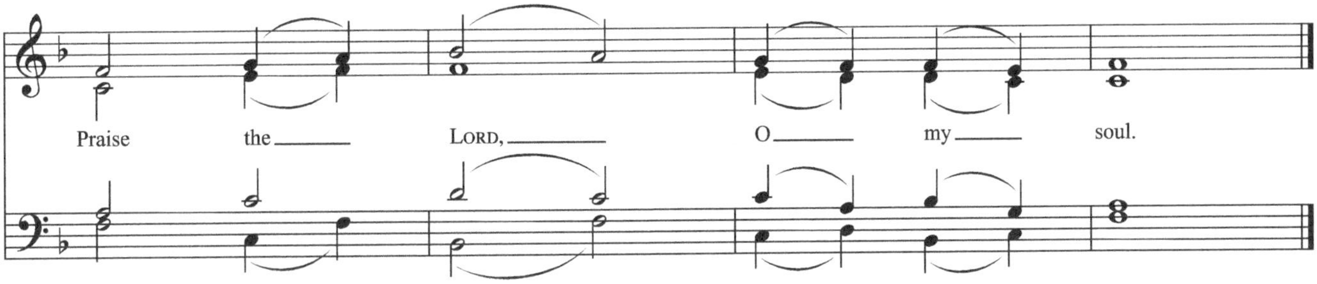

RCL Proper 22C (C Track) **A Song of Waiting**

RCL Proper 22C (C Track, alt.) **Psalm 137**

RCL Proper 22C (G Track) **Psalm 37: 1–10**

RCL Proper 23C (C Track) Psalm 66: 1–11

RCL Proper 23C (G Track) Psalm 111

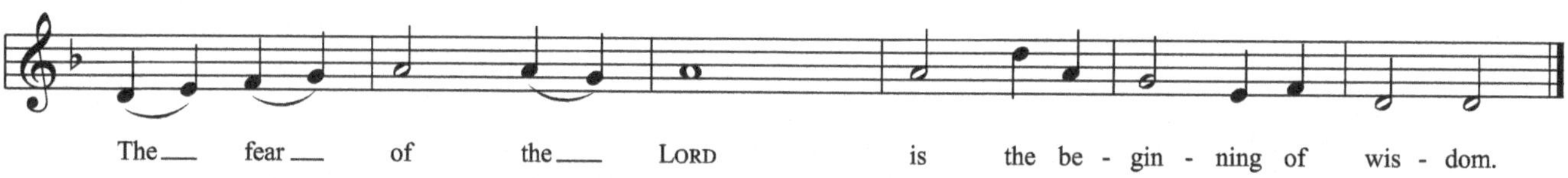

RCL Proper 24C (C Track) Psalm 119: 97–104

RCL Proper 24C (G Track) Psalm 121

RCL Proper 25C (C Track) Psalm 65

RCL Proper 25C (G Track) Psalm 84: 1–6

RCL All Saints' Day C Psalm 149

RCL Proper 26C (C Track) Psalm 119: 137–144

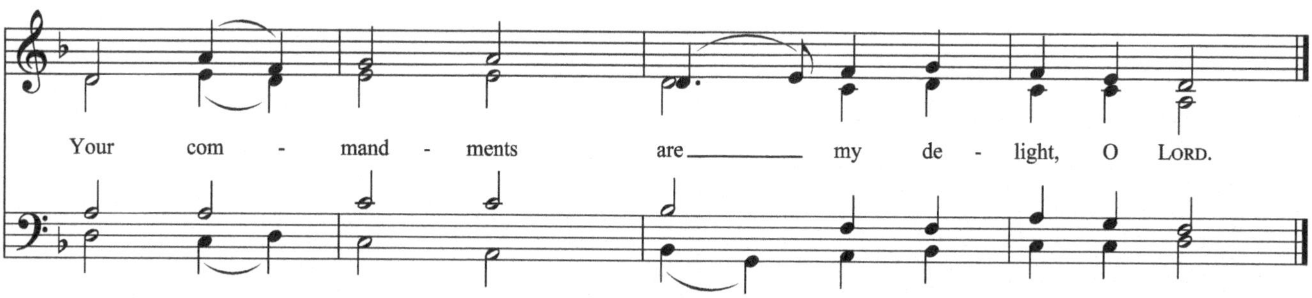

RCL Proper 26C (G Track) Psalm 32: 1–8

RCL Proper 27C (C Track) Psalm 145: 1–5, 18–22

RCL Proper 27C (C Track, alt.) Psalm 98

RCL Proper 27C (G Track) Psalm 17: 1–9

RCL Proper 28C (C Track) Canticle 9

RCL Proper 28C (G Track) Psalm 98

RCL Proper 29C (C Track) Canticle 16

RCL Proper 29C (G Track) Psalm 46

INDEX

PSALM	OCCURRENCES
1:1-6	Proper 25A; Easter 7B; Proper 20B; Epiphany 6C; Proper 1C; Proper 18C
2:1-13	Epiphany Last A
4:1-8	Easter 3B
5:1-8	Proper 6C
8:1-10	Holy Name ABC; Thursday in Easter Week ABC; Trinity Sunday AC; Proper 22B
9:9-20	Proper 7B
13:1-6	Proper 8A
14:1-7	Proper 12B; Proper 19C
15:1-7	Epiphany 3A; Proper 17B; Proper 11C
16:1-11	Easter Vigil ABC; Easter 2A; Proper 28B; Proper 8C
16:8-11	Monday in Easter Week ABC
17:1-7,16	Proper 13A
17:1-9	Proper 27C
19:1-14	Easter Vigil ABC; Proper 22A; Lent 3B; Proper 19B; Epiphany 3C
19:7-14	Proper 21B
20:1-9	Proper 6B
22:1-15	Proper 23B
22:1-30	Good Friday ABC

Psalm	**Occurrences**
22:18-27	Proper 7C
22:22-30	Lent 2B
22:24-30	Easter 5B
23:1-6	Lent 4A; Easter 4ABC; Proper 23A; Proper 11B
24:1-10	Proper 10B
25:1-8	Proper 21A
25:1-9	Lent 1B; Advent 1C; Proper 10C
26:1-8	Proper 17A; Proper 22B
27:1,5-13	Epiphany 3A
27:1-18	Lent 2C
29:1-11	Epiphany 1ABC; Trinity B
30:1-13	Epiphany 6B; Proper 1B; Proper 8B; Easter 3C; Proper 5C; Proper 9C
31:1-4,15-16	Holy Saturday ABC
31:1-5,15-16	Easter 5A
31:1-5,19-24	Proper 4A
31:9-16	Palm Sunday ABC: Liturgy of the Word
32:1-12	Lent 1A; Lent 4C; Proper 6C
32:1-8	Proper 26C
33:1-12	Proper 5A
33:12-22	Pentecost Vigil ABC; Proper 14C
33:18-22	Tuesday in Easter Week ABC
34:1-8	Proper 14B; Proper 25B

Psalm	**Occurrences**
34:9-14	Proper 15B
34:15-22	Proper 16B
36:5-10	Epiphany 2C
36:5-11	Monday in Holy Week ABC
37:1-12,41-42	Epiphany 7C; Proper 2C
37:1-10	Proper 22C
40:1-12	Epiphany 2A
41:1-13	Epiphany 7B; Proper 2B
42:1-15	Easter Vigil ABC; Proper 7C
43:1-6	Easter Vigil ABC; Proper 26A; Proper 7C
45:1-2,7-10	Proper 17B
45:11-18	Proper 9A
46:1-12	Easter Vigil ABC; Proper 4A; Proper 29C
47:1-10	Ascension ABC
48:1-13	Proper 9B
49:1-11	Proper 13C
50:1-6	Epiphany Last B
50:1-8,23-24	Proper 14C
50:7-15	Proper 5A
51:1-11	Proper 19C
51:1-13	Lent 5B; Proper 13B
52:1-9	Proper 11C

Psalm	**Occurrences**
54:1-7	Proper 20B
62:6-14	Epiphany 3B
63:1-8	Lent 3C
65:1-14	Proper 25C
65:9-14	Proper 10A
66:1-8	Proper 9C
66:1-11	Proper 23C
66:7-18	Easter 6A
67:1-7	Proper 15A; Easter 6C
68:1-10,33-36	Easter 7A
69:8-11,18-20	Proper 7A
70:1-6	Wednesday in Holy Week ABC; Proper 27A
71:1-14	Tuesday in Holy Week ABC
71:1-6	Epiphany 4C; Proper 16C
72:1-7,10-14	Epiphany ABC
72:1-7,18-19	Advent 2A
77:1-2,11-20	Proper 8C
78:1-4,12-16	Proper 21A
78:1-7	Proper 27A
78:23-29	Proper 13B
79:1-9	Proper 20C
80:1-2,8-18	Proper 15C

PSALM	OCCURRENCES
80:1-7	Advent 4C
80:1-7,16-18	Advent 4A; Advent 1B
80:7-14	Proper 22A
81:1,10-16	Proper 17C
81:1-10	Proper 4B
82:1-8	Proper 10C; Proper 15C
84:1-6	Proper 25C
84:1-8	Christmas 2ABC
84:1-12	Proper 16B
85:1-2,8-13	Advent 2B
85:1-13	Proper 12C
85:8-13	Proper 14A; Proper 10B
86:1-10,16-17	Proper 7A
86:11-17	Proper 11A
89:1-4,15-18	Proper 8A
89:1-4,19-26	Advent 4B
89:20-37	Proper 11B
90:1-6,13-17	Proper 25A
90:1-8,12	Proper 28A
90:12-17	Proper 23B
91:1-2,9-16	Lent 1C
91:1-6,14-16	Proper 21C

Psalm	Occurrences
91:9-16	Proper 24B
92:1-4,11-14	Proper 6B; Epiphany 8C; Proper 3C
93:1-6	Ascension ABC; Proper 29B
95:1-7a	Proper 29A
95:1-11	Lent 3A
96:1-9	Proper 24A; Proper 4C
96:1-13	Christmas Day IABC; Proper 4C
97:1-12	Christmas Day IIABC; Easter 7C
98:1-10	Christmas Day IIIABC; Easter Vigil ABC; Easter 6B; Proper 27C; Proper 28C
99:1-9	Epiphany Last AC; Proper 24A
100:1-4	Proper 6A; Proper 29A
103:1-8	Proper 16C
103:1-13,22	Epiphany 8B; Proper 3B
103:8-13	Proper 19A
103:8-14	Ash Wednesday ABC
104:1-9,25,37b	Proper 24B
104:25-32	Pentecost Vigil ABC
104:25-35,37	Pentecost Principal Service ABC
105:1-6,16-22,45b	Proper 14A
105:1-6,23-26,45c	Proper 17A
105: 1-6,37-45	Proper 20A
105:1-8	Wednesday in Easter Week ABC

Psalm	**Occurrences**
105:1-11,45b	Proper 12A
106:1-6,19-23	Proper 23A
107:1-3,17-22	Lent 4B
107:1-3,23-32	Proper 7B
107:1-7,33-37	Proper 26A
107:1-9,43	Proper 13C
111:1-10	Epiphany 4B; Proper 15B; Proper 23C
112:1-9(10)	Epiphany 5A
112:1-10	Proper 17C
113:1-8	Proper 20C
114:1-8	Easter Vigil ABC; Easter Day Evening Service ABC; Thursday in Easter Week ABC; Proper 19A
116:1,10-17	Maundy Thursday ABC; Proper 6A
116:1-3,10-17	Easter 3A
116:1-8	Friday in Easter Week ABC; Proper 19B
118:1-2,14-24	Easter Day Principal Service ABC
118:1-2,19-29	Palm Sunday ABC: Liturgy of the Palms
118:14-18	Saturday in Easter Week ABC
118:19-24	Monday in Easter Week ABC; Tuesday in Easter Week ABC; Wednesday in Easter Week ABC; Thursday in Easter Week ABC; Friday in Easter Week ABC; Saturday in Easter Week ABC
118:19-29	Easter 2C
119:1-8	Epiphany 6A; Proper 1A; Proper 26B
119:9-16	Lent 5B

Psalm	Occurrences
119:33-40	Epiphany 7A; Proper 2A; Proper 18A
119:97-104	Proper 24C
119:105-112	Proper 10A
119:129-136	Proper 12A
119:137-144	Proper 26C
121:1-8	Lent 2A; Proper 24C
122:1-9	Advent 1A
123:1-5	Proper 28A; Proper 9B
124:1-8	Proper 16A; Proper 21B
125:1-5	Proper 18B
126:1-7	Advent 3B; Proper 25B; Lent 5C
127:1-6	Proper 27B
128:1-6	Proper 12A
130:1-7	Lent 5A; Pentecost Vigil ABC; Proper 5B; Proper 8B; Proper 14B
131:1-4	Epiphany 8A; Proper 3A
132:1-13	Proper 29B
133:1-5	Proper 15A; Easter 2B; Proper 7B
136:1-9,23-26	Easter Vigil ABC
137:1-9	Proper 22C
138:1-9	Proper 16A; Proper 5B; Epiphany 5C; Proper 12C
139:1-5,12-17	Epiphany 2B; Proper 4B; Proper 18C
139:1-11,22-23	Proper 11A

PSALM	OCCURRENCES
143:1-12	Easter Vigil ABC
145:1-5,18-22	Proper 27C
145:1-8	Proper 20A
145:8-9,15-22	Proper 13A
145:8-15	Proper 9A
145:10-19	Proper 12B
146:1-9	Proper 18B; Proper 26B; Proper 27B; Proper 5C; Proper 21C
146:4-9	Advent 3A
147:1-12,21c	Epiphany 5B
147:13-21	Christmas 1ABC
148:1-14	Easter 5C
149:1-9	Proper 18A
150:1-6	Easter 2C

Canticle	**Occurrences**
Canticle 8	Easter Vigil ABC
Canticle 9	Easter Vigil ABC; Pentecost Vigil ABC; Advent 3C; Proper 28C
Canticle 13	Pentecost Vigil ABC; Trinity Sunday ABC
Canticle 15	Advent 3A; Advent 3B; Advent 4B; Advent 4C
Canticle 16	Advent 2C; Proper 29C
Exodus 15:1b-11,20-21	Proper 19A
1 Samuel 2:1-10	Proper 28B
Song of Solomon 2:8-13	Proper 9A
Lamentations 3:19-26	Proper 22C
Lamentations 3:21-33	Proper 8B
Wisdom of Solomon 6:17-20	Proper 27A
Wisdom of Solomon 7:26-8:1	Proper 19B
Wisdom of Solomon 12:13,16-19	Proper 11A